President
Carter

**Timely Reports to Keep
Journalists, Scholars and the Public
Abreast of Developing Issues, Events and Trends**

April 1977

CONGRESSIONAL QUARTERLY INC.
1414 22ND STREET, N.W., WASHINGTON, D.C. 20037

Congressional Quarterly Inc.

Congressional Quarterly Inc., an editorial research service and publishing company, serves clients in the fields of news, education, business and government. It combines specific coverage of Congress, government and politics by Congressional Quarterly with the more general subject range of an affiliated service, Editorial Research Reports

Congressional Quarterly was founded in 1945 by Henrietta and Nelson Poynter. Its basic periodical publication was and still is the CQ *Weekly Report,* mailed to clients every Saturday. A cumulative index is published quarterly.

The CQ *Almanac,* a compendium of legislation for one session of Congress, is published every spring. *Congress and the Nation* is published every four years as a record of government for one presidential term.

Congressional Quarterly also publishes books on public affairs. These include the twice-yearly *Guide to Current American Government* and such recent titles as *Origins and Development of Congress* and *Powers of Congress.*

CQ Direct Research is a consulting service which performs contract research and maintains a reference library and query desk for the convenience of clients.

Editorial Research Reports covers subjects beyond the specialized scope of Congressional Quarterly. It publishes reference material on foreign affairs, business, education, cultural affairs, national security, science and other topics of news interest. Service to clients includes a 6,000-word report four times a month bound and indexed semi-annually. Editorial Research Reports publishes paperback books in its fields of coverage. Founded in 1923, the service merged with Congressional Quarterly in 1956.

Editor: Margaret C. Thompson.
Contributors: Rhodes Cook, Mercer Cross, Alan Ehrenhalt, Ted Vaden, James R. Wagner, Laura B. Weiss.
Indexer: Diane Huffman.
Cover Design: Howard Chapman.
Production Manager: I. D. Fuller. **Assistant Production Manager:** Kathleen E. Walsh.

Book Department Editor: Robert A. Diamond.

Library of Congress Cataloging in Publication Data

Congressional Quarterly, Inc.
  President Carter.

  Includes index.

    1. Presidents—United States—Election—1976. 2. United States—Politics and government—1977. 3. Carter, Jimmy, 1924-
4. Mondale, Walter F., 1928- 5. Presidents—United States—Biography. 6. Vice Presidents—United States—Biography.
  I. Title.

E868.C66   1977   329'.023'730925   77-4222
ISBN 0-87187-109-2

Table of Contents

Editor's Note

President Carter presents an overview of the new President and his administration. The book provides in-depth political and biographical profiles of President Carter and Vice President Mondale, material on Carter's White House staff and detailed profiles of each cabinet appointee. It also includes an account of Carter's rise from political obscurity through his narrow election victory in November 1976, as well as a survey of the major policy initiatives of the first two months of the Carter presidency.

The appendix includes a selection of Carter statements tracing his views over a broad range of issues and a detailed chronology from Dec. 12, 1974, the day he announced his candidacy, to Jan. 20, 1977, Inauguration Day.

Introduction

From the standpoint of the American public, the 39th President must have been doing plenty of things right. Two months after his inauguration Jan. 20, 1977, Jimmy Carter enjoyed, according to public-opinion polls, a popularity rating of 71 per cent.

That was 20 per cent higher than the slim margin by which he was elected in 1976. Unless he broke all precedents, his popularity would decline as his administration progressed.

But Carter was no stranger to precedent-breaking. He was the first southerner to move into the White House since Zachary Taylor in 1849. He was the first former governor to become President since Franklin D. Roosevelt, 44 years earlier. He was only the third President of the century to turn out an incumbent. He was the century's fourth Democrat to take control when there were Democratic majorities in both houses of Congress.

Carter followed an unconventional path to the presidency. He had been governor of Georgia for one term, from 1971 to 1975. He laid some of the groundwork for his presidential campaign in 1974 when, as national coordinator for the Democrats' midterm campaign, he established a broad network of friends and acquaintances in the party.

But beyond the relatively narrow circles of his home state and a handful of party officials, Carter remained obscure. He was a peanut farmer from Plains, Ga., with a big grin, a lot of ambition and a talent for organization.

He put his organizational talents to telling use. The first test of the election year was the Democratic precinct caucuses in Iowa in January 1976. Carter outshone his rivals there, establishing himself as a serious candidate. A month later, he defeated all other Democrats in the New Hampshire primary, the first of the year. By the time he had won in Ohio June 8, a month before the national convention, it was all over. The nomination was his.

After the July convention in New York City had gone through the motions of making the nomination official, Carter struck one of the themes that would prevail through his campaign and into his presidency: concern for ordinary people. "We should make major investments in people, not in buildings and weapons," he said in his acceptance speech. "The poor, the aged, the weak and the afflicted must be treated with respect and with compassion and with love."

The focal point of the campaign was in the three televised debates between Carter and Gerald R. Ford, the incumbent Republican whose political career Carter would crush. The challenger did better than the challenged, the voters thought. They said so at the polls in November.

Carter often spoke in generalities, leaving much of what he said during the campaign open to interpretation. He was accused of being deliberately fuzzy on some issues. On the other hand, he was overly explicit at least one time too many. His admission, in a magazine interview, that he had mentally lusted after women almost cost him the election.

As Carter campaigned throughout the country, he had a team of bright young men and women at his Atlanta headquarters, out of the spotlight, planning the transition between administrations and developing positions on issues. By the time he had won the election, his transition team had done a considerable amount of the preliminary work on the major issues that Carter soon would present to Congress.

Carter ran against the Washington establishment, as an outsider taking on the insiders. His closest associates were Georgians who had worked with him in the state government. They came to Washington as the chief aides on his White House staff. Several of them were appointed to Cabinet-level jobs.

On his first visit to Washington after his election, Carter met with Ford one day and with congressional leaders the next. The transition period was one of extraordinary grace and tranquility, thanks largely to the cooperation extended by Ford.

Relations with Congress

Carter's relations with Congress were another matter. When he met with the leaders in November, he said that he wanted "almost unprecedented cooperation" with Congress. The honeymoon, predicted many Capitol Hill Democrats, would be long and tranquil.

It turned out to be shorter and more turbulent than expected. Scarcely had Carter and his family moved into the White House before the goodwill started to dissipate. The new President nominated a new Central Intelligence Agency director who later withdrew under pressure from Congress. Prior consultation with Senate Democrats could have prevented the unnecessary embarrassment, Carter was pointedly reminded. At about the same time, he tangled with the Speaker of the House over his unforeseen and unwelcome appointment of two Republicans to administration positions.

These were dismissed as transient spats, common to all honeymooners and repairable after the two branches of government got to know each other better. A more serious breach opened up in March, when Carter announced the deletion of $289-million in fiscal 1978 funds for 19 water resource projects. An aroused Senate voted to reject the President's plan, and the dispute showed signs of becoming a continuing battle.

It was evident long before Carter took office that he would, as President, place a premium on efficiency and tighter management of the government. During the campaign, he had said repeatedly that he would reduce 1,900 federal agencies to 200. One of his first acts after he was sworn in was to ask Congress to renew the reorganizational authority that had been granted to his predecessors. Congress agreed to his request.

Carter wanted to go further, to make statutory and not just administrative changes in the structure of the government. He sent Congress a proposal to create a new Energy Department that would consolidate functions previously scattered among numerous departments and agencies.

Aware of the lingering taint of Watergate in the minds of the electorate, Carter set another precedent in the stringency of the code of ethics he imposed on his appointees. Their personal and financial backgrounds were investigated in detail before the appointments were announced, so that the danger of scandal in the administration would be reduced to a minimum. Carter himself announced plans to place in trust his substantial personal holdings.

The thoroughness of the investigations of his appointees delayed the organization of his administration. Lack of sub-Cabinet officers created, at least temporarily, extra work for the Cabinet Secretaries. Defenders of Carter argued, however, that the delays were worth it if the end result were high-quality appointees.

An Open Administration

Frugality and openness were two of the early trademarks of Carter's administration. He announced plans to reduce the White House staff by one-third. At his first Cabinet meeting, he eliminated the use of limousines by the White House staff and suggested that his Cabinet officers follow his example. He was disdainful of the bureaucratic gobbledygook in the flood of executive-branch paperwork, and he ordered the language clarified and the paperwork reduced.

Before taking office, Carter had said he would hold news conferences every two weeks. During the first weeks of his administration, he was true to his promise. His performances at the conferences were relaxed, self-assured and occasionally witty, drawing comparisons with the style of John F. Kennedy.

But Carter went far beyond conventional news conferences in his efforts to cement his relationship with the American people. On Inauguration Day, he became the first President to walk, hand-in-hand with his wife, from the Capitol to the White House. He developed what was known as his "people program," a conscious reaching-out to the electorate.

Wearing a cardigan sweater, Carter sat before a fire in the White House during the record cold of the 1976-77 winter and talked informally to the people. He chatted with 42 people from 26 states during a phone-in broadcast nationally on network radio. He participated in a New England town hall meeting that was televised nationally. When the meeting was over, he spent the night in a private home. He had his energy adviser send letters to 450,000 citizens, soliciting their views on energy policy.

Carter's openness occasionally created concerns about the repercussions of what he said. At a news conference, for example, he discussed what appeared to be a new approach to resolving the dispute between Israel and Arab nations. He prompted criticism from the Soviet Union for his repeated emphasis on human rights in all nations. His critics, both at home and abroad, thought such matters should be brought up in the more conventional channels of secret diplomacy.

But these were not subjects that seemed to concern the people, and Carter had made clear his willingness to take his case to the people. He had shown himself to be a master of the political craft, and he was using it to best advantage as he began his new administration.

—Mercer Cross
March 1977

Carter: A Newcomer to Washington

The Democratic Party nominated a man it knew relatively little about. In national political terms, there was little to know. James Earl Carter Jr., 51, a former governor of Georgia, was not a typical presidential nominee. He was an outsider in control of a political party.

Jimmy Carter had never served in Congress. Except for seven years in the Navy, he had never worked for the federal government. He was not the product of any political machine and he had few ties to Washington, D.C. He came from a Deep South state that had little effect on presidential politics in modern history. He was not a lawyer. Nine months before he was nominated for President, three-fourths of American voters had not heard of him.

Carter's march through the primaries was not consistently smooth. He established his credentials as a front-runner in New Hampshire, Florida and Pennsylvania in the early spring, and took a clear lead in Texas and Indiana in May, but faltered a bit in the later primaries, challenged by Sen. Frank Church of Idaho and Gov. Edmund G. Brown Jr. of California. Carter lost nine of the last 12 primaries held outside the South.

By the time the Democrats reached their party convention in New York, however, the defeats were forgotten and all factions of the party were ready to unite behind Carter as the man to end eight years of Republican rule. He won an easy first ballot victory from a united convention.

Carter made it clear he would run as a national Democrat, moving left to pick Sen. Walter F. Mondale of Minnesota as his running-mate and speaking favorably in his acceptance speech of national health insurance, tax reform, and increased opportunity for minorities.

Starting From Scratch

Jimmy Carter began to consider running for President shortly after the 1972 Democratic convention. His drive began with his own belief that he might do the job as well as anyone else.

Before becoming governor, Carter had never met a President and he looked on the office with reverence and awe. "Then in 1971 and 1972," he wrote later, "I met Richard Nixon, Spiro Agnew, George McGovern, Henry Jackson, Hubert Humphrey, Ed Muskie, George Wallace, Ronald Reagan, Nelson Rockefeller, and other presidential hopefuls, and I lost my feeling of awe about Presidents."

With his family, staff and political friends, Carter began to assess his chances as a national candidate. He decided that some of the usual disadvantages—being a Southerner, a farmer, a state politician—could become advantages. Being politically unemployed in 1975 and 1976 would enable him to campaign full time. He began to emphasize certain duties as governor—administration of federal programs, long-range planning, budgeting procedures, criminal justice—that could be applied at the national level.

Carter's presidential campaign got a boost when he was named chairman of the Democrats' Campaign '74 Committee. In order to help the party's candidates he traveled all over the nation and studied the politics of all states and congressional districts. He met frequently with local leaders who ordinarily support Democratic candidates, and thus established a loose network of his own supporters. Carter himself campaigned in more than 60 congressional races. Working with four or five major pollsters, Carter's committee discovered the issues in the public's mind and prepared 30 background papers that were mailed to at least a thousand Democratic candidates.

On Dec. 12, 1974—one month after the mid-term elections and one month before his term as governor ended—Carter announced his candidacy for the 1976 presidential nomination. His speech before the National Press Club included most of the themes of his campaign: restoration of public trust in government; reforms to make government more open and more efficient; comprehensive energy policy; thorough tax reform; "a simplified, fair and compassionate welfare program"; a comprehensive national health program.

Three days after his announcement Carter appeared on NBC's "Meet the Press" and responded to the assumption that he was running in hope of being considered by a brokered convention. "The concept of a brokered convention is obnoxious to me," Carter said. "I don't believe that is the proper approach to take. I am going into the primaries and into the states that select delegates by conventions with the full intention of winning a majority of those delegates before the (national) convention."

With that, Carter set out on the road toward the White House. His strategy was to run everywhere and to win often. He spent most of 1975 on the road; he had planned to spend 250 days away from home but the actual count may have

Carter's Background

Profession: Farmer and businessman.
Born: Oct. 1, 1924, Plains, Ga.
Home: Plains.
Religion: Baptist.
Family: Wife: Rosalynn Smith Carter m. July 7, 1946; children: John William (Jack), b. July 3, 1947, James Earl (Chip), b. April 12, 1950, Donnel Jeffrey (Jeff) b. Aug. 18, 1952, Amy Lynn, b. Oct. 19, 1967.
Education: Georgia Southwestern College, 1941-42; Georgia Institute of Technology, 1942-43; U.S. Naval Academy, B.S., 1946; Union College, Schenectady, N.Y., 1952.
Offices: Chairman, Sumter County (Georgia) Board of Education; Georgia state senator, 1962-66; governor, 1971-75.
Military: Navy, 1946-53; discharged as lieutenant.
Memberships: Lions; American Legion; Baptist Brotherhood Commission; former state chairman, March of Dimes; past president, Georgia Seedsmen; Southern Peanut Warehousemen; past president, Georgia Planning Association.

been closer to 300. His travels took him to almost all states, and he often stayed in the homes of supporters. He came close to his fund-raising goal for 1975 of $750,000 and qualified for federal matching funds.

Local politicians and reporters began to write that Carter was a most effective face-to-face campaigner, but the national press paid little attention. A Gallup Poll in October 1975 found that less than 3 per cent listed him as their first choice for the Democratic nomination.

Even at year's end, national publications and broadcasters were giving Carter only a little space and time, usually emphasizing the novelty of his campaign. That changed dramatically on Jan. 19, 1976, when Carter's 28 per cent of the vote led all other candidates in the Iowa Democratic caucus, the first pre-nomination event of the election year. Suddenly, "Jimmy Who?" from Georgia was described in headlines and film as the front-runner. Critics were quick to point out, however, that his success depended on weeks of personal contact which would be impossible in larger states once the primaries began.

The Front-Runner

Then Carter won the New Hampshire primary Feb. 24 with 28.4 per cent in a field of nine candidates, including write-ins. Carter emphasized his distance from Washington and promised to bring morality back to the federal government. The voters liked it.

In Massachusetts on March 2, Carter ran behind Jackson, Rep. Morris K. Udall (D Ariz.) and Wallace but picked up 16 delegates. The same day, he won Vermont's advisory primary with more than 42 per cent against three other candidates.

Carter's first major test came March 9 in Florida, where he had vowed to defeat Wallace. In 1972 Wallace won nearly 42 per cent of the primary vote. Carter had to draw away some of Wallace's strength in the South to show that he was a national contender. When all the votes were counted, Carter had beaten Wallace 34.5 to 30.5 per cent. Jackson was third with 23.9. Carter cut into Wallace's lead in all parts of the state and ran strongest in central Florida and Jacksonville. Most observers felt that if Jackson had stayed out of the race Carter's victory over Wallace would have been much stronger.

The next week Carter went north to Illinois, where he surprised nearly everyone by winning 48 per cent of the popular vote—more than 20 points ahead of Wallace. Carter also won 53 delegates, although he did not have slates in all districts. Outside Chicago, he ran ahead of Sen. Adlai E. Stevenson III, the choice of the regular party organization.

Wallace Eliminated

In North Carolina on March 23, Carter became the first Democrat to receive a majority in any primary. He had 53.6 per cent against 34.7 per cent for Wallace, who had received a majority there in the 1972 primary. North Carolina was an important state for Carter because he knocked Wallace out of contention and demonstrated strength in all parts of the state. Carter ran especially strong among blacks and in urban areas. It was in this highly Protestant state also that Carter's evangelistic appeal first became evident. He was asked repeatedly about his religious beliefs and was eager to explain. "Jesus Christ is the most important thing in my life," he told one North Carolina audience.

Ethnic Purity

In early April, Carter made a mistake that caused his campaign to falter. Aboard a late-night flight a reporter for the *New York Daily News* asked Carter about subsidized low-income, scatter-site housing in the suburbs. He replied, "I see nothing wrong with ethnic purity being maintained. I would not force racial integration of a neighborhood by government action. But I would not permit discrimination against a family moving into the neighborhood."

His "ethnic purity" remarks got Carter into trouble with blacks and northern liberals, whose support he needed. Carter quickly and repeatedly apologized for the statement, and after a couple of weeks the furor died down. One reason it died down was the continuing support Carter received from leading black politicians, principally U.S. Rep. Andrew Young (Ga.) and the Rev. Martin Luther King Sr.

On April 6 in Wisconsin, Carter came from behind to win by 1 per cent after Udall had claimed victory. Carter's win boosted his campaign and sustained him through the "ethnic purity" controversy. Udall made an extensive effort in the state but lacked an emotional issue to bring out liberal voters. Carter benefited from Wallace's collapse, winning 22 of 23 counties Wallace had carried four years earlier.

Meanwhile, Carter was picking up delegates elsewhere. He won 35 in New York's complicated primary April 6, and kept working on the caucus states. By the April 27 Pennsylvania primary, Carter had 263 delegates to 176 for Jackson, his closest rival.

Jackson, who had done well in Massachusetts, claimed that Pennsylvania would prove Carter could not win in a northern industrial state. But Carter beat Jackson there, 37 to 24.6 per cent, and carried 64 of 67 counties. Jackson quit the race May 1.

Riding high, Carter won 92 of 98 Texas delegates on May 1 and easily won the May 4 primaries in the District of Columbia, Indiana and Georgia. As expected, Wallace won most of the Alabama delegates May 4.

Primary Problems

But Church upset Carter in Nebraska May 11, winning by less than 1 per cent. Church made an all-out effort to convince the party that his late-starting campaign was serious. His victory began some rough weeks for Carter.

On May 18, Brown beat Carter badly in Maryland, 48.4 to 37.1 per cent. The same day in Michigan, where Carter was expected to win overwhelmingly, he barely defeated Udall by 2,000 votes. Carter's Michigan campaign appeared to have been hurt by overconfidence within his organization and an effective television effort by Udall in Detroit.

There were six primaries May 25, and for Carter the results were mixed. He lost to Church in Oregon and Idaho and to Brown in Nevada. But Carter defeated Wallace and others overwhelmingly in Tennessee, Arkansas and Kentucky and added 165 delegates to his total.

June 1 was another mixed day for Carter. His delegates in Rhode Island lost to an uncommitted slate backed by Brown, and Church beat him by more than 2-to-1 in the Montana primary. But Carter won strongly in South Dakota, where Udall, supported by Senators James Abourezk and George McGovern, had been expected to achieve his first victory.

Carter's defeats in the late primaries did not prove as damaging as they at first seemed. For one thing, his base of support in the South absorbed the losses elsewhere. For another, the proportional division of delegates in most primaries allowed him to increase his convention support even in states where he was beaten. As he entered the last week of primaries Carter had 869 of the 1,505 delegates needed for nomination. Udall was a very distant second with 291 delegates.

The results on June 8 were decisive for Carter. It did not matter that he lost California to Brown, as expected, by a 3-to-1 margin. Nor was it important that in New Jersey, where Carter won more than 58 per cent in the preference poll, his at-large delegates lost badly to an uncommitted slate. What mattered most was that Carter won overwhelmingly in Ohio, with more than 52 per cent of the vote and 126 of 152 delegates.

Within hours Carter had won the nomination unofficially. He was endorsed by Mayor Richard Daley of Chicago, who had about 100 delegates at his disposal, and won the public support of both Wallace and Jackson. After that, Carter's nomination by the Democratic convention was merely a formality.

Carter ended the longest primary season ever with 39 per cent of all votes cast. In the 26 presidential preference primaries Carter finished first in 17 and second in eight. On the way to the nomination, Carter eliminated a dozen candidates who entered the campaign and showed enough strength to block his greatest potential rival, Sen. Hubert H. Humphrey.

New York In July

At the convention in New York July 12-15, Carter's principal concern was to prepare himself and his party for the nomination. He arrived two days early and held a rally outside his hotel. For six days he met with his staff, party leaders and other Democratic supporters, spoke quietly with delegations that were uncommitted or pledged to other candidates, soothed feelings in caucuses of women and black delegates, held press conferences, attended dinners and parties, and granted a few interviews. Carter urged Democrats not to be complacent about November and more than once he told delegates, "I never did intend to lose the nomination and I'll guarantee you I don't intend to lose the election."

Beyond all that, Carter had three important responsibilities: to select his running mate; to prepare and deliver his acceptance speech; and to discuss the fall campaign with party leaders the morning after the convention.

Running Mate

The procedure Carter established to select his vice presidential running mate illustrated the way he prepares himself for major decisions. He told a press conference in New York July 12, "It is undoubtedly the most important decision that I shall make this year, perhaps one of the most important of my whole life."

Carter began working on the problem two months before his final primary victories assured him of the nomination. On April 17 he began to review staff-prepared memos presenting alternative processes for selecting his running mate. On June 2, six weeks before the convention, Carter received a list evaluating Democratic mayors, governors and members of Congress.

A national poll conducted by Carter aide Pat Caddell to test the strength of 14 possible running mates was presented

What Makes Jimmy Run?

In a televised interview broadcast over PBS on May 6, 1976, Bill Moyers asked Jimmy Carter about his drive and self-discipline. Part of their conversation follows.

CARTER: I have a constant drive just to do the best I can, and sometimes it's disconcerting to other people. But it's not an unpleasant thing for me. I don't feel that I've got to win, or that I'd be terribly disappointed if I don't win. I feel a sense of equanimity about it. If I do my best and lose, I don't have any regrets.

MOYERS: What drives you?

CARTER: I don't know exactly how to express it. As I said, it's not an unpleasant sense of being driven. I feel like I have one life to live—I feel that God wants me to do the best I can with it. And that's quite often my major prayer: Let me live my life so that it will be meaningful. And I enjoy tackling difficult problems, and solving of solutions, and answering the difficult questions, and the meticulous organization of a complicated effort. It's a challenge—possibly, it's like a game. I don't know. I don't want to lower it by saying it's just a game, but it's an enjoyable thing for me.

to Carter June 12. It showed that Carter would not be helped or hurt significantly by any of the potential candidates. Senators Edmund S. Muskie (Maine) and John Glenn (Ohio) offered a slight advantage because their names were so familiar to the public.

Carter met at Jekyll Island, Ga., June 17 with adviser Charles Kirbo to plan preliminary discussions with the vice presidential candidates and to seek the counsel of more party leaders and elected officials.

Carter on June 20 compiled a list of persons to be interviewed by Kirbo and outlined the questions which Kirbo should ask. Kirbo, the only person authorized to speak for Carter, began the candidate interviews in Washington the week of June 28.

Kirbo requested information about any improper or illegal contributions received in the past and whether the candidate had ever been sued or arrested. It asked about health, including any psychiatric treatment. Several questions dealt with tax returns, personal finances and outside income. Carter requested a detailed financial statement and asked whether it could be made public if the person were nominated as Vice President. He also requested copies of federal tax returns for the last five years.

Carter met with Kirbo in Plains July 2 to receive detailed reports about the interviews. They decided then which persons Carter himself would interview the following week. In Plains, Carter saw Muskie on July 5 and both Glenn and Mondale on July 8. At his convention headquarters in New York, Carter saw Jackson on July 10, Rodino on July 11, and Church and Stevenson on July 12, the opening day of the convention. An eighth finalist, Sen. Abraham A. Ribicoff (Conn.), told Kirbo he did not want to be considered for the job.

At 8:30 a.m. July 15, the last day of the convention, Carter telephoned Mondale to ask him to be his running mate. He told no one else until two minutes before he called Mondale. Carter told the five remaining candidates (Rodino had dropped out earlier in the week) that they had not been picked. He announced the selection of Mondale at a 10 a.m. news conference.

Carter called the selection "one of the most difficult decisions that I have ever had to make." He said Mondale had not been his original choice and that he had changed his mind three times in 30 days as he gathered more information and conducted the interviews. "But I have absolutely no doubt that I have made the right decision," Carter said.

For future presidential nominees, Carter said he would recommend to the Democratic National Committee that conventions adjourn or recess to give the nominees an opportunity to follow a procedure similar to Carter's to select a running mate. After 30 days, Carter suggested, the convention could either reconvene or permit the 250-member DNC to confirm the vice presidential candidate chosen by the presidential nominee. Carter released an outline of the procedure he had followed, "for historical purposes."

A Confident Nominee

Carter spent much of the convention week working on his acceptance speech. The preliminary draft had been written in June by Patrick Anderson, a journalist and novelist who became Carter's principal speech writer late in the spring. Carter and his staff revised the speech considerably in Plains and New York, and Carter began rewriting the third draft at 6 a.m. July 14, the day he was nominated. He did not complete the speech until late in the afternoon on July 15, several hours before he delivered it.

In the speech Carter predicted that 1976 would not be a year of politics as usual. "Our country has lived through a time of torment," he said. "It is now a time for healing. We want to have faith again. We want to be proud again. We just want the truth again. It's time for the people to run the government, and not the other way around."

Throughout the primaries Carter said he would not make promises he could not keep. His acceptance speech made promises: a good working relationship between the President and Congress; more efficient government; complete overhaul of the federal income tax system; "a nationwide, comprehensive health program." He saluted Democratic Presidents of the past and pledged support for many traditional party goals. He also called for government economy and a balanced budget.

Much of the speech was populist in tone. "Too many have had to suffer at the hands of a political and economic elite who have shaped decisions and never had to account for mistakes nor to suffer from injustice," Carter said. "When unemployment prevails, they never stand in line looking for a job. When deprivation results from a confused and bewildering welfare system, they never do without food or clothing or a place to sleep. And when the bureaucracy is bloated and confused, the powerful always manage to discover and occupy niches of special influence and privilege."

Carter used the same tone in making an unspecified attack on the Watergate scandals and Ford's pardon of Nixon: "It's time for our government leaders to respect the law no less than the humblest citizen, so that we can end once and for all a double standard of justice. I see no reason why big shot crooks should go free and the poor ones go to jail."

Several times he cited the strength of American character and ideals. He said the United States can still have a President "who is not isolated from the people, but who feels your pain and shares your dreams, and takes his strength and his wisdom and his courage from you."

As he concluded the address, Carter spoke again of his vision for the nation. "I see an America on the move again," he said, "united, a diverse and vital and tolerant nation, entering our third century with pride and confidence—an America that lives up to the majesty of our Constitution and the simple decency of our people."

The speech was well received by the convention although it did not bring thunderous interruptions of applause. It seemed to be intended as much for television viewers—the largest audience Carter has ever had—with its quiet delivery and reassuring messages of national unity. The more arousing, partisan remarks were offered earlier in the evening by Mondale.

Fall Campaign

The following morning, when most convention delegates were starting home, Carter held a few meetings to prepare for the general election in November. He told party fund-raisers that he would conduct an extensive but economical campaign that would cost about $22-million. Much of the cost would be covered by public funds collected through the $1 income tax checkoff system. Other funds would be raised by the party, and Carter made it clear that he was happy to be free of that obligation.

The nominee met also with the Democratic National Committee. He made it clear that he wanted to win by a large margin and that he wanted a solid base of Democratic support in both chambers of Congress.

"I'm going to work just as hard, I am going to get up just as early, I am going to work just as late in October and September as I did in February and March," Carter said.

He told the national committee that he would run the campaign and that he and his staff would not waste time calling party officials to tell them to do what they already should be doing. Hamilton Jordan, Carter's campaign manager, presented the party leaders with a detailed plan for a nationwide voter registration effort.

His Georgia Roots

Anyone who wants to learn more about Carter might start with his 1975 autobiography, *Why Not The Best?* It is not a typical political book; it emphasizes his early years in Georgia as much as his political career. The title was inspired by Navy Admiral Hyman G. Rickover, Carter's commanding officer for a year, who used the words in dealing with his staff.

Early in the book Carter describes himself this way: "I am a Southerner and an American. I am a farmer, an engineer, a father and husband, a Christian, a politician and former governor, a planner, a businessman, a nuclear physicist, a naval officer, a canoeist, and, among other things, a lover of Bob Dylan's songs and Dylan Thomas' poetry."

Carter's family has been in Georgia for more than 200 years. His children will be the sixth generation to own the same land in the southwestern part of the state near Plains. Carter was born there Oct. 1, 1924. His father, a farmer and small businessman, died of cancer in 1953. His mother, usually known as "Miss Lillian," is a registered nurse and, at age 77, one of the more active campaigners in Jimmy Carter's large family.

The family home was three miles west of Plains in a rural community called Archery, which had two permanent families who were white and about 25 who were black. The house had no indoor plumbing or electricity until Jimmy, the oldest of four children, was in his teens.

Jimmy Carter was the first man in his family ever to graduate from high school. Since childhood he had planned on a naval career, and in 1942 he received an appointment to Annapolis through U.S. Rep. Stephen Pace. Carter first spent one year as a Naval ROTC student at Georgia Tech in Atlanta. He graduated from Annapolis in 1946, standing 59th in a class of 820.

In July 1946 Jimmy Carter married Rosalynn Smith, another fifth-generation resident of Plains who is about three years younger than he. She is his close adviser and an important member of the Carter campaign organization. The Carters have three married sons: Jack, 29; Chip, 26; Jeff, 23; and one daughter, Amy, 8.

Carter says that he liked the Navy. He advanced rapidly. Eventually he was assigned to Rickover's atomic submarine program and was the pre-commission commander of the U.S.S. Seawolf. He did graduate work in nuclear physics at Union College, but did not receive a degree. Carter's ambition was to become Chief of Naval Operations.

Home To Georgia

But the Carters returned to Plains in 1953, when Jimmy's father was dying. Soon afterward, Carter decided to resign from the Navy and go home to live on the farm. He wrote of his father: "I began to think about the relative significance of his life and mine. He was an integral part of the community, and had a wide range of varied but interrelated interests and responsibilities. He was his own boss, and his life was stabilized by the slow and evolutionary changes in the local societal structure."

Rosalynn Carter reluctantly agreed to the change. The family returned to Plains in the winter of 1953 with a few thousand dollars in savings and no assured income. They applied for and received an apartment in a public housing project.

Agriculture had changed so rapidly since Carter was a boy that he had to learn farming all over again. His first year he made a profit of less than $200. But gradually he expanded his peanut farm into a seed and fertilizer business, warehouses, a peanut-shelling plant, a cotton gin and a farm supply operation. He also acquired land, so that in 1976 Carter Farms Inc. owned or leased more than 3,100 acres. In 1974 Jimmy Carter listed his net worth as $588,698 and his total assets as $999,689.

Carter's maternal grandfather, Jim Jack Gordy, was a locally famous politician credited with originating the concept of rural free delivery of mail (RFD). His father, James Earl Carter Sr., also was active in Democratic politics, and shortly before he died he was elected to the Georgia House of Representatives. Jimmy Carter became involved in church and civic affairs when he returned to Plains, and was chairman of the Sumter County school board and first president of the Georgia Planning Association.

In 1962 Carter ran for the Georgia Senate in a district of seven counties. He eventually won the Democratic primary, which was the only contest, but not until Carter proved that his opponents had stuffed ballot boxes and violated other election laws in Quitman County. Carter was aided then by Kirbo, the Atlanta lawyer who became a top political adviser.

Carter was re-elected to the state senate in 1964.

Carter the Legislator

Since Carter held no other legislative positions, his state senate activities from 1963-66 are a particularly important record of his stands on various issues. Although less than 10 per cent of the state senate's votes during Carter's tenure were recorded roll calls, the record he established showed him to be an advocate of fiscal restraint but a progressive Democrat on most social issues.

As a member of the Senate Appropriations Committee, Carter sought new ways to control the state's budget. He developed a reputation as a tough-minded opponent of what he called "sweetheart legislation" to provide special tax relief for corporate interests. However, as a freshman in 1963, Carter introduced a resolution urging the United States Congress to retain a capital gains federal tax benefit for timber firms.

Carter's fiscal conservatism prevailed in his voting on tax relief for the disadvantaged. In 1964, he was one of only two senators against a bill to increase property tax relief for low income persons 65 years and older. In 1966, he voted against a similar tax relief bill for the disabled.

Education was an area in which Carter consistently abandoned his fiscal conservatism and to which he devoted considerable legislative energy. He drafted, sponsored and pressed for the passage of several pieces of legislation to improve the Georgia public education system. Those efforts included his work on a special commission which recommended a massive up-dating of the state school system. Among those recommendations, which Carter helped write into law, were a minimum standard for teacher training, an increased state education budget and a reduced pupil-teacher ratio.

Carter also recommended and served as the first chairman of a Senate subcommittee on higher education.

Civil Rights

Carter, whose presidential campaign benefited greatly from black support during the primaries, established a less conclusive record on the major civil rights legislation before the Georgia legislature from 1963-66. Those years of civil rights progress and racial strife throughout the country produced some legislative initiatives in Georgia to reduce racial discrimination and others to block implementation of federal civil rights orders. During a 1964 special session to re-write the state constitution, Carter voted for a freedom-of-association amendment aimed at blocking school integration. He also voted to prevent enactment of county-initiated open accommodation and fair employment laws.

However, Carter had a reputation of being generally supportive of modest civil rights legislation. He voted for bills to abolish separate listings of black and white taxpayers and to expand Atlanta's city limits to include an all black section, thereby increasing black voting power within the city.

Many of the personality traits noted by those who served with Carter in the legislature resemble characteristics exhibited during his presidential campaign. He was known as a diligent and well-informed legislator who did his best to uphold a pledge to read every bill which came before the legislature. He worked long hours, rarely socialized and relied on his soft-spoken personal appeal to win political friends and votes.

The most conservative aspects of Carter's record have been defended by former colleagues as an attempt to balance his desire to aid the underprivileged with his political need to keep in touch with his conservative constituency.

Statewide Gamble

In 1966 Carter decided to run for the U.S. House of Representatives against Republican incumbent Howard H. (Bo) Callaway. He announced his candidacy as soon as the state legislature adjourned in the spring and began making daily campaign visits in the district, followed by personal notes to the voters he had met. The routine continued from April to June, and Carter believed he was gaining on Callaway.

Then the Democratic front-runner for governor, former Gov. Ernest Vandiver, became ill and quit the race. Callaway decided to leave Congress and run for governor. Carter decided to enter the statewide race himself.

It was a reckless move because Carter was scarcely known in the state and he offended some of his supporters in the congressional contest. Moreover, the Democratic field quickly became crowded with former Gov. Ellis Arnall and several conservatives, among them segregationist Lester G. Maddox.

Carter's decision was important, because if he had gone to Congress he almost certainly would not have become the 1976 presidential nominee. The gubernatorial campaign also let Carter test some political rhetoric, including his rejection of ideological labels and his pledge to speak directly and truthfully to the voters.

Carter in 1966 ran what he called "an intensive and frantic campaign around Georgia." He did remarkably well in a short time. But Arnall and Maddox finished first and second in the primary; Carter, with 165,000 votes, missed the runoff by 21,000.

"This entire experience was extremely disappointing to me," Carter wrote. "I was deeply in debt, had lost 22 pounds (down to 130), and wound up with Lester Maddox as governor of Georgia. I waited about one month and then began campaigning again for governor."

He was successful the second time around, partly because in four years of campaigning he made 1,800 speeches and, with Rosalynn, shook hands with 600,000 people. But Carter's 1970 campaign became the most controversial event in his public life.

The 1970 Campaign

There were nine Democratic candidates, but the obvious leaders were Carter and former Gov. Carl E. Sanders (1963-67), both moderates. Carter moved to the right of Sanders in order to pick up some supporters of Maddox, who could not succeed himself and who was running for lieutenant governor. The campaign got rough, and Carter still stands accused of making racist appeals and using unethical tactics.

Carter ran on a populist slogan—"Isn't it time someone spoke up for you?"—and all but conceded the black vote to Sanders. He spoke out against federally imposed desegregation plans and school busing. He had occasional kind words for Maddox and Alabama Gov. George C. Wallace, and he apparently sought support from segregationist editors. *The Atlanta Constitution* opposed Carter and, he says, characterized him unfairly as, in his words, "an ignorant and bigoted redneck peanut farmer."

The same newspaper was the first to charge that the Carter campaign secretly distributed a leaflet showing Sanders celebrating a basketball victory with black members of the Atlanta Hawks, a team partly owned by Sanders. Later in the campaign Sanders charged that Carter's organization, through Gerald Rafshoon's advertising agency, financed radio ads for C.B. King, a black candidate for governor whose campaign drained votes away from Sanders.

Carter and his staff either denied the charges about racism and "dirty tricks" in the 1970 campaign or refused to comment on them. Carter later won the support of blacks and liberals but the six-year-old controversy continued. The Republican National Committee in 1976 sent out packets of 1970 Georgia newspaper clippings.

Carter defeated Sanders in the Democratic primary by 87,000 votes and almost won a majority. He then won the runoff by 161,000 votes, and trounced Republican Hal Suit in the general election.

Carter as Governor

Carter's four-year term began dramatically. For those voters who had considered him conservative, or possibly even racist, his inaugural address included a shocking statement: "I say to you quite frankly, the time for racial discrimination is over. Our people have made this major and difficult decision, but we cannot underestimate the challenge of hundreds of minor decisions yet to be made. No poor, rural, weak or black person should ever have to bear the burden of being deprived of the opportunity of an education, a job or simple justice."

The statement brought Carter national publicity, as did his later gesture of hanging portraits of Dr. Martin Luther King Jr. and other black leaders in the state capitol. During his term, Carter increased the number of black appointees on state boards and agencies from three to 53, and raised the total of state black employees from 4,850 to 6,684.

His greatest accomplishment as governor, in Carter's opinion, was to reorganize the state government. His first legislative proposal was for authority to order structural changes while giving the legislature power to veto his orders. He then formed a reorganization team of about 120 business and government executives. Their plan, which Carter eventually pushed through the legislature, abolished about 300 state offices, boards and commissions and consolidated their functions into 22 new agencies, each with unified budget, personnel, planning and accounting offices. Many other states reorganized in recent years, but Georgia's plan was one of the most ambitious.

In his presidential campaign Carter boasted about Georgia's improved efficiency and reduced administrative costs. Many state services were improved, but even state auditors had trouble pinpointing the savings. Carter did not claim that he made the government smaller. According to *The New York Times*, during Carter's term the number of state employees rose from 34,322 to 42,400, and the state budget increased 58.5 per cent from $1.06-billion to $1.68-billion, although much of the budget increase was due to inflation. The growth rates of both the budget and state employment were slower under Carter than under his predecessor, Gov. Lester G. Maddox.

Carter worked hard with a reluctant legislature to accomplish reorganization. He met frequently with opponents of the plan—often at breakfast or lunch in his office—and used jokes, sermons, persuasion and threats to win them over. Although he was stubborn he also compromised by avoiding the wholesale job cuts his planners had advocated.

Sunshine

Other features of Carter's term included passage of a "sunshine law" to open government meetings to the public, and reform of Georgia's outdated prison system. Carter also added thousands of acres of wilderness land for Georgia's parks. He either proposed or supported successful legislation to accomplish the following:

● Reinstate the death penalty in Georgia.

● Strengthen sentences for hard drug violations and reduce possession of less than an ounce of marijuana to a misdemeanor.

● Require candidates for state office to list all campaign contributions and expenditures in excess of $101.

● Limit pollution from automobile exhausts.

● Allow a woman and her doctor to make decisions on abortion during the first six months of pregnancy but require agreement from two more physicians for later abortions.

● Extend the use of electronic surveillance equipment by law enforcement officials.

● Provide special services for handicapped children and the retarded.

● Establish a state agency to issue revenue bonds to provide home mortgages to persons otherwise unable to obtain mortgages.

● Provide a statewide remedial reading program.

● Require judges to retire at age 70.

● Increase state taxes on cigarettes and gasoline.

● Require zero-based budgeting to force all state agencies to justify their total program annually.

● Establish community care centers for alcoholics and drug users.

● Permit a $10,000 homestead exemption from school taxes for elderly citizens making less than $6,000 a year.

Carter vetoed legislation to give local governments the option to levy a one per cent sales tax, and vetoed a bill to provide $50-million in property tax relief by allocating certain state funds to counties.

As governor, Carter increased the number of community centers for the mentally ill and retarded from 21 to 136. He created a nominating commission to screen candidates for judicial appointments and he was praised for selecting outstanding judges. He protected some of Georgia's wild rivers and established a trust program to save environmental, historical and scenic areas.

In most of his dealings with the legislature, especially the state senate, Carter was opposed by Lt. Gov. Lester Maddox. Segregationist Maddox never forgave Carter for his inaugural attack on racial discrimination, and the two men remain bitter enemies.

When he ran into strong opposition at the state capitol, Carter frequently went over the heads of the legislators with direct appeals to the public.

Writing in *The New York Times* in May 1976, James T. Wooten said that Carter as governor exhibited "a quick mind, eclectic intellectuality, enormous physical stamina, unabashed patriotism, a zealous instinct for reform, deep religious convictions and unflappable confidence in himself and his abilities." On the other hand, Wooten wrote, Gov. Carter also revealed "an unyielding stubbornness, a humorless and sometimes acerbic impatience with those less single-minded, a mastery of the use of people and institutions for his own purposes, and the willingness of an average politician to exaggerate on occasion."

The Vice President: A Consistent Liberal

The Senate record of Walter Frederick Mondale, Jimmy Carter's Vice President was one of orthodox liberalism and faith in government activism.

Mondale, 48, entered the Senate at the end of 1964 proclaiming that he was a liberal and "proud to join the Johnson-Humphrey team" that had been swept in that year, creating the opening that made possible his appointment to the Senate.

Mondale focused his attention as a legislator almost entirely on domestic issues, especially social welfare and consumer matters. Except to oppose military spending and foreign-aid programs that could drain money from domestic needs, he left foreign policy matters to his colleagues.

Mondale's major, though unsuccessful, legislative offering in the 94th Congress was a comprehensive child care bill that would have provided federal money for health care, nutritional aid, education and social services.

Mondale was regarded as one of the Senate's foremost civil rights advocates. He was the moving force behind passage of landmark open housing legislation in 1968. And he was a firm supporter of the use of busing to help speed school desegregation.

Political Career

Mondale's father, a Methodist minister, was the grandson of an emigrant from the Norwegian village of Mundal, from which the family took its name. Walter was born Jan. 5, 1928, in Ceylon, Minn., just north of the Iowa line. He lived in the area most of his childhood, attending schools first in Heron Lake and then Elmore as his father traveled from one Minnesota pastorate to another. Mondale said his upbringing by a liberal clergyman father and a socially activist mother steered him early to his interest in the underprivileged.

Mondale finished high school in Elmore in 1946 and then started college at Macalester College in St. Paul. He stayed there for two years, took a year off and then transferred to the University of Minnesota. He graduated *cum laude* in 1951 with a B.A. in political science.

After two years as an enlisted man in the Army, he returned to the University of Minnesota Law School. While there, he was on the Law Review and was a clerk to a Minnesota Supreme Court judge.

He was graduated in 1956 and joined the Minneapolis law firm whose alumni included former Democratic Minnesota Gov. and U.S. Secretary of Agriculture Orville Freeman, U.S. Rep. Donald M. Fraser (D Minn.) and former Federal Communications Commissioner Lee Loevinger. Mondale remained with the firm until 1960.

The only two elective offices Mondale held prior to his election as Vice President—Minnesota attorney general and U.S. senator—he acquired initially by appointment. But he never lost a political race, and he twice won easy re-election to each of his two elective posts.

His career also benefited from his long-standing friendship with Minnesota's junior but better-known senator,

Hubert H. Humphrey. The relationship went back to 1948, when Mondale, then a college student, managed Humphrey's successful Senate campaign in the state's 2nd Congressional District. Humphrey won the normally Republican district by 6,000 votes.

Mondale had been involved in liberal politics since the start of his career. In 1947 he invited Henry Wallace, the Progressive Party candidate for President in 1948, to speak at Macalester. Mondale's preference for President in 1948 was former Supreme Court Justice William O. Douglas.

To help finance his education, Mondale worked summers with migrant laborers in Minnesota fields and canneries, and one summer he helped organize the workers in an unsuccessful bid for better wages. He dropped out of college for a year in 1949 to work in Washington, D.C., for the now defunct Students for a Democratic America, the youth wing of Americans for Democratic Action.

While practicing law in Minneapolis, Mondale was active in the Democratic-Farmer-Labor (DFL) Party, working in a number of campaigns, including those of Orville Freeman and Eugene J. McCarthy. In 1958 he managed Freeman's successful gubernatorial re-election campaign.

In 1960 Freeman appointed Mondale, four years out of law school, to fill a vacancy as state attorney general. When the term expired a few months later, Mondale won election to the post with 58 per cent of the vote, and he was re-elected in 1962 with 59.6 per cent. As attorney general, Mondale established a reputation for consumer advocacy, and in 1961 the Minnesota Junior Chamber of Commerce named him "Outstanding Young Man of the Year."

Rise to National Prominence

In 1964 Gov. Karl Rolvaag appointed Mondale to the Credentials Committee of the Democratic National Committee. Mondale won national recognition as chairman of a subcommittee that, in settling a Mississippi delegate-selection dispute, set an unprecedented party requirement that future delegates be selected without regard to race, creed or color.

Humphrey's election as Vice President that year left Minnesota with a vacant Senate seat. Both Rolvaag and Sen. McCarthy were said to have their own preferences for the replacement, but Humphrey supported Mondale, and Rolvaag appointed him to the vacancy in December 1964.

In 1966, Mondale's opponent was Robert A. Forsythe, a former state Republican chairman who resigned from the Veterans' Administration to run. Forsythe contrasted his eight years of political and governmental experience in Washington to Mondale's two years in the Senate and attacked the Democratic administration for what he said were ineffective anti-inflation policies. Mondale, tied up in Washington by a lengthy Senate session, spent little time in the state until late in the campaign. Nevertheless, he won re-election with a comfortable 53.9 per cent plurality.

His 1972 opponent was Philip Hansen, a Lutheran minister and director of the alcoholism rehabilitation unit in a Minneapolis hospital. Hansen, a political newcomer, sought to tie Mondale to the controversial presidential candidacy of Sen. George McGovern (D S.D.), calling the two Democrats "the M&M boys, the radical twins." He also criticized Mondale for his opposition to the Vietnam War.

Mondale defeated the Republican handily with 56.7 per cent of the vote.

With Sen. Fred Harris (D Okla. 1964-73), Mondale was cochairman of Humphrey's 1968 presidential campaign. Four years later he was one of several Democrats who declined offers from George McGovern to replace Sen. Thomas F. Eagleton (D Mo.) as the party's vice presidential candidate.

Widely mentioned as a presidential prospect, Mondale spent much of 1974 traveling the country and speaking to Democratic groups, exploring his chances for a 1976 bid. In November 1974 he abandoned the run, saying, "I don't think anyone should be President who is not willing to go through fire."

Mondale's Senate Record

Youth and Aging

Mondale devoted much of his legislative energy to problems of the family, particularly children. He chaired the Senate Subcommittee on Children and Youth, which in 1973 and 1974 held hearings on "American Family: Trends and Pressures."

In 1974 he introduced legislation providing for a "family impact statement" that "would require the government to make a study of everything it does in light of what it does to families."

Mondale's most ambitious program for the young was his child-care section of the 1971 Economic Opportunity Act (S 2007), which President Nixon vetoed. The bill would have provided money for health care, nutritional aid, educational assistance and social services for the young.

Mondale introduced a similar measure in the 94th Congress. Although the bill (S 626) provided for extensive parent participation, critics contended that it would inject the federal government in the child-rearing process. Because of that heavy opposition and a considerable price tag, the bill languished in 1975 and 1976 without action.

Mondale was at the forefront of another child-care fight in 1976, to enforce strict staffing requirements for existing day-care centers. President Ford, arguing that staffing requirements should be left to states, in April vetoed legislation sponsored by Mondale that would have clearly imposed such standards. Attempting a compromise, Mondale rewrote the bill, delaying the standards but increasing funds for centers. Ford signed the compromise bill Sept. 7 (HR 12455—PL 94-401).

Welfare Reform

In 1974, Mondale was acclaimed for his role in forging an agreement among federal, state and local officials and welfare groups to win passage of a new social services program for welfare recipients and low-income families. Before that, the three governmental levels had been fighting over control and breadth of the programs, and welfare groups had been discontented with the level of services.

In 1973 Mondale sponsored a bill to provide $85-million over four years for the prevention and treatment of child abuse and neglected children. The bill was opposed by the administration, but, after some compromise, was passed and signed into law (S 1191—PL 93-247).

Mondale's Background

Profession: Lawyer.
Born: Jan. 5, 1928, Ceylon, Minn.
Home: Afton, Minn.
Religion: Presbyterian.
Education: Macalester College, St. Paul, Minn.; University of Minnesota, B.A. *cum laude*, 1951; University of Minnesota, LL.B., 1956.
Offices: Minnesota attorney general, 1960-64; Senate since Dec. 30, 1964.
Military: Army, 1951-53; discharged as corporal.
Memberships: Hennepin County, Minnesota and American Bar Associations; Moose; United Nations Association; American Veterans Association; American Legion; Sons of Norway; Eagles.
Family: Married Joan Adams, 1955; three children: Theodore Adams, Eleanor Jane, William Hall.
Senate Committees: Budget; Finance: chairman, Social Security Financing Subcommittee; Labor and Public Welfare: chairman, Children and Youth Subcommittee; Special Committee on Aging; Select Committee on Nutrition and Human Needs; Select Committee on Small Business.

Also in 1973, Mondale introduced a crib-death bill, subsequently passed and signed by the President (S 1745—PL 93-270), that provided funds for research into the sudden infant-death syndrome. In 1974, he sponsored legislation to increase financing of child-nutrition programs under the National School Lunch and Child Nutrition Acts.

Social Legislation

As chairman of the Labor and Public Welfare Subcommittee on Migratory Labor, Mondale in 1969 held widely publicized hearings into the plight of migrant workers in the hope that the publicity would prompt legislative relief. Over the years, he introduced or worked for legislation to provide migrant workers with unemployment benefits and legal services.

In 1965 Mondale was a cosponsor of the Johnson administration's Medicare bill, and he voted for the Appalachian Assistance Act (the first "Great Society" bill). He voted against efforts to remove the rent subsidies section of the HUD bill and to cut antipoverty funds.

In subsequent Johnson administration years he supported rent supplements, the school lunch program, the Economic Opportunity Act of 1966 amendments (earmarking funds for special programs) and the model cities program.

In 1967 Mondale introduced the Full Opportunity and Social Accounting Act, a bill to create a Council of Social Advisers modeled on the President's Council of Economic Advisers. The bill (S 3) passed the Senate in 1970 but died in the House.

Mondale also was an important figure in passage of legal services legislation. In 1969 he led successful opposition against an effort to give the governor of each state veto power over the Office of Economic Opportunity's legal services program. In 1974, after a three-year battle with conservatives, he and Sen. Jacob K. Javits (R N.Y.) won passage of their bill (HR 7824—PL 93-355) to establish an independent Legal Services Corporation in place of the more constrained OEO program.

In 1968 Mondale, then a member of the Senate Banking, Housing and Urban Affairs Committee, played a major role in passage of the comprehensive Housing and Urban Development Act (S 3497—PL 90-488). The bill that finally passed after a two-year effort embodied parts of several measures introduced by Mondale and other senators.

Civil Rights

Mondale was known for his liberal positions on civil rights. Observers cited as his greatest accomplishment his role in passage of the open-housing provisions of the Civil Rights Act of 1968 (HR 2516—PL 90-284).

In the midst of urban rioting that year after the killing of Martin Luther King Jr., Mondale argued on the Senate floor that such legislation was necessary to calm the black community. "We are fighting for the minds and hearts of the vast middle ground of responsible Negroes who have persevered in their commitment to progress through the courts and through the legislative process," he said in introducing an amendment to a civil rights bill that, without it, could expect safe passage. The Senate passed the open housing measure, the first in a century, after accepting a compromise that Mondale called "a miracle."

School Desegregation

In 1970 Mondale provoked even more controversy for his firm stand in favor of school desegregation, a stand that led a reporter on NBC's "Meet the Press" to refer to Mondale as "Mr. Busing."

Mondale stepped into the controversy in 1970 when he assumed chairmanship of the Senate Select Committee on Equal Educational Opportunity, a committee organized to make a thorough study of the school desegregation issue. In 1972, at the conclusion of the committee's study, Mondale urged the Senate to avoid "standing in the schoolhouse door" in its consideration of upcoming anti-busing legislation.

"Busing is the means—and at times the only means—by which segregation in public education can be reduced," he said. The Senate rejected a Mondale amendment to apply desegregation requirements uniformly across the country, but accepted anti-busing language weaker than that urged by conservatives and adopted by the House.

The next year, Mondale's committee issued its report, reaffirming the benefits of integrated education and urging a shift from "the misleading issues of busing and racial balance" to "quality integrated education."

He voted for the 1972 moderate anti-busing bill (S 659—PL 92-318) and for a similar bill (HR 69—PL 93-380) in 1974 opposing busing but leaving the decision to the courts. In 1971 he voted for an unsuccessful effort to have civil rights laws applied to *de facto* as well as *de jure* segregation, but in 1970 he voted against a similar effort, proposed by Sen. John C. Stennis (D Miss.). He said the Stennis amendment was a "hoax" designed to slow desegregation in the South.

Consumer Affairs

As a member of the traditionally conservative Agriculture Committee in his early Senate years, Mondale used his position to spotlight inspection practices in the meat and poultry industries. Partially as a result of his efforts, Congress passed the Wholesome Meat Act of 1967 (HR 12144—PL 90-201), which tightened federal regulation of state inspection standards.

Also during the 1960s, Mondale worked for passage of the Truth-in-Lending (S 5—PL 90-321) and Truth-in-Packaging Acts (S 985—PL 89-755). And although he was not a member of the Commerce or Public Works Committees, which are responsible for much consumer legislation, Mondale played a role in passage of auto-safety requirements. In 1966, the Senate accepted a Mondale amendment to the Highway Safety Act (S 3052—PL 89-564) requiring the government to study the effects of alcohol consumption on highway safety.

That year Congress approved a bill (S 3005—PL 89-563) with a Mondale provision requiring auto manufacturers to give notice of defects to owners and potential buyers. At Mondale's insistence, the Department of Transportation released a pamphlet listing defects as supplied to it by the manufacturers.

In 1968 Mondale teamed with consumer advocate Ralph Nader in assailing manufacturers for squeezing a profit from federally required safety devices. Although the Senate took no action on the charges, Mondale was successful in forcing the Bureau of Labor Statistics to release previously secret figures showing that manufacturers of 1968 and 1969 cars had raised prices an average of $180 for safety costs of $73.65.

Energy and Environment

Mondale's most controversial action in the environmental area was his attempt in 1973 to delay construction for at least a year of the trans-Alaska oil pipeline. An amendment offered by Mondale would have authorized study of an alternate route across Canada, with Congress then choosing one route after negotiations with Canada and an eight-month comparative study of the two routes by the National Academy of Sciences. Supporters, including environmentalists seeking delay of any pipeline, argued that the Canadian route would bring oil to the Midwest, where they said it was most needed. The amendment was defeated.

During the height of the 1973-74 oil crisis, Mondale offered an amendment to the emergency energy bill (S 2589) that would have limited price increases for crude oil and oil products to the cost of production. Criticizing the administration's plan of rationing oil through higher prices, Mondale said his amendment was necessary to keep prices within reasonable bounds. The amendment was defeated.

In 1974, in a move he said was designed to prevent large oil companies from expanding at the expense of independents, Mondale introduced a bill (S 3443) prohibiting any of the nation's 15 largest oil companies from acquiring refineries, pipelines or retail outlets they did not own before July 1, 1974.

The Economy

Mondale regularly called for reallocation of space and military funds to what he considered more pressing domestic needs. He was a persistent critic of NASA spending, arguing that unmanned flights could serve the same purposes as more expensive manned ones.

Mondale led unsuccessful opposition to authorization for and funding of the Skylab and space shuttle programs from 1970 to 1973. He also opposed funding the SST (a

Mondale's Ratings by Special-Interest Groups

Following are Mondale's annual ratings by special-interest groups during his first 11 years in the Senate:

	1965	1966	1967	1968	1969	1970	1971	1972	1973	1974	1975
ADA[1]	94	95	92	86	94	97	100	95	95	90	94
ACA	0	4	0	0	7	5	9	0	4	0	4
COPE[2]	100[3]	100[3]	100	100	100	100	83	90	90	82	95
NFU[2]	100	93	90	90	94	100	100	100	100	100	100

1. *Failure to vote lowers score.*
2. *Percentages compiled by CQ from information provided by groups.*
3. *Scores compiled for entire Congress (1965-66).*

Americans for Democratic Action (ADA)—ADA ratings are based on the number of times a senator voted, was paired or announced for the ADA position on selected issues.

Americans for Constitutional Action (ACA)—ACA ratings record the percentage of the time a senator voted in accordance with the ACA position.

AFL-CIO Committee on Political Education (COPE)—COPE ratings reflect the percentage of the time a senator voted in accordance with or was paired in favor of the COPE position.

National Farmers Union (NFU)—NFU ratings are based on the number of times a senator voted, was paired for or announced for the NFU position.

---

stand deeply resented by Minnesota's extensive scientific and engineering community) and participated in an unsuccessful battle in 1971 against guaranteeing loans to the Lockheed Aircraft Corp.

Mondale was the only Democratic senator who was a member of both the Finance and Budget Committees. His experience in economic issues was a factor cited by Carter as one of his qualifications for the vice presidency.

As a member of the Finance Committee, Mondale was a member in 1976 of a coalition of 15 senators trying to insert a package of amendments to the tax bill (HR 10612) written by the committee under the control of Chairman Russell B. Long (D La.).

While not the leader of the coalition, Mondale was the chief advocate, during Senate debate, of efforts to tighten the committee's recommendations in the area of minimum and maximum income taxes paid by the wealthy.

His proposals to tighten the minimum tax were defeated, but Mondale succeeded in killing a Finance Committee proposal that would have weakened the maximum tax law by making it applicable to investment income as well as "earned" income, such as wages and fees.

Although most of the other "reform" amendments proposed by the coalition were shot down by the Senate, Mondale withheld the bitter criticism of the bill that was voiced by some of his colleagues.

As a member of the Budget Committee, Mondale has pushed for higher spending levels for domestic programs—education, employment and social services—and supported cuts in defense spending.

Defense and Foreign Affairs

Generally, Mondale's foreign policy views were in line with Carter's. He espoused a new morality for America abroad, criticizing particularly this country's role as a major arms supplier to foreign countries. He favored detente with the Soviet Union, but with a call for greater Soviet responsibility in meeting the food and fuel needs of the developing nations. And he called for wider participation in the foreign policy-making process, criticizing the secretive and highly personal style of Secretary of State Henry A. Kissinger.

Mondale was a member of the Senate Select Intelligence Committee. He headed the panel's Subcommittee on Domestic Intelligence, and he emerged from the investigation urging tight checks on the activities—foreign and domestic—of the intelligence agencies.

Mondale came to the Senate supporting the American presence in Vietnam, at one time making the same arguments for "pacification" later made by the Nixon administration. But by 1968, after a visit to Vietnam, Mondale had reversed his position and was urging presidential candidate Humphrey, then tied to the Johnson administration war policy, to do likewise. "The worst mistake of my entire career was to remain silent so long against the war," Mondale told *The Wall Street Journal* in 1972. "Some people in Minnesota still haven't forgiven me, and I can't say I blame them."

After 1968 he supported all Senate efforts to limit fighting or military expenditures in Southeast Asia. In addition, in 1971 and 1973 he voted for two unsuccessful efforts to reduce U.S. troop levels in Europe and elsewhere overseas. In 1973 he offered his own bill to cut off funds for military activity in Cambodia. Also that year he proposed two successful amendments dealing with arms control—one providing for an international conference on arms control, the other prohibiting most sales of sophisticated defense weapons systems to underdeveloped countries.

An early proponent of increased trade between Communist and western nations, Mondale has urged that the U.S.S.R. assume greater responsibility for easing world economic burdens created by food and oil shortages. Noting the Soviets' growing reliance on industrial countries for its internal development, Mondale suggested in an October 1974 *Foreign Affairs* article that pressure should be applied to encourage such responsibility.

Young Georgians and Mondale Near Hub

Even before his inauguration, Carter revealed his preference for a decentralized White House staff arrangement.

This was a sharp departure from the practices of Ford and Nixon, who installed strong chiefs to head up their White House staffs. Carter said he would do away with a formally designated chief of staff, and instead rely strongly on his cabinet officers and on Vice President Mondale for advice and ideas.

But in other ways, Carter followed closely the precedents set by other Presidents in assembling their closest advisers. Like them, he chose to build his staff around a group of familiar faces, in this case, a cadre of bright, young Georgians, many of whom have been with him since his days as Georgia's governor.

An 'Unprecedented' Vice Presidency

One clear direction that Carter promised to follow was in the way he planned to use his Vice President, Walter F. Mondale, 48-year-old former senator from Minnesota. Carter had emphasized this intention from the outset.

At a news conference two days after the election, the President-elect said of Mondale: "I expect him to play a larger role in the next administration than any previous Vice President has ever played."

Carter made similar references repeatedly at subsequent news conferences, emphasizing his trust of Mondale and his personal closeness to him. Mondale's role, said Carter Dec. 23, will be "unprecedented in American history for a Vice President. I look on [him] as my top staff person."

Carter went on to say that Mondale would occupy an office in the White House. This would be a break with precedent; Vice Presidents usually have an office in the Executive Office Building next door.

Furthermore, Carter continued, Mondale will be privy to the same briefings and messages the new President himself will see, and he will represent Carter on some trips abroad. "I think the extent to which he will be actively identified as being very close to me and involved in the decision-making process will make his functions within our own country and abroad much more effective," Carter said.

He went even further Dec. 28 in a statement to his appointees to Cabinet posts and other key jobs. The group was holding planning sessions at a plantation on St. Simons Island, Ga.

Although Carter and his spokesmen had stressed earlier that he would have no chief of staff as such, he told his appointees that Mondale would serve as his "chief of staff person" and would have "unprecedented" authority. The President-elect said that he had informed his aides that Mondale "is their boss," who, "along with the other people who'll speak for me will be very careful to do just that, and will try to meld as much as possible his staff and my staff."

Mondale himself had some observations about his expanded role. In comments taped with Carter Dec. 27 for the ABC-TV "Good Morning America" program, he described his role in the transition as "historic" and added: "I've been through all the crucial decision-making processes establishing this government."

Comparing his pre-inauguration duties with the lesser ones of his fellow Minnesota Democrat, Sen. Hubert H. Humphrey, when Humphrey was Lyndon B. Johnson's Vice President, Mondale said, "The history of this office is nothing short of grim." But, he predicted, his function in the Carter administration will "break a lot of historic precedents.... We're working on suggested tasks for me in government that I think will be unique and to be announced later."

The Carter Approach

Throughout the transition period between the Ford and Carter administrations, Carter never left any doubt about who would be in complete charge of the White House. He will.

At the same time, he planned to rely heavily on his Cabinet officers. "I would never permit my White House staff to try to run the major departments of government," he said at his Nov. 4 news conference. He would, he said, choose Cabinet officers "who are completely competent to run their own departments.... The White House staff would be serving in a staff capacity only—not in an administrative capacity.

After he had clinched the Democratic nomination, Carter emphasized the procedures he would follow in choosing a running mate. He interviewed a half dozen persons, publicizing all their visits to Plains, Ga., but withholding the announcement of his decision until the nominating convention in July.

At a news conference Nov. 15, he said that he would follow the same system in selecting his Cabinet and top-level advisers. The process, he said, would be "careful and thorough and deliberate."

And so it appeared to be, for the most part, although Carter was subjected to pressures from several interest groups before making his final decisions. When he arrived at those decisions, the adjective he used most often to describe his choices was "superb." He worked closely with Mondale in selecting his Cabinet and several other key leaders. The first appointments were announced Dec. 3; the last, Dec. 23.

"I've been through all the crucial decision-making processes establishing this government."

—Walter F. Mondale

The Staff Jobs

Carter was slower in filling White House staff positions than in naming a Cabinet. His closest personal adviser, Charles Kirbo, a 59-year-old Atlanta lawyer, gave some insight into this during an interview with *U.S. News & World Report.* "I think he's going to depend more on his Cabinet than he is on his staff," said Kirbo. "I think he's going to appoint what he thinks are good men to the Cabinet and rely on them to get control of their agencies.

"He's going to give them a lot of rope. If they can't perform, he's going to change them."

That was the way Carter operated when he was governor of Georgia from 1971 to 1975. Some of his closest advisers then are his closest advisers now, and they were among the ones he brought into the White House.

By year's end, the only staff appointment Carter had announced was that of his White House press secretary, Jody Powell, 33. Powell, Carter's press secretary as governor and close associate since early in Carter's political career, was appointed Nov. 15. He immediately named several assistants.

January Appointments

Six days before the inauguration, Carter's other top White House aides were announced. As expected, most of them were young Georgians.

In announcing the staff appointments Jan. 14, press secretary Powell emphasized the open, informal nature of the new White House. "The idea is to insure free access to the President, to make sure that no one or two people will be able to cut him off from dissenting opinions," said Powell, whose own appointment was announced shortly after Carter's election.

In accordance with his earlier promise, Carter did not name a chief of staff to oversee the work of other aides. Powell said that each of the top aides would have equal access to the President.

There were no surprises in the list. All of the appointees had worked for Carter and most had played major roles in the transition between administrations.

Of the seven highest-level aides, only one, presidential assistant Margaret Costanza, was not a Georgian. None belonged to a minority group and only Costanza is a woman. Among the five second-level aides named were Martha M. Mitchell, who is black, and Joseph W. Aragon, who is an Hispanic-American.

Top Aides

Following are the seven chief assistants to Carter:

Robert J. Lipshutz, 55, counsel to the President. Lipshutz is an Atlanta attorney who has been close to Carter for 10 years. Oldest of the key staffers, he became associated with Carter during his unsuccessful 1966 campaign for the Georgia governorship. Lipshutz was treasurer to the Carter presidential campaign, which had its first headquarters in the offices of Lipshutz's law firm.

Hamilton Jordan, 32, assistant to the President. Jordan, who was director of the 1976 campaign, has been Carter's closest aide since 1970. Almost all of Jordan's adult life has been spent working for Carter, and his dedication to the man is total. "My commitment to politics," he has said, "is a commitment to Jimmy Carter."

Margaret Costanza, 44, assistant to the President in charge of contact with special interest groups. Costanza was one of Carter's earliest supporters in New York, when she was Rochester's vice mayor. She seconded Carter's nomination at the Democratic convention.

Jack J. Watson Jr., 38, assistant to the President for intergovernmental relations, and Cabinet secretary. Watson helped guide Carter's reorganization plan for the Georgia state government through the legislature when Carter was governor. He was in charge of planning and implementing policy for the presidential transition period.

Stuart E. Eizenstat, 34, assistant to the President for domestic affairs. Eizenstat is the only top-level aide with prior White House experience. He worked as a speechwriter in the last years of the Johnson administration, and was research director of Hubert H. Humphrey's 1968 presidential campaign. He was issues director in the 1976 Carter campaign, a position he also held in the earlier campaigns of Rep. Andrew Young (D Ga.) and Atlanta Mayor Maynard Jackson.

Frank Moore, 41, assistant to the President for congressional liaison. Moore is another veteran of Carter's gubernatorial administration, having worked as Carter's liaison with the state legislature, and later as his executive secretary. Appointed head of congressional liaison for the Carter campaign in February 1976, Moore was criticized for not being responsive enough to congressional Democrats. In a subsequent interview with Congressional Quarterly, Moore attributed the problems to the lack of a ready-to-go organization. He said the problems since have been eliminated. *(Moore's staff, p. 17)*

Jody Powell, 33, press secretary. Born not far from Carter's home of Plains, Ga., Powell is a young man whose career has been based almost entirely on his personal relationship with Carter. He has worked for Carter since the 1970 gubernatorial campaign. Powell's responsibilities include supervision of speech writing and presidential travel.

Special Assistants

Immediately below the top seven in the White House hierarchy are five special assistants to the President:

Tim Kraft, 35, special assistant for appointments. An experienced political operative, Kraft supervised Carter's crucial victories in the Iowa precinct caucuses and the Pennsylvania primary. He was director of field operations for the general election campaign. Kraft's White House position was originally intended for Greg Schneiders, who was disqualified because of his past financial difficulties.

Hamilton Jordan   **Jody Powell**

Two of Carter's Principal Staff Members

James E. King, 41, special assistant for personnel. A former official with the Massachusetts Bay Transportation Authority, King was in charge of transportation arrangements for the Carter campaign.

Dr. Peter Bourne, 37, special assistant for drug abuse prevention and mental health. Bourne, a psychiatrist who was health affairs adviser to Gov. Carter, was a member of the small group that first urged Carter to run for President.

Joseph W. Aragon, 35, White House ombudsman. Aragon, former director of Spanish-speaking affairs for the Democratic National Committee, handles citizen problems. His appointment followed criticism from Hispanic-American organizations that their people were being ignored for appointments to the new administration.

Martha Mallard Mitchell, 36, special assistant for special projects. Mitchell was director of information for the Drug Abuse Council.

Jordan's Role

Although Powell spoke of the equality of the top aides, it appeared that some would be more "equal" than others. Chief among these was Jordan, who was expected to continue the role of chief administrative assistant to Carter, which he had held since 1970. He would also have the responsibility of mobilizing political support for the President's policies.

Lipshutz would be, according to Powell, the "elder statesman" of the group. He was expected to chair the daily staff meetings in addition to being the chief White House lawyer.

As Cabinet secretary, Watson would be charged with ensuring that presidential policy was being properly implemented. As assistant for intergovernmental relations be would serve as liaison with state and local officials. While transition director, Watson became involved in an internal dispute with Jordan that could have weakened his influence in the new administration. Watson's transition plans allegedly slighted Jordan, who reacted strongly against the proposed diminution of his authority. When the dust settled Jordan's position as first among equals was confirmed, while Watson apparently lost influence.

Mondale Staff

Top staff aides to Vice President Mondale were announced Jan. 16. They are:

Richard Moe, 40, Mondale's Senate administrative assistant, chief of staff.

Michael S. Berman, 37, former Mondale administrative assistant, deputy chief of staff and counsel to the Vice President.

James Johnson, 32, deputy director of the vice presidential campaign, executive assistant.

Albert Eisele, 40, journalist, press secretary.

Gail Harrison, 29, of Mondale's Senate staff, assistant for issues development.

William Smith, former Mondale administrative assistant, congressional liaison.

Peter Kyros, 28, of the vice presidential campaign, deputy counsel.

Maxine Burns, 29, of Mondale's Senate staff, deputy press secretary.

Congressional Liaison Team

(as of March, 1977)

DIRECTOR

Frank G. Moore, 41, of Dahlonega, Ga. Bachelor's degree, University of Georgia. Public relations and sales jobs from 1959 to 1965, when he became a program developer in Gainesville for the Georgia Mountain Planning and Development Commission. In 1967, became executive director of the Middle Flint Planning and Development Commission in Ellaville, Ga. Special assistant to Gov. Carter for city and state reorganization, 1972. Governor's liaison with state legislature, 1972-73. Executive secretary to Carter, 1973-75. Carter campaign finance chairman and cochairman, 1975-February 1976. Southern states coordinator for Carter-Mondale campaign. Congressional liaison director for Carter during campaign and post-election transition.

SENATE

Dan Tate, 32, of Atlanta. Bachelor's degree, Emory University; law degree, University of Georgia. Legislative assistant to Sen. Herman E. Talmadge (D Ga.) for seven years.

HOUSE

Frederick T. Merrill Jr., 38, of Washington, D.C. Bachelor's degree, Cornell University; graduate studies, American University. Worked in international political youth organizations. New England coordinator for Eugene J. McCarthy at 1968 Democratic convention, then worked for Humphrey and Muskie at the Democratic National Committee. Legislative coordinator for the House Democratic Study Group, 1969-June 1976. Worked on Carter-Mondale campaign in Atlanta.

Valerie Pinson, 46, of Newburgh, N.Y. Bachelor's degree, Howard University. First Washington job at the Pentagon in 1952. On staff of former Sen. Thomas J. Dodd (D Conn. 1959-71) for four years. Worked on equal employment opportunities in the Johnson White House for one year. Various jobs, including congressional liaison, with the former Office of Economic Opportunity for six years. Administrative assistant to Rep. Yvonne Brathwaite Burke (D Calif.) for two years. Lobbyist for the National Association of Counties from June 1974 to December 1976, when she joined the Carter-Mondale transition staff.

James C. Free, 30, of Columbia, Tenn. Bachelor's degree, Middle Tennessee State University; master's in public administration, University of Tennessee. Administrative jobs in higher education for three years. Chief clerk of the Tennessee house for four years. Campaign chairman for Carter in the 1976 Tennessee primary. Carter-Mondale coordinator in Alabama, Mississippi and Tennessee in the general election.

Controversy Over Some Carter Nominees

Keeping his promise to complete his Cabinet selections before the end of the year, President-elect Carter finished the job Dec. 23, 1976.

On Dec. 3, he announced his first two Cabinet-level appointments: Cyrus R. Vance as Secretary of State and Thomas B. (Bert) Lance as director of the Office of Management and Budget.

Carter made the announcement at a news conference in Plains, Ga. The appointments climaxed several days of meetings with economic advisers.

In response to a question about his Cabinet, Carter said he was seeking "good geographical distribution," "fairly good distribution" of persons familiar and unfamiliar with Washington, and "good representation of women and minority groups as well." Vance and Lance qualified in two of those categories, he noted.

Vance, 59, a native of West Virginia, was practicing law in New York City, where he was president of the bar association. His federal government service dated back to the Kennedy and Johnson administrations. He was general counsel to the Defense Department under President Kennedy and deputy secretary of defense under President Johnson. He had considerable experience as a negotiator, participating in the Vietnam and Cyprus negotiations.

Lance, 45, is a Georgia native, an Atlanta bank president and a long-time political supporter of Carter.

Two more Cabinet secretaries and three other high-ranking federal officials were appointed by President-elect Carter during the week ending Dec. 18. They were:

● Secretary of the Treasury: W. Michael Blumenthal, 50, board chairman and chief executive officer of the Bendix Corp.

● Secretary of Transportation: Rep. Brock Adams (D Wash.), 49, chairman of the House Budget Committee.

● National security adviser: Zbigniew Brzezinski, 48, a Columbia University professor and Carter's presidential campaign adviser on foreign affairs.

● Chairman of the Council of Economic Advisers: Charles Schultze, 52, a senior fellow at the Brookings Institution in Washington, D.C.

● Ambassador to the United Nations: Rep. Andrew Young (D Ga.), 44.

Carter named the two Cabinet secretaries at a news conference Dec. 14 in Atlanta. He announced the other two appointments at a news conference Dec. 16 in Plains, Ga.

His top-level appointments were not announced as quickly as some previous Presidents announced theirs. At his Dec. 14 news conference, he opened with a statement that he was going through "a very slow and detailed and thorough and deliberative process.... It's very important that I devote a major part of my time to these selections, because I intend to let them play a role in the federal government perhaps exceeding that that members of the Cabinet have played in recent years."

At the Dec. 16 news conference, Carter emphasized, as he had before, the "very tight and continuing partnership" between himself and Vice President-elect Walter F. Mondale, who was on the platform with him, in deciding on appointees. "I don't believe it's ever been done before," he said, "but I've counted on and will continue to depend upon the sound judgment and good help of Sen. Mondale...."

The President-elect finished announcing his selections to top-level posts at a series of news conferences Dec. 18-23. This was the sequence:

● Dec. 18, Carter appointed Cecil D. Andrus, 45, the Democratic governor of Idaho, as Secretary of the Interior.

Dec. 20, he announced three Cabinet appointments:

● Griffin B. Bell, 58, an Atlanta lawyer and a former federal judge, as Attorney General.

● Juanita M. Kreps, 55, an economics professor and vice president of Duke University, as Secretary of Commerce.

● Rep. Bob Bergland (D Minn.), 48, as Secretary of Agriculture.

Dec. 21 Carter announced three more:

● Harold Brown, 49, president of the California Institute of Technology and a former Air Force secretary, as Secretary of Defense.

● F. Ray Marshall, 48, a University of Texas economist, as Secretary of Labor.

● Patricia Roberts Harris, 52, a District of Columbia lawyer and former ambassador to Luxemburg, as Secretary of Housing and Urban Development (HUD).

At the Dec. 21 news conference, Carter also announced his choice of Charles W. Duncan Jr., a Houston investment banker and former Coca-Cola president, as deputy defense secretary.

Carter rounded out his Cabinet and announced two other appointments at a final pre-Christmas news conference Dec. 23. His Cabinet choice:

● Joseph A. Califano Jr., 45, a District of Columbia lawyer and former aide to President Johnson, as Secretary of Health, Education and Welfare (HEW).

The other two appointments: Theodore C. Sorensen, 48, a New York City lawyer and former assistant to Presi-

---

Carter's Cabinet

Agriculture—Bob Bergland
Commerce—Juanita M. Kreps
Defense—Harold Brown
Health, Education and Welfare—Joseph A. Califano Jr.
Housing and Urban Development—Patricia Roberts Harris
Interior—Cecil D. Andrus
Justice—Griffin B. Bell
Labor—F. Ray Marshall
State—Cyrus R. Vance
Transportation—Brock Adams
Treasury—W. Michael Blumenthal

dent Kennedy, as director of the Central Intelligence Agency (CIA); and James R. Schlesinger, 47, a former CIA director and Defense Secretary, as a presidential assistant in charge of coordinating energy policy.

Carter made it clear that he was, in effect, appointing Schlesinger to what he envisioned as an expanded Cabinet. He repeated, in response to questioning, his intention to establish, through statute, a new Energy Department.

Reaction to Nominations

Carter's Cabinet fulfilled his campaign promise to appoint blacks and women. But, even as he was trying to placate various elements of his constituency, he managed to make a good many people unhappy.

The brunt of the initial criticism was directed at his selection of Bell as Attorney General. For 15 years, starting in 1961, Bell was a judge on the Fifth U.S. Circuit Court of Appeals, based in New Orleans. Early in 1976 he joined the Atlanta law firm of Carter's closest adviser, Charles Kirbo.

While Carter predicted that his friend Bell—they used to hunt quail together in Georgia—would be a "great" Attorney General and praised his choice as "superlative," the appointment came under immediate attack from civil rights groups and black organizations. A wire to Carter from the National Association for the Advancement of Colored People said that Senate confirmation of Bell "would be keenly resented by those of us deeply involved in the civil rights movement."

Bell's membership in organizations that excluded blacks and Jews was publicized as soon as he was nominated. At first he said he would prefer to "resign temporarily or become inactive" in order not to lose the initiation fees. But he issued a statement Dec. 22 saying that he would resign the memberships because "the Attorney General is a symbol of equality before the law."

Feminist groups had expressed dissatisfaction over the shortage of women among Carter's first appointments. They were appeased by his choice of Kreps and Harris. And Harris also pleased another interest group: she is black.

However, Harris was criticized for her lack of housing experience by the National Association of Home Builders and the U.S. Conference of Mayors. "In order to meet the legitimate demands of blacks and women," said John Gunther, executive director of the conference, Carter "has displayed a striking insensitivity to the problems of the cities."

Organized labor had its disappointments, too. AFL-CIO President George Meany had wanted Carter to name John T. Dunlop, President Ford's former Labor Secretary, to his old job. And Meany preferred Schlesinger as Defense Secretary, the post from which he had been pushed out by Ford.

Dunlop was opposed by women's and civil rights groups. Schlesinger was opposed by liberals who thought he was too much of a hard-liner on defense.

Meany expressed satisfaction with the selection of Marshall as Labor Secretary. And Schlesinger would clearly be one of the major figures in the new administration.

CIA Nomination Withdrawn

Although there was some criticism of Carter's selections, the Senate approved all the above nominations except that of Theodore C. Sorensen to head the Central Intelligence Agency.

Bowing to strong opposition from conservatives and some liberals of both parties, Sorensen Jan. 17 asked President-elect Carter to withdraw his nomination to head the CIA. Sorensen's announcement was made to an astonished Senate Select Intelligence Committee at the start of his confirmation hearings.

Opponents of the nomination had argued that Sorensen was inexperienced in intelligence and that he had demonstrated a casual attitude toward the use of classified information while serving as special assistant to President John F. Kennedy.

Sorensen insisted that the real reason for the opposition was that he was an "outsider" to the intelligence community and had called for limitations on covert overseas operations and disclosure of more information about CIA operations and those of other agencies. But he told the intelligence panel that since a "substantial portion" of the Senate would not support the nomination, he had decided to withdraw from the fray.

"To continue fighting for this post," he said, "would only handicap the new administration if I am rejected, or handicap my effectiveness as Director [of Central Intelligence] if I am confirmed."

Background

From the first disclosure of Carter's choice for intelligence director, support for Sorensen, one of the first prominent New York State Democrats to support Carter's bid for the presidency, had been less than enthusiastic. And conservatives immediately mobilized a campaign against the nomination, concentrating on Sorensen's inexperience, his dovish foreign policy views and his request in 1948 for draft classification as a non-combatant. On Jan. 7, Senate Republican leader Howard H. Baker Jr. (Tenn.), an ex officio, nonvoting member of the Senate Intelligence Committee, contended there was "significant opposition" to the choice.

But by all accounts, the decisive blow to the nomination was the revelation of affadavits filed by Sorensen in the Nixon administration's 1971 court case against publication by *The New York Times* of the Pentagon Papers and in its 1973 case against Daniel Ellsberg, who released those documents. In both affadavits, Sorensen argued that on the basis of his White House experience, arbitrary and excessive classification of information on national security grounds, without consideration of the possible harm that might result, was commonplace within the executive branch.

Although he conceded in the affadavits that there were legitimate national security grounds for keeping some secrets, he insisted that the nation would not be harmed from publication of the Pentagon Papers and might, in fact, be damaged by their continued concealment.

In the statement submitted in the Ellsberg case, Sorensen admitted that while serving on the White House staff, he often had used classified documents, at the direction of President Kennedy, in giving background information to the press. He also noted that on his departure from the White House in 1964, he had taken with him 63 cartons of documents—seven of them "classified"—which were regarded at the time by himself and various federal agencies as his property. He admitted using this material in writing his book *Kennedy,* which was published in 1965.

Opposition Mounts

The affadavits reached members of the panel during the week before the scheduled Jan. 17 hearing on his nomination, and by Jan. 15 opposition in the committee to Sorensen was widely reported. Republican committee member Jake Garn (Utah), in announcing his opposition to Sorensen, said he was "very concerned about someone who would leak classified documents out of the White House," a theme echoed in other, sometimes anonymous, comments by committee members.

On Jan. 16 newly elected Republican National Committee Chairman Bill Brock called the nomination of Sorensen "a major Carter blunder," saying that Sorensen had demonstrated "a total lack of fitness for the job."

Carter the same day defended his nominee. He said the "attacks on Mr. Sorensen's judgment and loyalty are groundless and unfair." He said that Sorensen's handling of classified documents in the early 1960s had been "consistent with what I understand to have been common practice in both parties." But some Democratic senators, including Spark M. Matsunaga (Hawaii), joined conservative critics in calling for withdrawal of the nomination. Perhaps most ominous was the warning from newly elected Senate Majority Leader Robert C. Byrd (W.Va.) that the nomination was in "serious difficulty" and that he could not commit himself to vote for confirmation of Sorensen to head the CIA.

According to Sorensen, Carter assured him by telephone on the night of Jan. 16 that "I will fight with you to the last vote." But Sorensen also said he and Carter realized that "confirmation would come only over a divided Senate which, he and I agree, would handicap my effectiveness, and it might very well be rejected."

Surprise Announcement

In brief statements at the opening of the committee hearing Jan. 17 several members of the panel indicated their concern over the implications of the Ellsberg trial affadavit. They also insisted that the new intelligence director command the "confidence" of the U.S. intelligence community and of allied intelligence agencies.

Sorensen, giving no indication that he would withdraw, then defended himself against what he called "the scurrilous and unfounded personal attacks which have been circulated against me." He insisted that he had used classified information while in the White House only as directed by President Kennedy.

His 1-A0 draft classification, he pointed out, did not bar his assignment to a combat zone. And he insisted that he had never let his preference for personal non-violence inhibit his advice to President Kennedy on foreign and defense policy.

He charged that these attacks against his suitability for the position were a facade for opposition based on disagreement with his views on foreign policy and intelligence. "There are those inside and outside of the intelligence establishment...who see no value for this post in a lawyer's sensitivities to civil liberties and lawful conduct," he said. "These people believe that only someone from inside the military or intelligence establishment has the experience necessary for the job."

He then announced his request to Carter that the nomination be withdrawn.

Several members of the committee, including some who had announced their opposition to Sorensen's nomination, assured him of their confidence in his integrity. Committee Chairman Daniel K. Inouye (D Hawaii) announced that the committee had received from the FBI a "four-star rating" attesting to Sorensen's fitness for any position, no matter how sensitive. He lamented that the report could not be put into the committee's public record.

Turner Approved for CIA

On Feb. 7, Carter announced his nomination of Adm. Stansfield Turner, then commander of NATO's southern forces, to the CIA directorship. No significant opposition to the nomination arose during confirmation hearings by the Senate Intelligence Committee Feb. 22, and he was unanimously approved 17-0 by the panel Feb. 23.

Turner assured the committee Feb. 22 that the work of the U.S. intelligence community would be conducted lawfully: "The greatest strength we have as a world power is our moral dedication to the rights of the individual," he said.

He expressed confidence that he could hold the various intelligence bureaucracies to a high standard. "If I ever have to come before this committee and say I didn't know what's going on because my subordinates didn't think I had to know every detail about any situation, there will be some fireworks out there.... I don't think I've ever failed to be in control of any mission I've commanded."

Turner called the disclosures of questionable intelligence activities over the past few years "quite necessary," but added that they had damaged the public standing of the intelligence community.

Turner also assured committee members that he would have direct access to the President and that Carter had intense interest in the role of intelligence. But he insisted that he would be independent of Carter if it became necessary: "If I felt the President acted contrary to moral principles or against the Constitution, I would feel responsible to make my views known to him extremely forcefully if necessary. If I were unable to reconcile our differences then I would resign," he said.

The only reservation expressed about Turner's nomination focused on his decision to retain his Navy commission. Turner pointed out that the law allowed a military officer to hold the post and that nine previous directors and deputy directors of central intelligence had been military men on active service. He said he wanted to retain the option of moving on to other military duty after his service as CIA head.

Committee member Gary Hart (D Colo.) expressed serious reservations about having a military man on active duty head an agency that had been set up specifically to be independent of the Defense Department. But Turner insisted that throughout his career he had transferred his loyalties to the job at hand and that he would not let his naval background affect his management of the intelligence community.

The Senate confirmed the nomination by voice vote Feb. 24.

Confirmations

A few hours after Carter was sworn in as the 39th President Jan. 20, the Senate by voice vote confirmed 10 of his nominees for the Cabinet and other high administration positions: Vance as Secretary of State, Brown as Defense Secretary, Blumenthal as Secretary of the Treasury,

Bergland as Secretary of Agriculture, Andrus as Secretary of the Interior, Harris as Secretary of HUD, Adams as Secretary of Transportation, Kreps as Secretary of Commerce, Lance as director of OMB, and Schultze as Chairman of the Council of Economic Advisers.

The Senate voted 95-1 Jan. 24 to confirm Califano as Secretary of Health, Education and Welfare. The "no" vote was cast by Robert W. Packwood (R Ore.) because of what he called Califano's "passionate" opposition to the use of federal funds for abortions. However, Califano said in his confirmation hearings that he would uphold the law regarding abortion.

Bell was confirmed as Attorney General on Jan. 25 by a vote of 75-21; Young as U.S. representative to the United Nations by a vote of 89-3 on Jan. 26; and Marshall to be Secretary of Labor, by a 74-20 vote on Jan. 26.

On Feb. 11, the Senate by voice vote, confirmed the nomination of Clifford Alexander, a 43-year old attorney, as Secretary of the Army, and W. Graham Claytor Jr., 64, who was president and chairman of the board of the Southern Railway Co., as Secretary of the Navy. Alexander was the first black secretary of one of the armed forces.

Other Appointments

In late January, Carter announced the following below-Cabinet level appointments:

Sidney Harman, 58, of New York City, chairman of Harman International Industries, as under secretary of commerce.

Richard N. Cooper, 42, a Yale University economics professor and a deputy assistant secretary of state in the Johnson administration, as under secretary of state for economic affairs.

Philip C. Habib, 56, as under secretary of state for political affairs, the job he already held.

John F. O'Leary, 50, administrator of the New Mexico Energy Resources Board, as administrator of the Federal Energy Administration.

Lyle E. Gramley, 50, research director of the Federal Reserve System, to the Council of Economic Advisers.

William Nordhaus, 35, Yale University economics professor, to the Council of Economic Advisers.

Kenneth S. Axelson, 54, senior vice president of J. C. Penney Co., as deputy secretary of the treasury.

Anthony M. Solomon, 57, assistant secretary of state for economic affairs in the Johnson administration, as under secretary of the treasury for monetary affairs.

Hale Champion, 54, financial vice president of Harvard University, as under secretary of the Health, Education and Welfare Department (HEW).

Ernest L. Boyer, 48, chancellor of the New York State University, as commissioner of education in HEW.

Named to Commerce Department posts were **Anne Wexler**, associate publisher of *Rolling Stone* magazine, as deputy under secretary for regional affairs; **Jerry Jasinowski**, former Carter campaign aide, as assistant secretary for economic policy; **Robert T. Hall**, director of the National Commission for Manpower Policy, as assistant secretary for economic development.

The administration's slowness in filling some 300 second-level positions provoked both criticism and defense. One critic was *The Washington Post*, which wrote in an editorial March 3 that "it's gone on long enough now to get in the way of the business of government."

A defender was Alan Cranston (D Calif.), assistant majority leader of the Senate. "I have great respect for the care being taken in the making of appointments," he told Congressional Quarterly. "If it slightly slows things down, it's well worth the time he's [Carter's] putting into it. There's never been this much care taken."

A Congressional Quarterly survey of 11 executive departments showed that at least 95 of the 145 sub-Cabinet positions at or above the level of assistant secretary had been filled as of March 2. Most of the nominees, however, were awaiting Senate confirmation and in many cases their names had not been announced by the Carter administration. Excluding Cabinet members, only 10 ap-

Carter's Well-to-Do Cabinet

The 11 members of the Carter Cabinet and four other Cabinet-level officials had 1976 earnings ranging from $43,000 to $681,748, based on information released by the administration.

The White House figures showed exact amounts of salaries, fees and capital gains, but they disclosed only general information about dividends. Both dividend income and statements of assets and liabilities were coded in five categories, the lowest from zero to $4,999 and the highest from $100,000 up. Following are income summaries compiled from the statements:

Brock Adams, Secretary of Transportation and former U.S. representative from Washington: $61,425.

Cecil D. Andrus, Secretary of Interior and former Idaho governor: $43,000.

Griffin B. Bell, Attorney General and former private attorney: $155,435.

Bob Bergland, Secretary of Agriculture and former U.S. representative from Minnesota: $76,505.

W. Michael Blumenthal, Secretary of the Treasury and former president of the Bendix Corp.: $681,748.

Harold Brown, Secretary of Defense and former university president: $149,829.

Joseph A. Califano Jr., Secretary of Health, Education and Welfare and former private attorney: $558,289.

Patricia Roberts Harris, Secretary of Housing and Urban Development and former private attorney: $102,600.

Juanita M. Kreps, Secretary of Commerce and former university vice president: $122,000.

F. Ray Marshall, Secretary of Labor and former university professor: $74,810.

Cyrus R. Vance, Secretary of State and former private attorney: $335,340.

Zbigniew Brzezinski, assistant for national security affairs and former university professor: $85,000.

Bert Lance, director of the Office of Management and Budget and former bank president: $300,000.

Charles Schultze, chairman of the Council of Economic Advisers and former private economist: $72,869.

Andrew Young, ambassador to the United Nations and former U.S. representative from Georgia: $61,125.

pointees had been confirmed. An additional 33 persons had been selected for the executive posts and were awaiting background checks. Twenty-three appointees from previous administrations were continuing in office and one of those, FBI Director Clarence M. Kelley, had been named to a committee to help find his successor.

As of March 2, the Carter administration had named a dozen blacks and a dozen women to secondary posts in the 11 Cabinet departments. There was some overlap because four of the women were also members of minority groups. One preliminary estimate—by *The New York Times*—showed that Carter's record on affirmative action hiring for high government positions could run as much as 80 per cent ahead of the record of the Ford administration.

Warnke Nomination

President Carter's selection of Paul C. Warnke as director of the Arms Control and Disarmament Agency as well as chief negotiator in the strategic arms limitation talks (SALT) with the Soviet Union provoked considerable controversy over the direction of the new administration's arms control policy. A former assistant secretary of defense for international security affairs in the Johnson administration, and before that the department's chief counsel, Warnke was a senior partner in the Washington law firm, Clifford Warnke Glass McIlwain and Finney.

The appointment of Warnke, announced Feb. 2, drew immediate criticism from members of the Senate fearful that his avowed commitment to nuclear arms reduction might let the Soviets tip the scale of nuclear superiority toward them. Carter, however, on Feb. 4 called the appointment of Warnke "crucial" to his administration, and on Feb. 8, he said he had "complete confidence" in Warnke and believed his proposals were "sound."

"There will be instances on nuclear weapons where each country has to take some initiative," Carter said. "But the overall balance of mutual restraint, cutting down on the overall dependence on nuclear weapons, is what counts." He added that Warnke's position "will be carefully coordinated with my own."

Warnke made the same point as the Senate Foreign Relations Committee opened hearings on the nomination Feb. 8. He would not be the policymaker, he said, he would be "part of a team." He said he favored arms reduction, but on a "collateral" basis, and he assured the committee that he believed the United States should keep strategic nuclear parity with the Soviets.

On Feb. 22, the Foreign Relations Committee overwhelmingly recommended approval of the nomination. Meanwhile, members of the Senate Armed Services Committee opposed to his nomination subjected Warnke to withering cross-examination during hearings Feb. 22-23. The opposition hoped to prove that Warnke, a prolific writer on strategic arms policy, had shown in the past a consistent bias against improvements in the U.S. arsenal.

Despite the controversy surrounding his nomination, the Senate March 9 confirmed Warnke as chief negotiator in the U.S.-Soviet strategic arms talks by a vote of 58 to 40 and as director of the Arms Control and Disarmament Agency by a vote of 70 to 29.

The votes followed four days of often heated debate. Critics, led by Sen. Henry M. Jackson (D Wash.), charged that Warnke had altered his previous "soft" views on the nuclear balance and on U.S. weapons needs only after being nominated in order to win confirmation. Warnke defenders contended that he had not been "soft." In effect, the substantial vote against him constituted, said Minority Leader Howard H. Baker Jr. (R Tenn.), a "signal" that Warnke should take a firm position in arms limitation negotiations.

Earlier on the day of the vote, President Carter in a news conference repeated his statement that he had "complete confidence" in Warnke. The President said he wanted "a substantial reduction" in nuclear weapons and that he thought many of those opposing Warnke "just don't want to see substantial reductions in nuclear weapons."

Biographical sketches of the Cabinet and other top-level appointees appear on pages 22 to 43.

Defense:

Harold Brown

Harold Brown's selection Dec. 21 to be Secretary of Defense in the Carter administration came in the 24th year of Brown's involvement with U.S. national security policy. Much of that career has focused on nuclear weaponry, from the earliest years of its development to the recent efforts to control it as a member of the U.S. delegation to the Strategic Arms Limitation Talks (SALT) with the Soviet Union.

The 14th man to head the Pentagon since the armed services were consolidated in 1947, Brown was the first Secretary to bring to the position the technical expertise of a weapons scientist. He also brought a public record of skepticism about the current policy of equipping U.S. forces to wage a limited nuclear war. Carter had suggested during the election campaign that he doubted the possibility of limited nuclear war, but he did not emphasize the issue. On the contrary, he fostered press reports of his keen attention to the advice of James R. Schlesinger, the former Defense Secretary, who publicly inaugurated the limited war policy in 1974.

But events, most prominent among them the continued deadlock in the SALT negotiations, likely would force Carter early in his administration to take a clear position on the awful complexities of nuclear strategy.

Brown's views on strategic arms, as he described them Jan. 11 at his confirmation hearings before the Senate Armed Services Committee, conflicted significantly with claims by some Pentagon sources and some members of Congress that the Soviet Union is approaching strategic superiority over the United States. "Presently," he insisted, "the Soviet Union couldn't attack the United States without our being able to deliver a devastating retaliatory blow that would destroy the Soviet Union as a functioning modern society."

Harold Brown

Brown said the Soviet Union probably would continue its heavy investment in upgrading its military capability in hopes of increasing its political leverage and that the United States should pursue an active weapons research program to have options ready should the need arise. But he cautioned that the U.S. response to the Soviet buildup should neither foreclose "peaceful, diplomatic options" nor leave the country open to "the naked use of force."

Carter's oft-repeated campaign promise of a $5-billion to $7-billion savings in defense spending was possible, he insisted, through improved management of the Pentagon.

Background

The 49-year-old president of California Institute of Technology was born in New York City Sept. 19, 1927. He graduated with honors from Columbia University in 1945 and remained at Columbia for graduate study in physics,

completing his M.A. in 1946 and his Ph.D. in 1949 at the age of 22.

After a year as lecturer at Stevens Institute of Technology in Hoboken, N.J., Brown in 1950 joined the staff of the Lawrence Radiation Laboratory of the University of California at Berkeley.

Nuclear Weapons Research

In 1952 he moved to the Livermore Laboratory, an offshoot of the Lawrence Laboratory dedicated to nuclear weapons research. At Livermore, Brown worked on development of a nuclear warhead small enough for the Navy's Polaris missile. He was also associated with Project Plowshare, a program of research on possible applications of nuclear explosions to such peaceful purposes as excavation and petroleum recovery.

Brown ascended rapidly through the Livermore hierarchy and in 1962, at age 32, he succeeded Dr. Edward Teller, the principal architect of the H-bomb, as director of the facility.

He was a member of the President's Science Advisory Board from 1958 to 1961 and served in 1958-59 as senior science adviser to the U.S. delegation at the Geneva negotiations on a nuclear test ban treaty.

After reviewing the results of U.S. nuclear tests in late 1958, Brown and other science advisers to the U.S. negotiating team warned that the Soviet Union could violate a test ban treaty with impunity by exploding nuclear weapons underground in a "big hole" that would absorb the seismic shock of the blast and thus circumvent the proposed test ban monitoring system. The problem of verification stymied until 1963 further progress toward a nuclear test ban.

Pentagon Whiz Kid

In 1961 Brown joined the band of relatively young economists, systems analysts and physicists with whom Robert S. McNamara set out to manage the Pentagon. At age 33 he was appointed to the Defense Department's third-ranking position, Director of Defense Research and Engineering, exercising general supervision over nearly half the nation's scientists and engineers.

McNamara and his aides, quickly labeled "whiz kids," earned the profound enmity of senior military officers and their congressional allies for vetoing weapons-related military recommendations on economic grounds or other considerations.

Commenting in 1962 on his role, Brown insisted on NBC's Meet the Press that he valued "military judgments based on the experience of decades in a military role." But he added: "We are talking in many cases about a kind of war in which we are all amateurs. In those considerations I think that technical people who have thought a great deal about them have a great deal to contribute [and] I think that the military people have a great deal to contribute."

As Pentagon research chief, Brown reportedly sponsored the TFX project that attempted, over the bitter opposition of the Navy and Air Force, to develop a single fighter-bomber for both services. He helped McNamara kill other weapons proposals: the Skybolt air-to-ground missile, the reconnaissance satellite called the Manned Orbital Laboratory and the B-70 bomber.

Brown said at the time that he favored a new manned bomber for the Air Force, but that the Rockwell-built B-70, designed to fly at very high altitudes, took the wrong approach to the problem. He favored research on a low-flying plane, which eventually evolved into the Rockwell B-1. Although Carter had expressed reservations about beginning production of the plane, Brown told Sen. William Proxmire (D Wis.) in a letter May 20 that he felt the Pentagon had "the best of the argument" over whether to produce the plane.

In 1965 Brown became secretary of the Air Force, succeeding Eugene M. Zuckert.

Vietnam Bombing

According to the Pentagon Papers, published by Beacon Press in 1971 after their release by Sen. Mike Gravel (D Alaska), Brown resisted, at least through 1968, any cutback in the bombing of North Vietnam. He insisted that was "an indivisible blue chip to be exchanged *in toto* for some reciprocity by the North Vietnamese." He also warned that it would be politically impossible to reverse any bombing cutback at a later date.

But over the course of the war, Brown appeared to lose confidence in the effectiveness of the U.S. bombing campaign in reducing enemy activity in South Vietnam by attacking its lines of supply in North Vietnam.

In a July 3, 1966, memo to McNamara on alternative strategies for the air war in the North, Brown rejected the options of 1) attacking the industries and ports of Hanoi and Haiphong, or 2) concentrating the attacks on infiltration routes from the North Vietnamese panhandle into South Vietnam. Instead, he endorsed a third option: stepping up the attacks against supply lines in the central part of North Vietnam except for a "sanctuary" area around Hanoi and Haiphong. With elaborate statistical analysis, Brown argued that, in comparison with a campaign against the infiltration routes, attacks deeper into North Vietnam would block a greater proportion of enemy supplies headed for South Vietnam and would require North Vietnam to divert a greater proportion of their imports to supply and service their air defense system.

But in the wake of the enemy's 1968 Tet offensive—less than two years later—Brown wrote a memo to Deputy Defense Secretary Paul Nitze in which Brown seemed uncertain that any of the three alternative forms of escalation of the air campaign could reduce Communist activity in South Vietnam below its 1967 level. He conceded in the memo, which was referred to in the Pentagon Papers, that he could not demonstrate "quantitatively" that such a result would follow even from a systematic attempt to "erode the will of the population" by lifting all restrictions on the bombing of North Vietnam in order to increase the casualties and destruction.

He added: "As long as they have the promise of continued Soviet and Chinese material support and substantial prospect of stalemate or better in [South Vietnam], the North Vietnamese government is likely to be willing to undergo these hardships."

Asked his general views on the Vietnam War in retrospect at the Dec. 21 press conference, Brown commented that it had been a "very, very catastrophic time in American history" and that the U.S. government had misjudged the political situation in Vietnam. He added that "we have become more cautious" about such interventions.

SALT Talks

In 1969 President Nixon appointed Brown, by then president of Cal Tech, to the U.S. delegation to the SALT negotiations with the Soviet Union. Unofficially, Brown was regarded as the scientific community's representative.

In an article that appeared in the March 1969 issue of *Foreign Affairs*, Brown had called for a ban on large anti-ballistic missile (ABM) systems and on multiple, independently targeted re-entry vehicles (MIRVs). He maintained that deployment of either weapon by the United States or the Soviet Union could undermine the stability of the strategic balance, which gave each nation the certain knowledge that an attack on the other would elicit a retaliatory strike wreaking "unacceptable damage" on the aggressor. Brown said that ABM systems of limited range to protect each nation's missiles and multiple warheads that were not separately targeted (MRVs) would not destabilize the deterrent system since they would only guarantee the effectiveness of a "second-strike" in case of enemy attack.

When the first round of SALT negotiations concluded in 1972 with the signing of an interim agreement limiting the number of strategic weapons and a treaty limiting the size of U.S. and Soviet ABM systems, Brown called it "a very substantial first step towards enhancing the security of both sides and of all the world." He has stoutly defended the first SALT agreements against charges that they favored the Soviet Union and, at the time of his selection by Carter, was still a member of the U.S. team seeking an agreement on SALT II.

Towards SALT II

In a March 1975 talk to a Soviet scientific group, Brown warned that progress toward a second SALT agreement would be "severely hampered and perhaps not possible" unless the two superpowers agreed that their nuclear arsenals could be used only for mutual deterrence of a direct attack and not for political coercion of other countries or to "win" a nuclear war. He noted that "many technologists were fascinated with new capabilities, [and] dedicated military men on both sides find it very hard to concede that they cannot protect the homeland." But he insisted that their views should be overridden by higher political authorities who realized that "the mutual hostage condition of our two countries is a fact" that precluded any political use of strategic forces.

He rejected the theory that the superpowers could wage a limited nuclear war, attacking each other's military forces while causing only modest levels of civilian casualties: "In the confusion of nuclear war, the distinction between classes of targets is very unlikely to be preserved." He warned that contingency planning for such a limited nuclear war could increase the chances of war by eroding the deterrent threat.

Brown maintained that a new arms limitation agreement would need to guarantee "some sort of perceived equivalence overall" between U.S. and Soviet forces, lest the apparent superiority of one dimension of one side's force fuel pressures on the other side for new deployments to redress the disparity. He said that the ceiling on the number of nuclear delivery vehicles in a new agreement should cover all bombers equal in range and payload to those defined as heavy bombers and all mobile intercontinental missiles.

He also proposed three measures to restrain the qualitative arms race by inhibiting the rate at which new weapons could be developed and deployed. Brown suggested limitations on the number of bombers and missiles that could be replaced or modernized each year, on the number of new weapons that could be introduced in a five-year period and on the number of missile tests that would be permitted in any year.

Treasury:

W. Michael Blumenthal

Werner Michael Blumenthal, choice of President Jimmy Carter to head the Treasury Department, will bring an expertise in international economics, great success in the corporate world and enormous energy to his new job.

That combination of qualities brought immediate praise from Capitol Hill. "The difficult trade and fiscal problems facing this nation require that the Secretary of Treasury be a person who understands commerce and knows what it is to meet a payroll," said Sen. Russell B. Long (D La.) in commending the selection of Blumenthal. Long is chairman of the Finance Committee, which approved the nomination.

Success Story

For lovers of rags-to-riches tales, Blumenthal is a perfect hero.

He was born Jan. 3, 1926, in Berlin, Germany, the son of a clothing store owner. After his father was imprisoned three months in Buchenwald in 1938 during Hitler's rise to power, the family escaped to China, where it spent most of World War II in Japanese-occupied Shanghai.

Blumenthal arrived in San Francisco in 1947, where he took a job as a billing clerk. He left that to go to college, and

W. Michael Blumenthal

supporting himself with odd jobs, graduated from the University of California at Berkeley in 1951 with a degree in international economics.

The following year he became a U.S. citizen and enrolled in the Woodrow Wilson School of Public and International Affairs at Princeton University. He received three degrees from there—a master of arts and master of public administration in 1953 and a doctorate in international economics in 1956. He taught at Princeton from 1954-57 and worked as a labor arbitrator for the state of New Jersey.

He turned down an opportunity to remain in academia, and in 1957 went with the Crown Cork International Corp. in Jersey City, a bottle-top manufacturer. He was vice president when he left in 1961 to join the Kennedy administration.

International Expertise

For two years Blumenthal was deputy assistant secretary of state for economic affairs, negotiating international commodity agreements. From 1963 to 1967, he and his family lived in Geneva while he was the President's deputy special representative for trade negotiations. With the rank of ambassador, he served as chief U.S. negotiator in the Kennedy Round of international tariff-reduction talks.

He remains a strong advocate of reducing international barriers. "We must work with trading partners on economic relations that would bring down trade barriers of all kind—tariff and nontariff barriers, including industrial and agricultural barriers," he said in an interview with *Nation's Business.* "The Kennedy Round helped to reduce barriers, and this benefited everyone."

Business Acumen

After completing the trade negotiations, Blumenthal left government in 1967 to become president and chief operating officer of Bendix International in New York, an operating group of Bendix Corp., where he stayed until 1970. He then became vice-chairman of the corporation, which is headquartered in Southfield, Mich., outside Detroit, and rose to his present position as chairman, president and chief executive officer.

The company under Blumenthal has built an enviable reputation. It has four basic divisions—automotive, aerospace-electronics, shelter and industrial goods—and does not, contrary to popular conception, manufacture washing machines. The firm was chosen as one of the five best-managed companies in the United States in 1976 by the business magazine *Dun's Review* because its balanced diversification has helped it achieve record earnings for the past four years despite the nation's economic difficulties. The magazine described Blumenthal as "a perpetual-motion machine sporting a cigar," and said that as a business leader he "relishes taking progressive positions on social issues" but has a "strictly no-nonsense" management style. That style was reflected in his comment on Bendix's performance: "Nothing works if you don't make money."

Similarity of Views

Blumenthal's knowledge of international economics is a departure for Treasury secretaries who frequently come from Wall Street or the banking world. It is an area, however, about which Carter has expressed deep concern, particularly the need for better coordination of U.S. economic and foreign policy.

On other matters, too, Blumenthal seems to share the attitudes of President Carter. On the Humphrey-Hawkins employment-economic planning legislation, he told *Nation's Business:* "The bill calls for too much detail and too elaborate a structure. It would result in too much bureaucracy, and it would hamper the functioning of a free economy in ways that I would regret. However, I do believe some kind of economic planning is necessary for the nation, as it is for individual companies. This national planning should look to estimating options and alternatives and providing a general direction for the economy.

In the same interview, he took a hard line on illegal foreign payments by corporations to make sales and described what his firm had done: "You set down clear policies against kickbacks and bribes, you set up policing procedures, you let people know you mean what you say. If you do these things, executives will refrain from giving kickbacks and bribes, even if it means losing some business. We have, I think, convinced our executives that we want them to pass up business rather than commit illegal acts." He also has proposed a watchdog group to establish professional standards for business conduct as a way of ensuring "the business community maintains standards that are above reproach."

He married the former Margaret Eileen Polley in 1951, and they have three daughters in college. His wife is studying for her doctorate and is a professor at Mercy College in Detroit.

Attorney General:

Griffin B. Bell

Griffin B. Bell, 58, emerged as the most controversial of President-elect Jimmy Carter's Cabinet appointments, stirring opposition primarily from civil rights and minority groups, but also from "public interest" advocates of many stripes.

Announced as Carter's choice for Attorney General on Dec. 20, Bell overcame a final hurdle on his lengthy path to the post when the Senate voted Jan. 25 to confirm his nomination, 75-21.

The opposition to Bell stemmed in part from his extensive record as a federal judge. For 15 years, beginning in 1961, Bell served as one of the 15 judges on the Fifth Circuit Court of

Griffin B. Bell

Appeals. That circuit embraces the Deep South, stretching from Texas to Georgia and Florida. In that period, the Fifth Circuit was the battleground for the major civil rights fights of the entire nation. At the press conference announcing his appointment, Bell urged reporters to refer to one of his 1972 cases, *Cisneros* v. *the Corpus Christi Independent School District*, to ascertain his position on the ever-

divisive issue of busing. In that decision by a badly split court, Bell laid out a series of efforts which Corpus Christi officials had to pursue before they could resort to substantial levels of student transportation. In separate dissents that variously characterized Bell's remedy as "absurd," "enigmatic" and "astounding," the more liberal judges of the circuit objected vehemently that the local efforts already had covered that ground without alleviating the fact that two-thirds of the city's blacks and Mexican-Americans continued to be "victims of unconstitutional ethnic and racial segregation." The dissents opined that Bell's approach "will produce no substantive changes...except delay."

That split in the court appears characteristic, with there being, as one recent clerk for a Fifth Circuit judge stated, "no question that he was part of the conservative wing of the court." His role on the court is thought by some to have been a powerful one. Another recent clerk said that he is "an aggressive and intimidating man. He's gruff and blunt, and he has the reputation for striking fear in the hearts of his colleagues and the clerks."

Public interest advocates other than minority representatives were troubled by another aspect of Bell's legal career—his long-term association with the prestigious Atlanta law firm of King & Spalding. A top Washington public interest lawyer lamented: "I had hoped that we wouldn't have to dip into the corporate defense bar for Attorney General this time. Bell is that kind of lawyer, and he brings that range of attitudes to the job."

Bell has been associated with the Atlanta firm, also that of Carter confidant Charles Kirbo, for much of his professional life.

Appointed by Kennedy

Bell received his law degree, with honors, from Mercer University of Macon, Ga., in 1948. He then practiced law in two other Georgia cities, Savannah and Rome, before graduating to Atlanta and becoming a King & Spalding partner in 1953. He remained with that firm until his 1961 judicial appointment by President John F. Kennedy, having served as its managing partner from 1959-61. He returned to the firm after leaving the federal bench in the spring of 1976.

Despite having lived a lawyerly life, Bell is no stranger to politics. While in law practice, he served as chief of staff to Georgia Gov. Ernest Vandiver from 1959-61, a parallel to the later association of Kirbo with Carter as governor. Bell also served as Georgia campaign manager for John Kennedy in 1960. He has been frank in ascribing his judicial appointment to that political link. In a recent published interview, Bell humorously acknowledged that "becoming a federal judge wasn't very difficult" since he not only led Kennedy's campaign, but "two of my oldest and closest friends were the two senators from Georgia" [Democrats Richard B. Russell (D 1933-71), and incumbent Herman E. Talmadge].

Such political associations combined with a near life-long association with Carter to make him a familiar and trustworthy choice for the President-elect. Bell was born in Americus, the town just 12 miles from Plains, Ga., on Oct. 31, 1918. He attended Georgia Southwestern College, and served five years in the Army during World War II, attaining the rank of major. He married the former Mary Foy Powell during the war, in 1943. After demobilization, he returned to law school in Macon.

Carter's Pledges

Those same political and personal ties troubled observers who recalled Carter's campaign pledges. In Iowa last January, Carter proposed making the Attorney General an independent officer with a five-to-seven-year term to protect it from political influence. In his June presentation to the Democratic Party platform committee, Carter's main comment on the Attorney General was that he "must be removed from politics...[and] barred from all political activity." In Oregon in September, Carter deplored the Washington leadership as being ingrown because its members "go to the same restaurants, they belong to the same clubs, they play golf on the same golf courses...." That remark proved embarrassing to Carter when it was disclosed that Bell belongs to three Atlanta clubs that have discriminated on the basis of race and religion. Bell said Dec. 22 he would resign from all three.

Even though the Bell nomination created consternation among several interest groups, no genuine confirmation battle was waged. Lawyers interviewed were unanimous in stating that Bell's judicial work is quite competent, if not scholarly, and that he could not be opposed as being inadequate to the job, as G. Harrold Carswell, whom Bell supported, was for a Supreme Court appointment. Also no hint of impropriety energed that tainted Bell's nomination as it did that of Clement F. Haynsworth Jr's nomination to the Supreme Court.

The vote on Bell's confirmation came after a day of debate, marked by continuing disagreement over the nominee's civil rights record and sensitivity. The day before the vote, Bell had conceded that the arduous process of gaining the Senate's consent to his nomination might have been a healthy experience because it had made him more aware of certain issues and interest groups.

State:

Cyrus R. Vance

The new Secretary of State, Cyrus R. Vance, brings to the Carter administration a broad background of experience in foreign policy and crisis management. A solidly establishment figure—Wall Street lawyer, former Pentagon official and international troubleshooter—he offers to foreign governments the reassurance of a well-known and widely respected figure in charge of U.S. diplomacy.

Vance's selection was looked upon as particularly important in light of foreign unease over the presidency of a one-term Georgia governor with little experience in foreign affairs. News of the appointment was greeted with enthusiasm by Western European diplomats, who are familiar with Vance's participation in international crises from the Panama riots of 1964 to the Paris peace talks on Vietnam in 1968.

Vance served as a foreign policy adviser to Carter during the presidential campaign. In announcing the appointment Dec. 3, Carter praised Vance as a "superb adviser and negotiator—a level-headed, competent, good manager." Vance's reputation as a manager and organization man, rather than an academic conceptualizer in the Kissinger mold, is in line with Carter's determination to be personally in charge of foreign policy. Carter told the Chicago Council on Foreign Relations in May that "the foreign policy spokesman of our country should be the President and not the Secretary of State."

Vance was born on March 27, 1917, in Clarksburg, W.Va. He attended Kent School in Connecticut, graduated from Yale University in 1939 with a B.A. in economics and received his law degree from Yale in 1942. Like Carter, he was a Navy man, serving as a lieutenant in several combat operations during World War II.

In 1947 Vance joined the New York law firm of Simpson, Thatcher and Bartlett. He has maintained his association with the firm, with time out for government service, ever since.

Missiles

Vance began his government career in 1957 as special counsel to the Preparedness Investigating Subcommittee of the Senate Armed Services Committee. The subcommittee was chaired by Lyndon B. Johnson (D Texas). Spurred by the Soviet launching of the first man-made satellite in October 1957, the subcommittee undertook an investigation of the U.S. missile program, which led to the establishment in 1957 of a Special Space and Astronautics Committee with Johnson as chairman and Vance as consulting counsel. In 1959 and 1960, Vance served as counsel to Senate investigations of the Pentagon budget and the comparative strength of U.S. and Soviet missile systems. During the period he became known as a protege of Johnson.

Cyrus R. Vance

Vance was appointed general counsel of the Defense Department by President Kennedy in January 1961, and in that capacity he worked closely with Defense Secretary Robert S. McNamara in studying recommendations for reorganizing and streamlining the department.

The close working rapport between Vance and McNamara led to Vance's appointment in 1962 as secretary of the Army. Observers at the time stressed the harmony between McNamara and Vance in their mutual emphasis on efficiency and precise thinking. Vance became a loyal associate of McNamara; McNamara was to reciprocate by urging that Vance be appointed Defense Secretary when McNamara left in 1968.

As Army secretary, Vance continued his efforts at bringing "cost effectiveness" to the Army. He also worked to mediate the deteriorating relations between McNamara and the military establishment.

Foreign Crises

President Johnson appointed Vance deputy secretary of defense in January 1964. Immediately thereafter he was sent to Panama as part of a four-man peace mission to restore relations severed in the wake of Panamanian rioting over the U.S. presence in the Canal Zone. The peace-seeking team recommended "an integral revision of the treaties that govern relations" between the two countries. Vance later charged that Cuban agents were responsible for the Panamanian violence. Diplomatic negotiations arising from the crisis were to become the subject of intense controversy during the 1976 presidential campaign.

In 1965 Johnson sent the Marines to the Dominican Republic to protect American lives endangered by the outbreak of civil war. Vance accompanied a presidential fact-finding mission, headed by national security adviser McGeorge Bundy, to the strife-torn nation.

Vance was forced by a chronic back problem to resign his Defense Department post in June 1967, but it did not mean the end of his government service. He became Johnson's trusted personal representative, a troubleshooter in times of crisis.

Vance's first assignment was in a domestic crisis: the Detroit riots of July 1967. Johnson sent Vance to Detroit to assess requests by state and local authorities for the use of federal troops to quell the disorders. He was credited by observers with maintaining a calm perspective in the face of a chaotic situation.

Vance also served as Johnson's representative during the riots in Washington, D.C., after the assassination in April 1968 of Martin Luther King. It was later revealed that Vance, together with Attorney General Ramsey Clark, had formulated the government policy for dealing with the disorders. The strategy called for "overwhelming law enforcement manpower," combined with restrictions on the use of gunfire.

In November 1967, the long-standing antagonism between the Greek and Turkish communities on the island of Cyprus led to a major confrontation between Greece and Turkey. Alarmed by the threat of hostilities between two NATO members, Johnson sent Vance on a round of shuttle diplomacy to Athens, Ankara and Nicosia in an attempt to mediate the dispute. Eventually an agreement providing for force reductions in the area was reached.

In February 1968, Vance was sent to reassure the South Korean government of American support in the face of North Korean provocations. Vance brought with him an offer of $100-million in military aid and the promise of "immediate consultation" in the event of an attack, but apparently he was unsuccessful in allaying Korean doubts.

In the spring of 1968, with his Vietnam policy in crisis, Johnson called together a group of advisers from outside the government, including Vance, to help decide on future policy toward the war. Vance was among those urging a gradual termination of the war and the beginning of negotiations. In response, Johnson ordered a halt of bombing against the heavily populated areas of North Vietnam, and he chose Vance to help begin the negotiating process by serving as deputy to Ambassador-at-large W. Averell Harriman at the peace talks with the North Vietnamese in Paris.

Vance served as deputy chief of the American delegation from May 1968 to February 1969. Little was accomplished during that period beyond an agreement to halt bombing of all North Vietnam. Most of the discussions centered around procedural matters and the shape of the conference table. By the time Vance left, he had only been able to lay the groundwork for continued negotiations under the Nixon administration.

Unlike his predecessor, Henry A. Kissinger, who is a prolific author and theorist on international relations, Vance has not written a great deal about his view of America's role in the world. He is described by observers as favoring Democratic orthodoxy on most questions. An issue of particular concern to Vance is the world trade in weapons. He served as vice chairman of a United Nations Association policy panel on conventional arms control, which released a study in 1976 deploring the continued growth in the world arms race.

In a *New York Times* article in May 1976, Vance strongly opposed President Ford's veto of the International Security Assistance and Arms Export Control Act of 1976, which would have strengthened congressional control of American arms sales.

In his Dec. 3 news conference with Carter, Vance also stressed the importance of talks with the Soviet Union aimed at limiting the growth in nuclear weaponry. He told *Newsweek* magazine shortly after his selection that he considered moving the strategic arms limitation talks "out of the doldrums" to be his first priority.

At the news conference, Vance also stressed a subject repeatedly emphasized by Carter in his presidential campaign: the importance of morality in the conduct of foreign policy. "I think that one has to deal also with the practicalities of the situation as they exist, but the underguiding principle must be a concern, and a deep concern, for human rights and the problem of human rights, and that certainly would be a factor in considering how we deal with other nations," he said.

Office of Management and Budget:

Thomas Bertram Lance

Thomas Bertram (Bert) Lance is the president of the sixth-largest bank in Georgia. But he still refers to himself as a "country banker."

His professional roots may indeed be in a country bank. But the affable millionaire has come a long way since he started his career as a $90-a-month teller in a Calhoun, Ga., bank in 1951.

By 1963, he was president of the Calhoun National Bank. In 1974 he and two other men bought the controlling interest of the Atlanta-based National Bank of Georgia, and Lance became president.

Lance, 45, chosen by President-elect Carter Dec. 3 to be the next director of the Office of Management and Budget, is a self-described "fiscal conservative." His banking background will bring comfort to the nation's conservative business community.

Thomas B. (Bert) Lance

In a newspaper interview a few days before his appointment to the Cabinet-level job, Lance said he saw no need for wage and price controls. "Voluntary restraints are really what we're all about," he added. He told another interviewer that he would not now advise Carter to seek a reduction in income taxes.

Lance worked in Carter's first, and unsuccessful, campaign for governor in 1966 and again in 1970, when Carter won. During Carter's administration, Lance was state commissioner of transportation.

As commissioner, he reorganized what had come to be known as the "Department of Paving and Politics." Lance was credited with ridding the transportation department of corruption, expanding the Georgia roadbuilding program and removing excess personnel from the bloated department.

He also assisted Carter in extensive reorganization of the state government, doing considerable lobbying in the legislature. This experience may prove valuable when Lance becomes OMB director. He undoubtedly will be a key figure in trying to sell Congress whatever federal reorganization plans Carter proposes.

The 6-foot-4, 240-pound banker has run for public office himself only once. In 1974, he was Carter's personal choice for governor. He finished third in the three-man Democratic primary.

Apparently in an effort to avoid future embarrassment, Carter's transition staff announced Nov. 25 that the family peanut warehouse business owed $4.7-million to Lance's bank. The loans were described as routine business transactions.

Lance was born June 3, 1931, in Gainesville, Ga. He attended Emory University, the University of Georgia and the graduate schools of banking at Louisiana State University and Rutgers University. He married LaBelle David in 1950; they have four children.

Interior:

Cecil D. Andrus

While some of Jimmy Carter's choices for Cabinet-level posts might be called equivocal, his decision to name Idaho Gov. Cecil D. Andrus, 45, as his new Secretary of the Interior could not. Andrus is a conservationist who was a sure bet to please environmentalists and displease mining, logging and other development interests.

Andrus' second race for governor (he ran unsuccessfully in 1966) in 1970 centered on one environmental issue. His opponent, incumbent Governor Don Samuelson (R) favored a proposal by the American Smelting and Refining Company (ASARCO) to extract molybdenum from an open-pit mine in the White Clouds area, one of the state's most beautiful mountain vistas.

Andrus opposed the plan while Samuelson contended that the mining operation would bring needed industry to the predominantly agricultural state. Although arguments over taxes and state support of education played a role in the 1970 race, the White Clouds issue was widely regarded as the deciding factor in Andrus' slim 52-to-48 per cent victory over Samuelson. In 1970 Andrus was helped by a $5,000 contribution from the League of Conservation Voters.

Once in office, Andrus continued to oppose the mining and logging interests in his state. He supported federal legislation (HR 6957—PL 92-400) that placed the White Cloud and other areas in the newly established Sawtooth National Recreation Area. Both the recreation area and a related wilderness area were removed from future new mining operations and put under strict environmental regulations by the new law. The legislation was strongly opposed by logging and grazing interests and supported by the major environmental lobbies.

Cecil D. Andrus

Actions as Governor

In addition to supporting federal legislation to protect scenic parts of his state, Andrus used the power of the statehouse to impede the progress of developers.

"Even with the wilderness act (PL 88-577) people have until 1984 to explore for minerals on most federal land," he pointed out in 1973. "I can't stop that. But through access restrictions and a lot of other means I can make it very tough for them trying to get anything out. And that's just what I intend to do."

In 1971 Andrus joined Govs. Tom McCall of Oregon (R) and Daniel J. Evans of Washington (R) in opposing proposed hydroelectric dams in Hells Canyon on the Snake River in those three states. In a letter to the Federal Power Commission (FPC), all three said the area was a national treasure and should not be despoiled. Hells Canyon was made a national recreation area in 1975.

In 1976 Andrus' opposition to a proposed 1,000-megawatt coal-fired electric-generating plant near Boise that he said would turn on the "growth switch" was credited with killing the proposal.

Little is known about Andrus' stance on environmental issues that the Interior Department deals with that he did not encounter as governor, such as offshore oil leasing. But on western-oriented environmental issues ranging from land use to clean air the partnership struck between Andrus and environmental groups has been consistently strong.

In 1973 Douglas Scott, northwestern representative of the Sierra Club, commented on Andrus' first years in office: "Andrus has been absolutely excellent. I can't say enough in his praise."

Andrus had his own comments that year on his role in mediating Idaho's environmental disputes: "About 10 per cent of our people are what I call preservationists—the way-outs. They criticize me for not being tough enough. About 15 per cent are the rape-and-run people, who only want to despoil our natural blessings. They hate me. But 75 per cent of our people are concerned about our environment, in various degrees, and I think I'll have them with me."

Indeed he did. In the 1974 gubernatorial election Andrus overwhelmed his Republican and American Independent opponents, winning 70.9 per cent of the vote despite the normally conservative Republican voting patterns in Idaho.

As a result of the state's Republican tradition, Andrus was forced to work with Republican legislatures throughout his career as governor. He had no luck with his proposals to provide state funding for kindergartens or enact comprehensive land-use planning, but he ultimately succeeded in revising the state's income tax laws, specifically eliminating a state tax deduction for federal taxes and boosting corporate taxes from 6 to 6.5 per cent. These changes added an estimated $1-million each year to the state revenues. Like Jimmy Carter, Andrus reorganized the state government, reducing 268 agencies to 20.

In 1974 Andrus and many other northwest officials opposed a Pentagon plan to launch Minuteman missiles from Malstrom Air Force Base in Montana over western portions of the United States. The flight path of the missile would have taken it over Idaho and Oregon on its way to a target in the Pacific. The first stage of the missile, weighing 4,800 pounds and measuring 28 feet long, was to be jettisoned over federal forest land in Idaho. Four smaller sections were to be dropped 50 miles further downrange. As a result of high-powered opposition, the proposed test was never made.

Andrus was born Aug. 25, 1931, in Hood River, Ore., the son of a sawmill operator. He attended Oregon State University in 1948 and 1949 and served in the Navy from 1951 to 1955. When discharged he held the rank of aviation electronic technician second class. He married the former Carol May in 1949, and has three daughters.

His political career began in the Idaho State Senate, where he served from 1961 to 1966 and again from 1968 to 1970. He was a member of the executive committee of the National Governors Conference in 1971-72 and chairman of the Federation of Rocky Mountain States during the same period. Andrus' business and professional experience includes a position as assistant manager of the Workmen's Compensation Exchange from 1963 to 1966. He also maintained several positions with the Paul Revere Insurance Companies during his political years.

His memberships included the Elks, the Masons, the American Legion and the VFW. He has also served in voluntary capacities with the Idaho Mental Health Association, the Associated Taxpayers of Idaho and the Idaho Mental Retardation Task Force. He is a Lutheran.

Agriculture:

Bob Bergland

When President-elect Carter chose Bob Bergland, he fulfilled his campaign pledge to appoint a farmer as Secretary of Agriculture. Bergland, 48, grew up in the bleak but fertile farmland of Roseau County, Minn., near the Canadian border. He has spent all his adult life either farming or working with farmers.

Since 1971, Bergland—he never uses his first two names, Robert Selmer—has been the Democratic U.S. representative from Minnesota's huge 7th District, one of the most rural in the country. He was a member of the House Agriculture and Small Business Committees.

Bob Bergland

He still raises spring wheat and lawn seed on a 600-acre farm near Roseau. His son-in-law manages the farm.

At the televised ceremony at which his appointment was announced Dec. 20, Bergland promised that he would be a "farmer's advocate" as Agriculture Secretary. This would be consistent with his record in Congress, where he is respected for his conscientious attention to complex and politically delicate agricultural problems. He had strong bipartisan backing for the Cabinet post, including that of nearly every Republican member of the Agriculture Committee.

Bergland has developed a reputation as something of an ambassador between rural and urban interests in the House. In 1973, for example, he helped negotiate a compromise leading to passage of a farm bill. "When I talk to the urban liberals," he said at the time, "I don't try to explain the intricacies of the farm bill. I explain to them about sections they are particularly interested in—conservation, food for peace or food stamps."

Bergland's approach has paid off in support not only from farm groups but from consumer and environmental organizations. Spokesmen for all three interest groups had words of praise for Carter's choice of Bergland. "Now the food stamp program will be administered by a Secretary who wants to make it work rather than someone who wants to see it fail," said Carol Tucker Foreman, president of the Consumer Federation of America.

Liberal Background

Similar praise came from the president of the National Farmers Organization, of which Bergland is a member. Bergland also has been associated with the National Farmers Union for nearly 30 years. From 1948 to 1950, he was a field representative for the Minnesota chapter.

His relationship with the more conservative American Farm Bureau Federation is not as warm. The federation president, Allan Grant, spoke against Bergland's nomination, arguing that he could be expected to favor higher price supports that might lead to crop surpluses and lower farm prices.

During his three terms in the House, Bergland said, his goal has been to "be part of the effort to establish a permanent farm program that will truly preserve and protect the family farmer and the communities which rely on him for their existence." This approach placed Bergland in regular

opposition to former Agriculture Secretary Earl L. Butz, whom he regarded as a partisan of corporate agricultural conglomerates.

Bergland's ratings by interest groups reflect his liberal voting record. He has scored between 80 and 100 with the Farmers Union, Americans for Democratic Action and the AFL-CIO Committee on Political Education. His percentages with the conservative Americans for Constitutional Action never have risen above 14.

In the 94th Congress, Bergland chaired the Agriculture Subcommittee on Conservation and Credit. He has supported higher price supports and subsidies for agricultural commodities.

Bergland occasionally has tangled with environmentalists over the use of pesticides; the advantages in many cases, he claims, outweigh the disadvantages. In 1975, however, he played a conciliatory role on pesticides. His amendment to the omnibus farm bill that year—in opposition to the House Agriculture Committee position—kept authority for enforcing the pesticide provisions of the Occupational Safety and Health Act in the hands of the Labor Department instead of transferring them to the Agriculture Department.

Bergland has voted for federal inspection of grain shipments. In 1976, in the wake of the previous year's inspection scandals, he offered an amendment to the Grain Standards Act that would have required federal rather than state inspection of grain shipments. The amendment was defeated in the House. When the bill went to conference, Bergland led the way in reaching a compromise between the House and Senate.

Political Activist

Bergland's appointment was recommended by Vice President-elect Walter F. Mondale, a fellow Minnesotan for whom Bergland served as an adviser on farm issues during the 1976 campaign. But Bergland's political activism predates that association by decades. Since his early 20s, he has worked in the Minnesota Democratic-Farmer-Labor Party (DFL), and has served as county DFL chairman.

He has spent most of his life in the same area. He was born July 22, 1928, in Roseau, the son of Norwegian immigrant parents. After studying agriculture for two years at the University of Minnesota on a scholarship, Bergland returned to the Roseau area. He began farming on his own in 1950, buying 280 acres from a neighbor. That year he married Helen Elaine Grahn. They have six children.

Their first years on the farm were hard ones. For a time, they lived in a house that had no plumbing. Several winters in the 1950s they spent in Florida, where Bergland worked as a construction laborer and carpenter.

In 1961 and 1962, Bergland was chairman of the Minnesota State Agricultural Stabilization and Conservation Service (ASCS) Committee, part of the U.S. Agriculture Department. After former Minnesota Gov. Orville L. Freeman was named President Kennedy's Secretary of Agriculture, he appointed Bergland the Midwest regional director of ASCS. Bergland held the job from 1963 to 1968.

Bergland ran for Congress and lost in 1968, kept campaigning during the next two years and defeated Republican incumbent Odin Langen (1959-71) in 1970. Bergland's margin last Nov. 2 was 73 per cent.

Commerce:

Juanita M. Kreps

Approved by the Senate on Jan. 20 as Secretary of Commerce, Juanita Morris Kreps, a labor economist with blue-chip corporate connections, was expected to confront early in her term the tough question of U.S. business compliance with the Arab boycott of Israel

A bill to outlaw observance of the boycott died at the end of the 94th Congress, largely the victim of a hostile Commerce Department under departing Secretary Elliot L. Richardson. But anti-boycott legislation was almost certain to reappear in the first months of the 95th Congress. And there was pressure on the department to release confidential reports by businesses that would reveal the extent of their cooperation with the Arab boycott.

Kreps was vice president for academic affairs at Duke University, where she was a faculty member since 1955. Her academic interests have been in labor and manpower, gerontology, income distribution and women in the workforce.

Though she has not specialized in foreign trade, she may be expected to bring to the boycott question the same social concerns that have made her ask corporate boards to deal with issues they might otherwise bypass—"like minority hiring and pricing policies," as she recently told a *Forbes* interviewer.

Unlike most consumer and minority advocates, Kreps has been able to raise questions of corporate responsibility from within the board room. She was a director of the J.C. Penney Co., Western Electric Co., Eastman Kodak Co., and the North Carolina National Bank. She also was a public member of the board of the New York Stock Exchange, reorganized in 1972 to include a sizable "public interest" contingent. By all accounts, Kreps' gracious southern accent has failed to mask a penetrating style and notable independence in her corporate dealings.

Even President-elect Carter was not immune to a critical, public appraisal of his selection process by the first woman named to his Cabinet. At the Dec. 20 news conference where he announced her appointment, Kreps challenged Carter's claim that it was difficult to locate "the best" Cabinet members among the ranks of blacks and women. "I think it would be hard to defend the proposition that there are not a great many qualified women," she declared, adding, "We'll simply have to do a better job of looking."

Juanita M. Kreps

Kentucky Native

Kreps' independence probably derives from her childhood in the coal-mining community of Lynch, Ky., where she was born Jan. 11, 1921. She has traced her interest in economics to "the Depression and World War II...economic affairs were very much in the front of our minds as college students. I felt economics would give me more insight into what was going on."

After earning a B.A. in 1942 from Berea College, a pioneer in work-study programs for impoverished Appalachian students, Kreps studied at Duke. She received a Ph.D. there in 1948.

Married to Clifton H. Kreps Jr., an academic expert on banking whom she met as a graduate student, she is a confirmed family woman. For years she meshed part-time teaching assignments with raising three children. She joined the Duke faculty after having taught in Ohio and New York. Her appointment as vice president came almost 20 years later, in 1973.

Kreps' major publications began appearing in the early 1960s and her books include a basic economics text written with a colleague, and studies of manpower and retirement, allocation of work and income, and the provocatively titled *Sex in the Marketplace,* a study of women's employment. She has identified herself with the liberal philosophy of economist Paul A. Samuelson, who advocates an active role for government in economic and social affairs.

Public Service

As her career matured, Kreps' 16-hour days increasingly reflected her own interest in shaping public policy. In addition to her corporate and academic posts, the economist has served on the National Council on Aging, the North Carolina Manpower Commission and the National Commission for Manpower Policy. The last of these recently recommended special programs, costing an estimated $4.5-billion in fiscal 1977 and 1978, to deal with unemployment.

Kreps was a member of a Twentieth Century Fund task force that in 1974 recommended creation of a nonprofit data bank to analyze the financial status of state and local governments. And she served on the Commission on the Operation of the Senate (the "Culver Commission," so called because Iowa Sen. John C. Culver (D) had urged its creation) which recently recommended a major overhaul of Senate operations.

Ombudsman

As Commerce Secretary, Kreps is responsible for much of the federal government's statistics apparatus—including the Bureau of the Census, the Bureau of Economic Analysis and various science and technology information services.

Traditionally the Secretary of Commerce has acted as a federal ombudsman for the U.S. business community. In recent years the post provided a base for Republican political operatives such as Rogers C. B. Morton and Maurice H. Stans. Richardson's appointment marked a departure from that precedent, and Kreps' continued the trend away from businessman-politicians. Though not regarded as a major innovator in economic thought, Kreps brought to the job an unprecedented academic background.

Kreps herself envisioned an expanded role for the department. She told the Dec. 20 news conference that American business was "being tested globally" and that Commerce "should encourage business to perform well all tasks that improve human welfare."

Kreps, a Democrat, was the first woman to serve as Secretary of Commerce since the department was created in 1913. She was the fourth woman Cabinet member ever (or the fifth including Patricia Roberts Harris who was approved as Secretary of Housing and Urban Development).

Labor:

F. Ray Marshall

With the choice of labor economist F. Ray Marshall for Secretary of Labor, Jimmy Carter took steps to repair a major rift developing among his supporters. A professor at the University of Texas specializing in problems of disadvantaged workers, Marshall, 48, had broad appeal to key elements of Carter's coalition—unions, civil rights groups and the South.

Organized labor, which obviously considers the Labor post a crucial one, responded to the selection with enthusiasm. "He's obviously a top-notch labor economist...and a sound and sensible man," said an AFL-CIO spokesman, noting that Marshall and the federation had worked together on job training programs for the underprivileged in the past. "We'll be looking forward to working with him again as Secretary of Labor," the spokesman said.

F. Ray Marshall

Dunlop Controversy

Marshall began to emerge as a "dark horse" possibility for Labor Secretary after civil rights groups publicly urged Carter to appoint a person with "proven" commitment to the concerns of minorities and women. Led by the Congressional Black Caucus, the National Women's Political Caucus and the National Organization of Women, these interests specifically pressed Carter not to appoint Harvard Professor John T. Dunlop, who served as Secretary of Labor briefly under President Ford and was widely thought to be the leading contender for the same job under Carter. Generally they alleged that Dunlop, both as Secretary and in a previous administrative position at Harvard, opposed certain affirmative action policies intended to improve employment opportunities for blacks, women and other victims of discrimination.

Dunlop, who quit Ford's Cabinet in protest of the President's veto of picketing legislation extremely important to the construction trades, clearly was organized labor's top choice for the job. When Carter's staff pressed the AFL-CIO for other suggestions earlier this month, Meany reportedly indicated that there was no second choice.

At a press conference Dec. 21, however, Carter basically dismissed the idea that opposition to Dunlop had forced him to settle on Marshall as a compromise. Carter apparently had known Marshall for years and he insisted that all along he had had "no doubt" that he wanted Marshall for the job.

Southern Roots

Born in Oak Grove, La., on Aug. 22, 1928, Marshall has spent most of his eventful life and career in the South. He was raised in a Baptist orphanage, from which he ran away at age 15. Soon after, he overstated his age in order to enlist

in the Navy during World War II, and went on to college after the war on the GI bill.

Marshall began his studies in economics at Millsaps College in Jackson, Miss., where he was graduated in 1949. The following year he earned a master's degree in economics from Louisiana State University and received a Ph.D. in economics from the University of California at Berkeley in 1954.

He began teaching economics as an instructor at San Francisco State in 1952 and moved on to a position as an associate professor of economics at the University of Mississippi in 1953. After two years as a Fulbright scholar in Finland in 1955-56, Marshall taught at Louisiana State for five years, 1957-62, during which time he rose to the rank of full professor.

Except for two years at the University of Kentucky from 1967 to 1969, Marshall has held his current position as professor of economics at the University of Texas since 1962. In 1970 he became the first director of the Center for the Study of Human Resources, a foundation-supported research institution at the university to which he devoted half his time.

Marshall's research has focused increasingly on rural manpower problems and, according to colleagues, his work on rural poverty in the South first drew Carter's attention several years ago. He consulted with Carter on these and other labor issues while Carter was governor of Georgia. More recently, Marshall wrote speeches for Carter's presidential campaign.

Most of Marshall's earlier work involved employment problems of blacks—particularly their exclusion from labor unions. His major writings on these subjects include *The Negro in Organized Labor* (1965) and *The Negro Worker* (1967).

Not in Government

Unlike most of Carter's Cabinet-level choices, Marshall has not served directly in the federal government. Since the mid-1960s, however, he has done considerable work for advisory commissions on manpower issues. He was chairman of the Federal Committee on Apprenticeships and a member of the National Council on Employment Policy, which in 1973 superseded the National Manpower Policy Task Force as an organization seeking to identify the nation's manpower needs.

Marshall also was president of the National Rural Center in Washington, D.C., president of the Industrial Relations Research Association and chairman of the American Economic Association's Committee on Political Discrimination, which is investigating the firings of a number of radical economists from university faculties.

Marshall was the author or co-author of several recent books, including *Rural Workers in Rural Labor Markets* (1974), *Human Resources and Labor Markets* (last revised in 1975), *Labor Economics: Wages, Employment and Trade Unionism* (last revised in 1976) and *The Role of Unions in the American Economy* (1976).

George Washington University Professor Sar A. Levitan, who with Marshall wrote *Human Resources and Labor Markets*, called the nomination "excellent." In addition to high marks from organized labor, Levitan noted, Marshall has established very good relations with blacks, minority groups and, above all, with Jimmy Carter. Marshall also is a friend of Juanita M. Kreps, Carter's Secretary of Commerce, which Levitan said could usher in a "new era" of cooperation between business and labor.

HEW:

Joseph A. Califano Jr.

Membership in the Cabinet of a U.S. President may have its frustrations, but it is seldom a step down from a position of greater power held in the past. For Joseph A. Califano Jr., announced Dec. 23 as President-elect Carter's choice for Secretary of Health, Education and Welfare, it might be considered that.

Califano first came to national prominence when he succeeded Bill Moyers as the top White House staff aide to President Lyndon B. Johnson. From 1965 until 1969, Califano was the chief presidential adviser on domestic issues. With Johnson's mind and energies increasingly consumed by the Vietnam War, Califano had a responsibility for shaping governmental programs that was extraordinary even for a uniquely placed aide. Cabinet officers at times found that they first had to go to Califano to reach the ear of the President.

Vance Protege

That unusual grip on power came early in Califano's career. Califano, born May 15, 1931, in Brooklyn, N.Y., was only 34 when he became an LBJ deputy. His rapid rise had been facilitated by his ability to impress important superiors in office whose protege he then became. His first protector in this skein, Cyrus R. Vance, will join him in the Carter Cabinet as Secretary of State. In 1961 Califano was tiring of the staidness of law practice in the firm then led by former New York Gov. Thomas E. Dewey (R). After three years of tax and securities work, he was interested in government service. A letter to Vance produced the opportunity. He became "special assistant" to Vance, then the general counsel of the Defense Department. In 1962 Vance was promoted to secretary of the Army and Califano was advanced in stride, remaining special assistant. The next year, Califano was made Army general counsel. By that time, he had entered the orbit of Secretary of Defense Robert S. McNamara, and in 1964 he became special assistant to both McNamara and Vance, who was then deputy secretary of defense.

Joseph A. Califano Jr.

Link to White House

Califano's work under McNamara dealt with a broad range of issues, including both the development of the supersonic transport (SST) and the use of federal troops in the civil rights-related strife in Selma, Ala. The bulk of his work was as liaison between the Pentagon, where he had served three years as a Navy legal officer (1955-58), and the White House. As a result, he soon came to be known by Johnson, Moyers and others on the White House staff. When Moyers resigned his White House post in July 1965, the Holy Cross (1952) and Harvard Law (1955) educated Califano was chosen to be groomed as his successor.

Reorganization Battles

Califano's responsibilities in the White House made him peculiarly well-suited for the pursuit of one of Carter's most-promised goals: bureaucratic reorganization. Califano arrived at the Johnson White House at a time when the proliferation of federal programs was first generating the impulse to reorganize and rationalize the bureaucratic structure. During his stint there, he was heavily involved in a reorganization of the Budget Bureau (now the Office of Management and Budget), in the creation of the Department of Transportation and in Johnson's ill-fated effort to merge the Departments of Labor and Commerce.

The scorecard for those Johnson reorganization fights inevitably taught Califano volumes on the political difficulties and the complexities of any such plans. Even the successful creation of the Transportation Department had its tinges of defeat. The vested interests of several of the independent agencies the White House sought to bring together into the department managed either to exempt themselves outright, as in the case of the Maritime Administration, or to retain the significant pieces of their regulatory power. Consequently, the reorganization altered the formal structure far more than it affected the realities of power and policy in the transportation field.

'A Doer, A Manager'

Califano's years of service to LBJ say much about his style and his capabilities for aiding a President. Based on his own descriptions of what he wants out of his Cabinet, Carter apparently found these qualities attractive. Califano seldom was considered an ideologue, always seen as a doer, a manager. Patrick Anderson, the former journalist who was the top Carter speechwriter, wrote extensively about Califano when he was under LBJ, and he referred to Califano as "the President's instrument." He quoted a Califano friend as saying that "there aren't many stories about Joe; he just gets things done." Among the things he got done in the White House was the institution of the McNamara-inspired program of systems analysis throughout the executive branch. In 1977, many observers were more jaundiced about the ultimate worth of such devices in value-laden decision areas, but the Johnson-decreed move was seen at the time as a healthy attempt to rationalize the budgeting and planning process of the government, akin to the virtues ascribed to the Carter proposal of zero-based budgeting.

When the war forced Johnson from office, Califano left the White House and its power, but he did not leave Washington. Teaming with well-known defense lawyer Edward Bennett Williams, he set up the litigating law firm where he continued to practice. That legal practice included constitutional work on behalf of prominent journalistic clients, such as *The Washington Post* and Daniel Schorr in his 1976 appearance before the House ethics committee regarding the leaking of the Pike committee report on the CIA. Califano was also active in the political sphere, serving as general counsel for the Democratic National Committee for two and a half years, ending in August 1972. Seeking a return to power along with the Democrats in 1976, he volunteered to help Carter as an adviser on matters relating to the family, a long-time interest of Vice President-elect Walter F. Mondale's which was shared by Carter. Mondale was said to have been one of Califano's strongest backers inside the Carter camp.

HUD:
Patricia Roberts Harris

Washington lawyer and Democratic loyalist Patricia Roberts Harris has always played to mixed reviews. Her nomination to head the Department of Housing and Urban Development (HUD) was no exception.

Hours after President-elect Carter announced his choice of Harris as the first black and second woman for his Cabinet, housing, civil rights and other special-interest groups registered reactions ranging from icy disapproval to warm praise. Although conceded to be exceptionally bright and able, Harris, 52, has had no experience in housing or urban affairs, a fact not lost on the National Association of Home Builders and the United States Conference of Mayors. Both groups deplored her selection, with the mayors complaining that Harris had shown "a striking insensitivity to the problems of the cities."

While Rep. Parren Mitchell (D Md.), head of the Congressional Black Caucus, called the nomination "great," the National Association for the Advancement of Colored People pointedly refused to comment. Feminist Gloria Steinem said only that Harris could "bridge the gap between the old and new" faces in the women's movement. What these comments reflected was the mixture of admiration and distrust that Harris' career and establishment connections have always elicited. Personally she is perceived variously as abrasive, warm, aloof, principled and perfectionistic. She is not, apparently, an easy person to know.

Patricia Roberts Harris

Harris was born May 31, 1924, in Mattoon, Ill., where her father, a railroad dining-car waiter, was based. After a brilliant undergraduate performance at Howard University, which awarded her a B.A. *summa cum laude* in 1945, she returned to the Midwest, studying industrial relations at the University of Chicago for two years. At the same time she served as program director of the Chicago YWCA, becoming an executive with the American Council on Human Rights after ending her graduate studies. In the mid-'50s she became executive director of Delta Sigma Theta, a national black sorority. She also married lawyer William Beasley Harris. They have no children.

In the next decade her career took off professionally and politically. Harris had been active in local Democratic politics since 1948. With the encouragement of her husband, now an administrative law judge at the Federal Maritime Commission, Harris earned a law degree with honors from George Washington University in 1960. Four years later she was seconding the nomination of Lyndon B. Johnson at the Democratic national convention, telling delegates that for the first time "we who labor under the double handicap of race and sex see at hand a time when interest and ability, not sex or race, are the criteria by which individuals are judged and permitted to make their contribution to our society."

Within a year Johnson had appointed her U.S. ambassador to Luxemburg—the first black woman to hold that rank—and in 1966 and 1967 she served as an alternate delegate to the United Nations.

Back to Howard

In 1967 Harris returned to Howard, becoming dean of the law school for an abortive 27-day term in 1969. She resigned from her post rather than concede to student demands at the predominantly black school, telling one protestor that she had not stopped "being a white man's nigger to become a black man's nigger."

Harris angers groups that, because of her race, sex or background, expect more sympathy than she usually provides. She said students should be excluded from curriculum planning and other policy decisions at Howard because "the final decisions must be made by people who have a long-range commitment to the institution."

She has been criticized for her move from the embattled university to a major Washington corporate law firm, where her fellow partners include mainline Democrats Sargent Shriver and Max M. Kampelman, a close associate of Sen. Hubert H. Humphrey (D Minn.). Her establishment credentials include directorships of International Business Machines, Chase Manhattan Bank, Scott Paper Co. and the Twentieth Century Fund. She is also a member of the Council on Foreign Relations and the executive board of the NAACP Legal Defense Fund.

Harris is, at best, impatient with the suggestion that she has forgotten her roots. In 1971, when she became the focal point of internecine warfare between reform and regular Democrats, Harris declared herself firmly in favor of reform rules that aimed at bettering representation of minorities and women at the 1972 convention. "Let's face it," she snapped, "25 years ago I couldn't have walked in here through the back door."

Credentials Chairman

The remark came shortly after she had been elected temporary chairman of the 1972 convention credentials committee.

Hand-picked by Democratic Chairman Lawrence F. O'Brien and heavily backed by organized labor, distrustful of the new delegate-selection rules, Harris beat out a reformer, Sen. Harold E. Hughes (D Iowa 1969-75), for the post. Under her direction, the committee in 1972 upheld a challenge to the California winner-take-all primary law that cost front-runner Sen. George McGovern (D S.D.) 151 convention delegate votes.

The committee also unseated some 59 Chicago-area delegates for failure to observe the new selection procedures. This action was a major affront to one party kingpin, Chicago Mayor Richard J. Daley.

In 1976 Harris, a national committeewoman-at-large, presented to the convention the platform section on relations with the U.S.S.R., and she subsequently served as vice chairman of the Carter-Mondale coordinating committee.

Confirmed by the Senate on Jan. 20, Harris faced a stiff first year in office. Virtually every federal mortgage credit and housing program was due to expire in September 1977, as was a community development block-grant program. Even Harris' detractors in housing and urban affairs gave her high marks for ability and enterprise and not all shared the gloomy view of mayor's conference official John J. Gunther that she will need two years of "on-the-job training."

Transportation:

Brock Adams

When Washington Democrat Brock Adams finished his term as chairman of the House Budget Committee, he spoke with relish of returning from "the billion-dollar world of macroeconomics to what has been a long-standing interest, our national transportation system."

But instead of returning to his position as second-ranking Democrat on the Interstate and Foreign Commerce Committee's Transportation and Commerce Subcommittee, Adams will be serving as Transportation Secretary in the Carter administration.

Adams began his new job with an established reputation as one of the leading congressional experts in the field of transportation. When House Speaker Carl Albert (D Okla.) appointed Adams to the National Transportation Policy Study Commission in August 1976, he praised Adams' "truly outstanding record of accomplishment in the field of national and regional transportation legislation." Adams has been a prime mover behind important transportation legislation such as the Airport and Airways Development Act of 1970 and the Regional Rail Reorganization Act of 1973.

Budget Chairman

But transportation has not been Adams' only specialty during his 12 years in the House. In the 94th Congress, he gained a national reputation as chairman of the House Budget Committee, leading efforts of reformers to assert congressional authority over the federal budget as a whole.

Brock Adams

He took charge of the committee during the crucial first two years of the new congressional budget process, at a time when there was widespread doubt that the disparate interests in Congress would be able to agree on overall spending levels. Through close cooperation with committee chairmen and a solid background in the facts-and-figures of the budget, he helped guide Congress successfully through the first full exercise of the budgetary process.

Adams should be particularly helpful in establishing good relations between the new administration and Congress. He was one of its most popular and respected members. The next Speaker of the House, Thomas P. O'Neill Jr. of Massachusetts, echoed the prevailing sentiment when he called Adams "one of the most talented and hardest working members of Congress." The House leadership was so pleased by his performance as Budget chairman that they considered changing the law to allow him to serve more than two years as chairman. There was even talk of supporting him for majority leader in the 95th Congress. Both ideas were eventually dropped at Adams' own request.

It was widely known that Adams was ready to leave the House. He was poised to run for the Senate in 1976, had Washington Sen. Henry M. Jackson won the Democratic presidential nomination. The term of Sen. Warren G. Magnuson (D), who is 71, expires in 1980, and some observers feel that Adams views the transportation post as an ideal base from which to launch a campaign.

Adams was born in Atlanta on January 13, 1927. During the Depression his family moved West, finally settling in Seattle in 1940. He served in the Navy from 1944 to 1946, and graduated from the University of Washington in 1949. He received his law degree from Harvard in 1952. Soon after returning to Seattle to practice law he met and befriended young Sen. John F. Kennedy (D Mass.). Adams worked on the Kennedy campaign in 1960, and in 1961 he was appointed United States Attorney for the Western District of Washington. In 1964, he was elected to the House from the 7th District, defeating K. William Stinson, a conservative Republican. He has been re-elected with increasingly more comfortable margins ever since.

Voting Record

In the House, Adams has compiled a consistently liberal, pro-labor voting record. His ratings from the liberal Americans for Democratic Action have never dipped below the 79 per cent he received his first year, while his scores from the conservative Americans for Constitutional Action have seldom reached double figures. He broke with the Johnson administration over the Vietnam War in August 1967, and was the first member of Congress to announce his support for the presidential campaign of Robert F. Kennedy.

Adams was an early supporter of the wave of congressional reform. In 1968, he joined a small group of liberal Democrats and Republicans pushing to force a vote on changes in campaign spending laws and congressional procedures. In 1971, he led the fight to remove John McMillan (D S.C.) as chairman of the District of Columbia Committee. McMillan was re-elected by the Democratic Caucus on a 126 to 96 vote.

Adams was a leading liberal member of the District Committee at that time, and after McMillan was defeated in a primary run-off in September 1972, he joined with chairman Charles C. Diggs Jr. (D Mich.) in pushing District legislation that had been blocked by McMillan. He served as chairman of the government operations subcommittee that drafted the legislation giving home rule for the District.

It was as a member of the transportation subcommittee of the Commerce Committee that Adams acquired his wide-ranging expertise in transportation problems. His most important achievement came in 1973, when, along with Richard G. Shoup (R Mont.), he developed legislation reorganizing the bankrupt railroads of the Northeast and Midwest. The massive reorganization consolidated the bankrupt firms into one corporation, ConRail, and provided government loan guarantees and operating subsidies. Adams was applauded by conservatives for his efforts to, in his words, "save these railroads from government ownership."

Boeing Corp. is the largest employer in Adams' district, and he has, along with the rest of the Washington delegation, been a supporter of the aerospace industry. In 1971, he voted to continue funding the SST. In 1976, he opposed efforts to halt the landing of the supersonic Concorde at New York and Washington, D.C., airports.

Adams was defeated by Al Ullman (D Ore.) for the chairmanship of the new Budget Committee in August 1974. Ullman resigned to become chairman of the Ways and Means Committee, and Adams was elected to fill his place in February 1975. As chairman, he steered a centrist course, with an emphasis on realism in government programs. He stressed fiscal responsibility, telling *The Washington Post* that "the new reality is that we have to live within our revenues." At the same time he supported Democratic orthodoxy on social issues; in his March 1976 proposal on the fiscal 1977 budget he denounced President Ford's restrictive economic policies as reflecting "a callousness toward the unemployed which Congress must reject."

Transportation Policy

Adams brings to the Transportation Department a commitment to reorganization of government transportation agencies. In October 1976 he called for the combination of all government transportation offices into one agency, and for the consolidation of all regulatory functions into a single "transportation court." In 1975 he came out in support of the establishment of a congressional Select Committee on Transportation.

Though he is a critic of the current structure of transportation regulation, Adams did not support the Ford administration plan for loosening government control of the industry. He favors practical reform of the system, rather than abolition. One reform he has proposed would be to require the regulatory agencies to establish wide-ranging rules, rather than to make decisions on a case-by-case basis.

One issue certain to arise in the 95th Congress will be the continuation of the Highway Trust Fund, long a sore spot with urban members who want to use the funds for mass transit. Adams supported an unsuccessful move in 1973 to allow the cities to spend up to $700-million from the fund for mass transit. He now favors the creation of a "combined transportation account," which would allow selection of the best method of financing for each mode of transportation. Under this proposal, mass transit, as a public service, would be financed out of general government revenues.

UN Ambassador:

Andrew Young

The choice of Rep. Andrew Young (D Ga.) to head the U.S. delegation to the United Nations signaled a clear change in the style of U.S. foreign policy, particularly toward Third World nations. It was less sure that Young, who was openly sympathetic to the economic aspirations of developing nations, would be able to affect the substance of foreign policy from his post on the East River.

A skilled negotiator who forged major desegregation plans in southern cities during the 1960s, Young has called for a moral dimension in U.S. alliances, and he dislikes the politics of confrontation that have recently split the international forum.

An ordained minister and top aide to the late Martin Luther King Jr., Young himself has deplored aspects of U.S. foreign policy. "We've come down on the wrong side of too many issues," he told a Foreign Policy Association meeting in New York. In a clear reference to South Africa, where he had recently toured, Young said that the United States had

"unwittingly supported the worst leadership groups and as a consequence we have become party to a vast network of oppression. We have ignored the real human needs."

The 44-year-old black Georgian also told the group that he had felt "very much at home in South Africa—it was just

Andrew Young

like traveling in Mississippi or Louisiana or Georgia when I was a child." But the congressman from the "New South" added that he couldn't write off South African whites because he had learned "how far people can go if they have to."

Cool and articulate, Young's style reflects a comfortably middle-class childhood in New Orleans—far from the harsh realities of rural racism—and a thoughtful education. With a degree from Howard University (1951), Young decided upon the ministry largely, he has said, because of the independence church leaders seemed to have within the community.

After graduating from Hartford Theological Seminary (1955), where he was much influenced by the writings of Gandhi, Young served as a pastor of several Georgia and Alabama churches.

By 1957, Young had become youth activities director for the National Council of Churches. Three years later he moved directly into civil rights work, joining the Southern Christian Leadership Conference's (SCLC) voter education project, which prepared unregistered southern blacks for state literacy tests.

For the next decade Young's career paralleled the dramatic unfolding of the civil rights movement and the young activist was among those present at the major desegregation demonstrations in the South. At Birmingham, Selma and other violent confrontations, Young marched, was beaten and went to jail with his mentor, King. In 1964 he became executive director of King's SCLC. But he spent more days at the bargaining table than behind bars, gaining a reputation as a shrewd and effective conciliator.

One of Young's first successes came in Birmingham in 1963 when he secured from the white power structure important commitments on desegregating schools and public facilities. The agreement came only after Young and King appealed to Roger Blough of U.S. Steel—a major employer in the racially torn city—to gain a hearing with recalcitrant local officials. In 1969, Young was instrumental in resolving a long and bitter hospital strike with racial overtones in Charleston, S.C., reportedly when he appealed as a minister to the hospital administrator, himself the son of a missionary.

The year after the Charleston agreement, Young turned his sights to national politics, running for Congress from Atlanta's 5th District. Despite the district's sizable black population, Young lost badly to Republican incumbent Fletcher Thompson in a campaign which featured film clips in which Young seemed to endorse the militant Black Panther organization and the "destruction of western civilization." While waiting for another chance to run, Young served as chairman of the Atlanta Community Relations Commission.

By 1972, court-ordered redistricting had lopped off the most conservative white sections of the old 5th, and Thompson left the seat to run for the Senate. Young spent a lot of time with white voters, campaigning against an unpopular freeway proposal and for cleaning up the Chattahoochee River. He finished with 53 per cent of the vote to become the first black man since Reconstruction elected to Congress from the old Confederacy. (Rep. Barbara Jordan was elected from Texas the same year.) Young easily was reelected to the House in 1974 and 1976.

Ford Vote

Once in Congress, Young showed a quick aptitude for the unwritten rules of the game. His closeness to the congressional establishment has occasionally discomfited members of the Black Caucus, who object particularly to his vote—the only one of the Caucus—to confirm Gerald Ford as Spiro Agnew's successor. Young recently told *The Washington Post* that he had revised his earlier view of Ford, who he originally thought a "harmless conservative." But he added that Atlanta had received close to a billion dollars in federal funds, adding that, "Whenever I can, I cooperate with an administration."

On the record, Young's votes have supported busing for desegregation of schools and extension of the Voting Rights Act. The liberal Americans for Democratic Action consistently has considered Young's voting record near-perfect. More typically, Young during his first term quietly took the problem of under-funded black land-grant colleges to Rep. Jamie L. Whitten (D Miss.), chairman of the Agriculture Appropriations Subcommittee. Whitten, one of the most outspoken segregationists in the House, ended by including funds for the hardpressed colleges in a routine bill which passed without comment. Such tactics have earned Young general recognition as a "man of sweet reason," a fact not lost on the House leadership which, in 1975, seated him on the powerful House Rules Committee.

Young's record in Congress, however, is far from parochial. Committee assignments put him in touch with consumer issues, mass transit, and foreign economic policy. One of his first floor victories came when he succeeded in amending a foreign aid bill to provide for suspension of aid to Portugal if the money were funneled to that nation's African wars. He was an early and outspoken opponent of American involvement in Southeast Asia. "We had that war," he has said, "because we had a racist Congress who thought the Third World was to be manipulated." Young voted for the Turkish arms cutoff and the ban on American aid to anti-Soviet factions fighting in Angola.

Young has stated that he does not believe African nations are opposed to Israel. He voted in 1975 to condemn a U.N. resolution equating Zionism with racism.

Pushing Carter

Young took probably the biggest risk of his career when he decided to put his reputation on the line for a south Georgia peanut farmer with questionable liberal credentials and an extremely long shot at the presidency.

Young and Carter had met on the campaign trail in 1970 when Carter stumped successfully for the Georgia governorship. Though not close then, they stayed in touch and Young made a conditional commitment in 1976 to support Carter in the Florida primary, largely because he thought his fellow Georgian had the best chance of knocking off Alabama Governor George C. Wallace.

Young appealed to other moderate and liberal Democrats to leave the Florida race to Carter. His support, coupled with his unquestioned status among black voters, is credited with turning out more than 75,000 crucial black votes for Carter.

What Young did in Florida with such effect he repeated on a national level, crisscrossing the country, orchestrating his contacts with black religious leaders and speaking on Carter's behalf at churches where, as Young says, "you can still meet a lot of the right people." At the same time Young, who received a 100 per cent rating from the AFL-CIO in 1975, was building bridges to skeptical white liberals.

When Carter tangled himself in the "ethnic purity" gaffe, Young publicly termed the statement a "disaster" and insisted that Carter apologize. Young's seconding speech at the Democratic National Convention gives a clue to his evident trust of the white southerner. The South, he said, had "laid down the burden of race" and had been "liberated."

From Young's foreign policy positions and his carefully nurtured contacts with the African diplomatic community, he may be expected to use the U.N. post to push for a comparable "liberation" of U.S. policy. He will be a decided change from the flamboyant Daniel Patrick Moynihan, the newly-elected senator from New York. The former U.N. ambassador's provocative speeches infuriated Third World nations and often embarrassed U.S. allies.

Young's version of a new U.S. foreign policy combines ethical and practical considerations. On the one hand, he has declared that "Once we get on the right side of moral issues in this world, then we can have an orderly approach to the problems of the Middle East and a genuine dialogue on the international economic order." On the other hand, he has urged higher payments for Third-World raw materials because he believes that the money would be returned in the form of increased orders from developing nations for U.S. products—and thereby create more jobs for the unemployed. He disparages U.S. deference to the white-minority government of South Africa and a concomitant lack of interest in Nigeria which, he states, "is now a larger trading partner" of the U.S.

Confirmed by the Senate Jan. 26, Young became the first black to head the U.S. delegation to the United Nations, and the first to be named to a Cabinet-level position in the Carter administration.

He is married to an instructor at an Atlanta junior college and has four children.

National Security Council:
Zbigniew Brzezinski

Carter's choice for assistant to the President for national security affairs and director of the National Security Council, Zbigniew Brzezinski, 48, in many ways reminds one of his well-known predecessor, Secretary of State Henry A. Kissinger. Kissinger held those posts from 1969 to November 1975.

Despite some similarities, their world outlooks differ substantially, and Brzezinski could play an important part in reshaping the Kissinger foreign policy as formulated and carried out during the past eight years.

Background

Brzezinski was born March 28, 1928, in Warsaw, the son of a Polish diplomat. In 1938, a year before Russian and German armies divided up Poland, Brzezinski's father was assigned to Montreal as consul general. Brzezinski remained in Montreal and graduated from McGill University with honors in economics and political science in 1949 and with an M.A. degree in political science a year later.

In 1953 Harvard awarded him a Ph.D. degree and offered him a position as an instructor and research fellow at its Russian Research Center. In 1960 he accepted the post of associate professor of government and public law at Columbia University; in 1962 he became a full professor, a position he currently holds.

In 1964 Brzezinski worked for President Johnson's re-election as a member of the Young Citizens for Johnson. In 1966 he took his first government job, serving until 1968 as a member of the State Department's Policy Planning Council.

Zbigniew Brzezinski

Aside from numerous magazine articles, which he annotated and distributed to public figures, he is the author of several books, including *The Permanent Purge-Politics in Soviet Totalitarianism* (1956), *The Soviet Bloc—Unity and Conflict* (1960) and *Between Two Ages* (1970).

During the 1976 campaign, at least five Democratic candidates other than Carter received his advice.

Kissinger Critic

In an article appearing in the summer 1976 issue of *Foreign Policy,* Brzezinski argued that the foreign policy pursued by Nixon and Kissinger "seemed committed to a largely static view of the world, based on a traditional balance of power, seeking accommodation among the major powers on the basis of spheres of influence, and more generally oriented toward preserving the status quo than reforming it."

Writing in the same journal two years earlier, he had conceded that the two men had scored some impressive achievements, including the ending of the Vietnam War, the opening to China, initial steps toward detente with the Soviet Union and initial progress toward a Middle East settlement. But Brzezinski insisted that by 1974 the process of detente was proceeding to the disproportionate advantage of the Soviet Union, while U.S. relations with its principal allies, Western Europe and Japan, were at a low ebb.

In part, Brzezinski argued, the fault lay with President Nixon's and Kissinger's conduct of diplomacy as a secretive duet, with the result that foreign policy—notably detente—had been manipulated to serve their domestic political requirements. But he maintained that the policy's basic flaw was its basis in an obsolete conception of world politics.

World Order Transformed

Contrary to the assumptions of the old policy, said Brzezinski, the great powers have been losing their dominance of world politics. The newer, developing countries, with their demands for greater benefits from the international economy, are assuming greater importance, he emphasized. Meanwhile, Western Europe and Japan have been challenging U.S. leadership of the world political system, although they themselves are unable to substitute for that leadership.

He concluded: "Relations among the most advanced societies, notably in Western Europe, Japan and the United States, call for a new political framework. New cooperative arrangements are needed with the *nouveaux riches*—especially the [Middle East] oil producers—who must be given a creative stake in the global system. Finally, the [developing countries], some of which are rapidly becoming...the global equivalents of our black ghettos, cannot be left out of any effort to refashion existing relations."

Brzezinski's voluminous writings are short on details about the new global political system toward which the United States should strive. He has maintained repeatedly that economic relations will loom much larger in the future than in the period since World War II. In addition, he has called repeatedly, usually without elaboration, for U.S. policymakers to reverse their current priorities and assign the highest importance to U.S. relations with its western European and Japanese allies rather than with its adversaries: the Soviet Union and China.

A New Kissinger?

Sensitive to comparisons between himself and Kissinger, Brzezinski emphasized at a Dec. 16 press conference that he did not envision "policy-making" as part of his new job. In addition, he described Secretary of State-designate Cyrus R. Vance as Carter's "primary advisor on foreign affairs."

The strongest force working against Brzezinski's emergence as the Kissinger of the Carter administration could be the precedent itself, which was strongly condemned by both Carter and Brzezinski, the latter having labeled Kissinger's domination of foreign policy-making under Nixon a triumph of "the personal over the politic" and an "acrobatic" juggling act.

Even if Brzezinski tried to assert control over the Carter foreign policy, he would likely find Vance a formidable opponent, since Vance has far more experience in the conduct of foreign affairs than did Nixon's first Secretary of State, William Rogers, over whom Kissinger rode roughshod.

But the ultimate factor in how foreign policy is to be made in the new administration could be the least predictable ingredient of them all: the character of Jimmy Carter as President of the United States.

Council of Economic Advisers:

Charles L. Schultze

Charles Louis Schultze so impressed President-elect Jimmy Carter and his advisers that a position for him in the new administration was considered a certainty. The question was which one.

Since Carter's election, Schultze had been mentioned as a possible Secretary of the Treasury, Secretary of Defense, Chairman of the Council of Economic Advisers (CEA) and other jobs. Carter proposed Schultze Dec. 16 for the CEA post.

It was Schultze's second job with the council and a dramatic step up from his position as a staff economist from 1953-59.

A member of the Democratic "shadow cabinet" during the Nixon-Ford era, Schultze, who turned 52 Dec. 12, left his positions as a senior fellow at

Charles L. Schultze

the Brookings Institution, an independent research organization, and as economics professor at the University of Maryland to take the CEA post.

Schultze has been described as a liberal Democrat and a Keynesian economist who believes that government can actively influence the economy through fiscal policy to assure healthy expansion. But he also is known as a hard-headed skeptic when it comes to assessing the value of government spending programs. His objections to details of the Humphrey-Hawkins full-employment bill (S 50) helped sidetrack the measure in 1976.

Background

Schultze was born in the Washington, D.C., suburb of Alexandria, Va., Dec. 12, 1924. He graduated in economics from Georgetown University in Washington in 1948.

For the next 12 years Schultze studied part-time for graduate degrees in economics, obtaining his M.A. from Georgetown in 1950 and his Ph.D. from the University of Maryland in 1960.

Schultze began his government service in 1952 as a staff economist at the Office of Price Stabilization, where he served a year before moving over to the Council of Economic Advisers, again as a staff economist. He left the job in 1959 to become an associate professor of economics at Indiana University in Bloomington and then became a professor of economics at Maryland in 1961. He resumed government work in 1962 as assistant director of the Bureau of the Budget.

At 40, Schultze in 1965 became the youngest ever to hold the position of director of the Budget Bureau. It was reorganized and renamed the Office of Management and Budget in 1970. He resigned in January 1968 to take the positions he held before his CEA appointment.

Original Thinker

Schultze's innovative ideas elevated him to a position as a principal economic architect of the Kennedy and Johnson administrations. While at Indiana University, he developed a concept known as the "full employment surplus," a gauge for measuring the impact of federal tax and spending programs on the economy by relating them to the economy if it were operating at a full-employment level. President Kennedy's Budget Bureau Director David E. Bell adopted Schultze's concept and hired him as an assistant director in 1962.

Upon becoming Budget Bureau director in 1965, Schultze implemented for all federal departments cost-effectiveness techniques introduced at the Pentagon by then-Defense Secretary Robert S. McNamara. The procedure was called "planning-programming-budgeting system" (PPBS). *Forbes* magazine in its Feb. 1, 1967, issue, praised Schultze's budgetary effort as "the first attempt of the U.S. government to figure out in detail what it really is spending the tax dollar for."

Fiscal Views

A leading spokesman for the Kennedy-Johnson programs of federal economic stimulus, Schultze was recruited by unsuccessful Democratic presidential candidates Hubert H. Humphrey (Minn.) in 1968 and George McGovern (S.D.) in 1972 to advise them on the economy.

For the future, OMB director Thomas B. (Bert) Lance is likely to find Schultze an ally in urging tax cuts in 1977. Testifying before the Senate Budget Committee in December 1974, Schultze advised tax cuts to pull the economy out of its deep recession. In an October 1976 interview on NBC-TV's *Today* program, Schultze suggested economic stimulus might be necessary.

"I don't think we ought to rush in with an immediate dose of stimulus, but we are getting closer and closer and closer to the point where that might be necessary," he said. Schultze also said he attributed the Fall 1976 pause in economic recovery in part to government spending falling short of the levels anticipated in the fiscal 1976 budget. The spending reduction offset the positive effects of tax reductions, Schultze said.

Military Spending

Since leaving government service in 1968, Schultze has been critical of the nation's military policies and defense spending. At a March 1969 Conference on Military Budget and National Priorities in Washington, he said, "The general attitude of the American people is that if you wrap it in a flag and call it 'national security,' you can't question it." While acknowledging his failure to scrutinize soaring Vietnam-era defense budgets during his Budget Bureau directorship, he urged that future Pentagon budgets be as closely questioned as other civilian agencies.

In an April 1973 article in *Foreign Affairs,* Schultze argued that most of the popular views connecting the economy with national security were wrong or misleading. "Our military strength does not depend, to any significant degree, on the size or rate of growth in our economy...," he wrote.

Schultze was married in 1947 and has six children. Known for his 18-hour work days as Budget Bureau director, he once told a reporter all his spare time was devoted to sleep. "With six kids and a house to take care of, and some reading to do, there isn't much time left for anything else," he explained. ∎

Central Intelligence Agency:

Stansfield Turner

President Carter's nomination Feb. 7 of Adm. Stansfield Turner as Director of Central Intelligence encountered little opposition in the Senate, which confirmed the nomination by voice vote Feb. 24.

The selection of a career naval officer did not arouse the ire of foreign policy hardliners, who in January opposed the confirmation of Carter's first choice for the intelligence post, Theodore C. Sorensen.

Senate Intelligence Committee member Gary Hart (D Colo.), a liberal who had supported Sorensen, initially expressed concern about a military man heading the CIA since that agency had been "designed to be independent of the military." But Hart said he had been impressed by Turner's performance in his most recent post of NATO forces commander for southern Europe and would not oppose the nomination because of Turner's military background.

Under fire from liberals and conservatives alike for his handling of the Sorensen nomination, Carter took pains to consult with Intelligence Committee Chairman Daniel K. Inouye (D Hawaii) and other members of the panel before announcing the Turner appointment.

The Turner Approach

In a January 1977 *Foreign Affairs* article on the U.S.-Soviet naval balance, Turner provided some clues to his assumptions about the role of military forces in global politics and about the process of assessing relative military strength. He argued that the symbolic importance of U.S. forces must be weighed as well as their combat effectiveness. And he said the basic criteria of U.S. military adequacy depended not on technical military judgments, but on political judgments of the scope of U.S. global interests and the acceptable degree of risk to those interests.

Adm. Stansfield Turner

Symbolic Force. Turner said that one of the Navy's major missions was the exertion of psychological leverage on allies, neutrals and opponents by demonstrating a naval "presence" in areas of interest to the United States. The question of the psychological impact of weaponry is basic to the current debate over the U.S.-Soviet strategic nuclear balance.

Former Defense Secretaries James R. Schlesinger and Donald H. Rumsfeld maintained that Soviet advantages in the number and size of its intercontinental ballistic missiles (ICBMs) could embolden Moscow while eroding the morale of the Western democracies in a political showdown. The current Pentagon chief, Harold Brown, and President Carter's nominee to head the U.S. arms control agency, Paul C. Warnke, argued that the so-called Soviet advantages were militarily insignificant and would take on political importance only if exaggerated by U.S. leaders.

In his article on naval power, Turner maintained that military forces might have a political impact that depended not on the fleet's power but, rather, on the audience's "subjective perceptions" of that power. These perceptions, he said, "may be based on numbers, on superficial appearances (size of ships, new versus old, etc.), on techniques of employment, or simply on the rhetoric that accompanies the fleet's arrival."

But Turner also warned, as did Harold Brown during his Jan. 12 confirmation hearings, that U.S. officials might contribute to the perception of Soviet strength by alarmist statements: "A doomsday picture convincingly drawn for a congressional budgetary committee may negatively influence other nations' perceptions of our naval effectiveness. And a few extra ships in the budget or at sea may not be enough to overcome an inaccurate perception of weakness."

Combat Effectiveness. Turner dismissed static comparisons of the numbers of U.S. and Soviet weapons as the source of a "fruitless debate on the wrong issues." He insisted: "What one navy requires may not be what another needs if their missions differ." Whether U.S. forces were becoming more able or less able to carry out their assigned missions depended not only on changes in the number of weapons, but also on "technological developments which increase vulnerability or potency and such tempering factors as extension or loss of base facilities, national resolve and alliance solidarity."

With that attitude, Turner, as director, might lessen the disputes over numbers of missiles, ships and tanks that have accompanied recent congressional deliberations on the defense budget. The controversy over the fiscal 1977 Pentagon budget, for example, took as its starting point a January 1976 study of the U.S.-Soviet military balance compiled by the Library of Congress. That study warned against reliance on mere quantitative comparisons and said the real question was whether U.S. forces could perform assigned missions. But the numerical comparisons were a

---

Director's Intelligence Role

Under President Ford's executive order of Feb. 18, 1976, reorganizing the U.S. government's foreign intelligence agencies, the director of central intelligence not only heads the CIA but also serves as the President's "primary adviser" on foreign intelligence. He is responsible for setting national intelligence requirements and priorities and, as chairman of the Committee on Foreign Intelligence, has authority over the budget requests and management policies of those agencies that produce "national intelligence" (excluding military tactical intelligence).

The executive order also made the director responsible for protecting intelligence sources and methods and for ensuring that each intelligence agency had a strong inspector general's office to prevent any illegal or improper actions by the agencies. He also was made the intelligence community's spokesman before Congress.

At the insistence of the House Appropriations Committee, the final version of the fiscal 1977 defense appropriations bill (HR 14262—PL 94-419) included an appropriation of $5.6-million to ensure that the staff through which the director carried out his oversight of the intelligence community would be separated from the CIA bureaucracy.

powerful weapon in the hands of those opposed to major cuts in the Pentagon's budget.

Political Judgments. The basic decisions that must be made about U.S. military preparedness, according to Turner, require political judgments rather than technical military knowledge. Because of growing Soviet naval power, "we are moving into a shrinking range of political options and a higher level of risk." But the acceptability of this situation "depends on judgments which transcend the power of military men."

If Turner emphasizes that point of view as Director of Central Intelligence, debate over the U.S.-Soviet military balance might be directed to underlying assumptions about U.S. foreign policy goals. Despite an abortive attempt to hold a "great debate" on U.S. global policy during the Senate's consideration of the fiscal 1976 weapons authorization bill, attention usually focused on narrow military comparisons, with little systematic attention to the political context in which the United States would face the question of using force.

Turner Background

Besides suggesting an intellectual bent, the 53-year-old admiral's career indicates a degree of iconoclasm that is uncommon in the Navy, generally regarded as the most tradition-bound of the armed services.

After joining the Naval Reserve at Amherst College, which he attended from 1941 to 1943, Turner entered the Naval Academy class of 1947, (which graduated in 1946 because of an accelerated schedule during World War II). Turner graduated 25th in the class of 820; Jimmy Carter ranked 59th. Reportedly, the two were not personally acquainted at Annapolis.

After an initial tour of sea duty, Turner won a Rhodes scholarship and, in 1950, received a Masters degree in philosophy, politics and economics from Oxford University. He served principally on destroyers and commanded the guided missile frigate Horne off the coast of Vietnam in 1967. In 1970, while concluding a two-year tour as military aide to the Secretary of the Navy, then-Captain Turner spent six weeks assisting Adm. Elmo R. Zumwalt Jr. plan a reorganization of Navy shipbuilding and personnel regulations that were to be the central theme of Zumwalt's tour as Chief of Naval Operations (1970-74). After two years commanding a carrier task force in the Mediterranean, Turner returned to Washington to head the Navy's Office of Systems Analysis.

War College Chief. As President of the Naval War College (1972-74), Turner radically reformed the curriculum. He placed greater emphasis on historical analysis of military strategy. He greatly increased the

Military Officers at CIA

Confirmed by the Senate Feb. 24, Adm. Stansfield Turner became the sixth military officer to head the Central Intelligence Agency or its immediate predecessors. The others were:

Rear Adm. Sidney W. Souers. A Missouri businessman who served in the naval reserve during and after World War II. Souers was the author of the 1946 intelligence reorganization plan that eventually led to the establishment of the CIA. Souers was the intelligence chief from January through June 1946.

Lt. Gen. Hoyt S. Vandenberg (USAF). The chief of Army intelligence in 1946 (before the creation of a separate Air Force), Vandenberg was the unanimous nominee of the Army, Navy and State Departments to replace Souers. He was a nephew of Sen. Arthur H. Vandenberg (R Mich. 1928-51), who was the architect of the bipartisan foreign policy of the late 1940s. Vandenberg served through May 1947.

Rear Adm. Roscoe H. Hillenkoetter. Director of Central Intelligence from May 1947 through October 1950, Hillenkoetter came under heavy congressional fire for allegedly failing to warn of the North Korean attack on South Korea June 25, 1950.

Gen. Walter Bedell Smith. Well-known as Gen. Dwight D. Eisenhower's chief of staff during World War II, Smith was ambassador to Russia from 1946 to 1949. He headed CIA from October 1950 to March 1953.

Vice Adm. William F. Raborn Jr. Raborn had retired in 1963 after receiving high praise for his direction of the Polaris missile development project. He lacked any background in intelligence, and President Lyndon Johnson was strongly criticized for submitting the nomination. Raborn served for only 14 months, April 1964-June 1965, as CIA Director.

By law, only one of the top posts in CIA (director and deputy director) can be held by a military officer.

number of reading assignments and the writing demands placed on the students. In 1972 he told a *New York Times* reporter that he intended to implant an understanding that the Navy's resources were limited and that "tough decisions must be taken if we come to grips with the Soviet Navy." He also said he hoped to encourage senior officers to develop open minds so they could understand hostile points of view and to counter the overconfidence that, he felt, affected some branches of the Navy, including the air arm.

In 1974 Turner assumed command of the Second Fleet, based in the Atlantic, and in 1976 he became commander of NATO forces in southern Europe and the Mediterranean.

Energy Policy Coordinator:

James R. Schlesinger

James R. Schlesinger's appointment as the nation's next "energy czar" drew fire from environmentalists who feared he is too rigidly committed to nuclear power as the answer to America's energy crisis.

Schlesinger's record stamps him beyond dispute as a believer in nuclear power. But he also holds solid—if less visible—credentials of concern for the environment and support for development of non-nuclear energy sources, such as solar power.

"I consider this to be one of the most important appointments that I shall make," commented President-elect Jimmy Carter in naming Schlesinger coordinator of all federal energy programs Dec. 23. Carter, who had won enthusiastic support from environmentalists during his race for the White House, was asked at a press conference that day why he had picked "the strongest booster of nuclear power" to be his energy czar.

"I don't believe that I have," Carter replied.

Schlesinger's claim to expertise in energy affairs stems from his stint as chairman of the old Atomic Energy Commission (AEC) from August 1971 until January 1973.

Shortly after assuming the post, he found himself deep in controversy. The AEC was to supervise the underground test explosion of a five-megaton nuclear bomb Nov. 6, 1971, on Amchitka Island in the Aleutians off Alaska's coast. The test was opposed vigorously by environmentalists.

Convinced that the test did not threaten the environment, Schlesinger arranged to personally witness the blast accompanied by his wife and two of their eight children.

Nuclear Power Supporter

As AEC director, Schlesinger's support of nuclear-powered electricity generation was unqualified. "I personally would very much prefer to live next door to a nuclear power plant," he said in response to a hypothetical question in a Feb. 14, 1972, *U.S. News & World Report* interview. "It is clean and attractive. The risk of an accident...is exceedingly remote."

Schlesinger also said then that radiation from a nuclear power plant is "exceedingly small" relative to radiation from everyday sources such as medical X-rays.

In the same interview, Schlesinger said he saw "no real alternative" to nuclear generation of electricity—but he keyed that view to a concern for the environment. "Without nuclear plants we would be faced with massive use of fossil fuels—coal, oil, natural gas—and the impact on the environment would be much greater." He also conceded that nuclear plants were not without environmental threats of their own. "Thermal pollution of our streams and rivers by a power plant's heated discharge is the most complicated of all our questions," he said.

Environmentalists Cited

His appreciation of environmentalists' concerns perhaps was best shown in his first major speech as AEC chairman. Addressing an audience of nuclear industry executives in Bal Harbour, Fla., Oct. 20, 1971, Schlesinger said: "Environmentalists have raised many legitimate questions. A number have bad manners, but I believe broadside diatribes against environmentalists to be not only in bad taste but wrong."

His speech went on to alert the nuclear industry that the AEC would be different under his tenure.

James R. Schlesinger

"You should not expect the AEC to fight the industry's political, social and commercial battles," he told the industry's captains, admitting the AEC had done as much in the past. But now, he said, "The AEC exists to serve the public interest."

Schlesinger followed his words with action. One of his first moves was to retain the Arthur D. Little management firm to examine the AEC for structural flaws. The Little firm's report led to the most sweeping internal reorganization in the AEC's history. He juggled the agency's top management, created new decision-making procedures and, perhaps most importantly, formed a new division for environmental and safety affairs. Another Schlesinger innovation put the AEC into the business of developing non-nuclear energy sources for the first time.

He also decided that the agency would not appeal a controversial federal court decision directing the commission to consider the environmental impact of all nuclear power plant site selections.

Energy Views

Schlesinger often has spoken on energy-related questions of public policy. He conceded on "Meet the Press" Dec. 17, 1972, that nuclear power had received a disproportionate share of federal energy research money. "Within the government, energy technology should receive even-handed treatment," he said.

He also has called repeatedly for extensive reorganization of the energy bureaucracy, putting forth conceptual proposals very similar to Jimmy Carter's expressed intent.

Regarding the liquid metal fast breeder nuclear reactor, Schlesinger once said: "The fast breeder is a priority item, but we must keep a very careful watch over its environmental effects."

On the question of nuclear wastes, Schlesinger told *U.S. News & World Report* Feb. 14, 1972, that "we are confident that the salt mines provide a safe storage place." He also noted, however, that proposals such as shooting nuclear wastes by rocket into the sun had been considered as possible future solutions.

Role Under Carter

Carter said Schlesinger would work within the White House to coordinate federal energy policies, a job not subject to Senate confirmation. However, Carter intended to persuade Congress to create a Cabinet-level Department of Energy that Schlesinger presumably would head, a post that would require Senate confirmation.

Apparently, the nuclear industry welcomed Schlesinger's return to a position of energy authority. Former Rep. Craig Hosmer (R Calif. 1953-75), once the ranking Republican on the Joint Committee on Atomic Energy, predicted in an atomic industry newsletter that

Schlesinger will "rev up the nuclear business once again."

Schlesinger Background

James Rodney Schlesinger was born in New York City Feb. 15, 1929. He is a *summa cum laude,* Phi Beta Kappa graduate of Harvard University (1950), where he also earned his masters (1952) and doctorate (1956) degrees, all in economics.

From 1955 through 1963 he taught at the University of Virginia and during those years also served terms as a consultant to the Naval War College and the Federal Reserve System's Board of Governors.

In 1960 he published *The Political Economy of National Security: A Study of the Economic Aspects of the Contemporary Power Struggle.* The book was "based on the contention that the East-West schism will stay unresolved and that this country's position in the western influence sphere must be held at any cost," according to a contemporary review by *Library Journal.*

Officials of the Rand Corporation, a national security think tank in Santa Monica, Calif., were impressed enough to invite Schlesinger in 1963 to become a senior staff member, and by 1967 he was Rand's director of strategic studies.

From 1965 to 1969 he doubled as a consultant to the federal Bureau of the Budget. He entered that agency as an assistant director in 1969 and became assistant director with responsibilities in the areas of national security and energy when the agency became the Office of Management and Budget (OMB).

In August 1971 Schlesinger was named chairman of the Atomic Energy Commission, where he stayed until he became director of the Central Intelligence Agency (CIA) in February 1973. Although only at CIA about three months, Schlesinger launched an ambitious reorganization of "the company." Most analysts credit him with firing about 10 per cent of the total staff. Richard Nixon saved the CIA from Schlesinger by making him Secretary of Defense. Schlesinger took over the Pentagon July 2, 1973, and it was there that he rose to his greatest fame.

Although he was widely credited with trimming $6-billion from the Pentagon's budget while at OMB, once in the top defense job he became an adamant and articulate advocate for beefing up America's defense.

He was vocally skeptical of detente and hostile to cuts in the defense budget. He warned that the Russians were building a huge military machine while America—under President Ford and Secretary of State Henry A. Kissinger—was having the wool of a false detente pulled over its eyes.

Schlesinger's carping proved too much for President Ford and he fired him in November 1975. His dismissal was seen a victory for Kissinger and as a reflection of Ford's discomfort with intellectuals. The act was applauded by few. Even foes of the military on Capitol Hill had respected Schlesinger, a man who "puts things into perspective," as Rep. Les Aspin (D Wis.), an outspoken defense critic, said.

After his curt dismissal Schlesinger served on an academic study project jointly funded by Johns Hopkins and Georgetown Universities, biding his time until he might return to government service.

Adjectives commonly used to describe Schlesinger include brilliant, tweedy, pipe-smoking, arrogant, rumpled, principled, philosophical, professorial, conservative and efficient.

Arms Control and Disarmament Agency:

Paul C. Warnke

President Carter's choice of Paul C. Warnke as chief U.S. delegate to the strategic arms limitation (SALT) talks with the Soviet Union highlighted the ongoing debate over U.S. nuclear arms policy. After the press reported Jan. 31 that Warnke would be nominated to head the Arms Control and Disarmament Agency (ACDA) as well as lead the SALT negotiating team, some members of Congress charged that he would be too "soft" a bargainer with the Russians.

Opponents of the nomination, in arguing that Warnke should not be given the post to conduct negotiations with

Paul C. Warnke

Moscow, cited a 1975 article he wrote on national security policy. In it, Warnke proposed a six-month moratorium on the development of some U.S. strategic weapons in hopes of inducing a similar Soviet response.

Warnke said the U.S.-Soviet strategic balance was sufficiently stable to permit such an initiative. There would be no risk to U.S. national security if the Russians did not reciprocate, he said. The Pentagon's arms programs quickly could be resumed if necessary.

The nomination was formally made Feb. 4. Carter's choice had been disclosed on Feb. 2 by presidential assistant Hamilton Jordan. The delay was due to completion of an FBI security check, according to White House aides.

The Warnke nomination to the SALT job was another blow to those who maintained that the continuing expansion of the Soviet nuclear arsenal demands accelerated development of new U.S. strategic weapons. Carter's strong emphasis on the importance of reaching a new SALT agreement and his selection of Harold Brown as Secretary of Defense already had disturbed some congressional hardliners. They were certain to challenge at least Warnke's appointment to head the SALT bargaining team when the Senate considered the ACDA nomination.

Views on Strategic Weapons

Warnke has argued that the only value of U.S. and Soviet strategic nuclear weapons is to forestall each other's use of such arms by the threat of devastating retaliation. This deterrent threat, he maintained, would be effective even if the Soviet Union had a greater number of nuclear weapons because a sufficient U.S. retaliatory force would survive any imaginable Soviet attack. The force of 656 submarine-launched missiles, some of which carry 10 or more separately aimed warheads, represented a more than adequate nuclear deterrent, according to this view.

This mutual hostage relationship between the two superpowers ruled out the use of strategic nuclear arms as levers of political influence since their use could not credibly be threatened. Moreover, it was his position that the United States need not match every Soviet weapon development; it could defer its own arms program, up to a point, without undue risk while seeking arms limitation agreements with Moscow.

The opposite position, held by former Secretary of Defense James R. Schlesinger, among others, insists that the strategic balance is inherently unstable and that if the Soviet Union is allowed to develop a large lead in the quantity of weapons, it could derive massive political advantage. They warn that with a large enough force of intercontinental ballistic missiles (ICBMs), the Russians could destroy most of the U.S. ICBM force while retaining enough missiles to hold U.S. cities hostage against a U.S. retaliatory strike. They maintain that this view has become even more plausible since the Soviets stepped up development of their civil defense system, which is intended to protect their population against U.S. retaliation.

If such a Soviet advantage were perceived, the Russians, according to the Schlesinger group, would be emboldened to pursue a more adventurous course against U.S. allies and non-aligned countries while brandishing the tacit threat of their massive conventional military might. These states, believing that the United States could give them no assistance, would cave in to Soviet demands.

This situation could result, they maintain, even if the Soviets erroneously concluded that, on the basis of cuts in Pentagon spending, the United States lacked the will to counter the Soviet threat.

But Warnke has maintained that the Soviet Union could capitalize on perceived "advantages" that had no basis in fact only if they were given credibility by unduly pessimistic assessments of U.S. strength.

Carter's initial decisions in the nuclear arms field appeared to go against the hardliners. In his inaugural address and in press interviews, the President repeatedly placed the highest priority on conclusion of a new SALT agreement. He said he would not let the two outstanding arms control issues, the U.S. cruise missile and the Soviet Backfire bomber, stand in the way.

Support/Opposition

On Feb. 1 an anonymous memo was circulated to several members of Congress charging, on the basis of selective quotations from his writings, that Warnke supported unilateral U.S. arms reductions "to levels far below anything being proposed in current arms limitation talks."

At a Senate Armed Services Committee hearing later that day, Sam Nunn (D Ga.) asked Air Force Chief of Staff Gen. David C. Jones to comment on an excerpt from a 1972 memo in which Warnke argued that "substantial nuclear superiority, short of nuclear monopoly, could not be a decisive factor in any political confrontation between the United States and the Soviet Union."

Jones disagreed strongly with this statement, insisting that U.S. nuclear superiority in October 1962 had contributed to the Soviets' decision to withdraw their missiles from Cuba. Nunn then identified Warnke as the author of the statement and urged Armed Services Committee Chairman John C. Stennis (D Miss.) to ask Warnke to appear before that panel as well as Foreign Relations.

In a House speech Feb. 2, Samuel S. Stratton (D N.Y.) charged that Warnke favored unilateral disarmament and that, as SALT negotiator, he "would be likely to give away the store in a mistaken mood of guilt and good will." Stratton maintained that the U.S. negotiator needed "a hard-nosed, realistic attitude" toward the U.S.S.R. that would alert him to Soviet efforts to insert loopholes in any accord.

He observed that, although only the Senate would vote on the nomination, "strong opposition in the House to an individual could well imperil support for any SALT treaty that might subsequently be presented to the House for approval." The 1972 SALT agreement limiting strategic offensive weapons, which was not a treaty requiring Senate ratification, was submitted to both houses of Congress for approval in the form of a joint resolution (H J Res 1227—PL 92-448).

Warnke's supporters began to counterattack Feb. 2. Senate Majority Whip Alan Cranston (D Calif.) told the Senate he had assurances from the White House that the nomination would be made. "ACDA should have a strong voice at its head," he said, "to compete with the powerful bureaucratic forces that drive defense budgets ever higher...." Four other senators voiced support for Warnke.

Secretary of State Cyrus R. Vance, who had been deputy secretary of defense during part of Warnke's Pentagon tenure, spoke up on behalf of his former colleague Feb. 3. He called Warnke "superbly qualified" and condemned the anonymous anti-Warnke memo as "a gross misstatement of his views."

The Senate Foreign Relations Committee Feb. 22 voted overwhelmingly to recommend Warnke's confirmation to the two posts, calling his nomination an "excellent choice." However, in the Armed Services Committee, Warnke was opposed by a margin of two to one during hearings on the nomination. The panel decided not to take a formal position on the nomination since Armed Services lacked jurisdiction.

Floor debate on the nomination began March 4 and lasted four days; on March 9, the Senate voted to confirm Warnke as the top arms negotiator and as director of the Arms Control and Disarmament Agency.

Carter's Inauguration, His Style, Early Priorities

Jimmy Carter was sworn in as the 39th President of the United States Jan. 20. He called for a "new national spirit of unity and trust" and the leadership of a government "both competent and compassionate."

Chief Justice Warren E. Burger administered the oath of office to the 52-year-old Georgian two minutes after noon, the constitutionally designated time for the passing of power from one administration to the next. A crowd estimated at 150,000 cheered as Carter repeated the 35-word pledge.

Then he began his 14-minute inaugural speech, one of the shortest ever. "For myself and for our nation, I want to thank my predecessor for all he has done to heal our land," Carter began. The newly installed Democrat turned and shook the hand of Gerald R. Ford, the Republican he had replaced. Ford acknowledged the applause of the crowd, and Carter continued.

He reiterated his campaign themes of "a new beginning, a new dedication within our government and a new spirit among us all." But he admitted, as the first President of the nation's third century, that "I have no new dream to set forth today, but rather urge a fresh faith in the old dream."

Faith, in fact, was an important thread running through the message of Carter, a Baptist whose two-year campaign for the presidency emphasized his religious beliefs. He took his oath with his left hand on a Bible that has been in his family for four generations. It was open to a page containing the admonition of the prophet Micah "to do justly, and to love mercy, and to walk humbly with thy God."

"Let us learn together and laugh together and work together and pray together, confident that in the end we will triumph together in the right," said Carter in one of the seven statements that was interrupted by applause during his speech.

Like most inaugural speeches, Carter's was built on generalities. Domestically, he said, "more" is not necessarily "better," even the United States has limits and "we can neither answer all questions nor solve all problems."

Carter cited a rising "passion for freedom" around the world. He said that "there can be no nobler nor more ambitious task for America to undertake on this day of a new beginning than to help shape a just and peaceful world that is truly humane."

American strength should be based, he said, "not merely on the size of an arsenal, but on the nobility of ideas." The enemies to be fought, he continued, are poverty, ignorance and injustice.

The Common Touch

Throughout the inaugural observances, Carter seemed to be doing everything he could think of to make it a celebration of the people. One such touch was in the way he dressed. For the swearing-in ceremony at the Capitol, he wore a dark-blue suit instead of the traditional formal morning coat. He was hatless, as were the other men beside

him on the platform: Ford, Vice President Walter F. Mondale and former Vice President Nelson A. Rockefeller. Ford wore a black suit with a vest.

Carter broke another precedent after the inauguration ceremony. Instead of riding at the head of the inaugural parade to the White House, he and his family walked the mile and a half down Pennsylvania Avenue from Capitol Hill. They smiled and waved to the cheering throng—and, by their 40-minute exposure, created great uneasiness for the Secret Service men responsible for protecting them.

Upwards of a half-million people were expected in Washington for the five-day inaugural celebration. They came, apparently undeterred by the record-breaking cold spell that threw much of the eastern United States into semi-paralysis and transformed many of the streets and sidewalks of the capital into skating rinks.

The overflow crowd on the Capitol grounds for the swearing-in was well bundled-up against the cold. The skies were clear when the program began at 11:30 a.m., but the temperature was in the high 20s and the wind was brisk, especially for the members of Congress, the diplomats and other dignitaries occupying choice seats on the elevated platform.

Before Carter was sworn in, House Speaker Thomas P. O'Neill Jr. (D Mass.) administered the oath of office to Mondale, the 42nd Vice President. All the principals were protected by a transparent shield of bulletproof glass.

The Methodist bishop of Atlanta delivered the invocation. The Catholic archbishop of St. Paul pronounced the benediction. A Jewish cantor from Atlanta sang the national anthem, at least partly placating leaders of the Jewish and Eastern Orthodox faiths, who had complained before the ceremony that they had been excluded.

Early in the morning of inauguration day, some 5,000 worshipers showed up at the Lincoln Memorial for an interdenominational prayer service. Participating in the service were Carter's Baptist pastor from Plains; Carter's evangelist sister, Ruth Stapleton; and the Rev. Dr. Martin Luther King Sr. of Atlanta, father of the assassinated civil rights leader who had delivered his "I had a dream" speech from the steps of the Lincoln Memorial in 1963.

Carter and Mondale did not attend the early-morning service. They and their wives worshiped later that morning at the First Baptist Church in Washington.

Carter did not ignore the people from his home state who had worked to elect him. A large share of his time, both on inauguration day and the day after, was spent at receptions and parties. One of the social functions Jan. 21 was a White House reception for Carter's fellow Georgians.

But the other festivities were for the public as well as the privileged. After his narrow victory over Ford in the Nov. 2 election, Carter had invited the American people to Washington to celebrate his victory. Some 300,000 invitations were sent out by the inaugural committee.

Admission was charged for many of the events, but prices were deliberately kept modest and frequent comparisons were made with the far more expensive tickets to events at the second Nixon inaugural in 1973. Besides the paid events, there were dozens of free concerts, fireworks displays and other festivities that the public was invited to attend.

The spirit of egalitarianism also pervaded the seven inaugural parties—they were not called balls, as in the past—the night of the inauguration.

Before their ride to the Capitol for the inauguration, the Carters stopped at the White House and had coffee with Ford and his wife, Betty. Ford appeared to be genuinely moved by Carter's opening words of praise. As soon as the ceremony was over, the Fords and the Rockefellers flew by helicopter to nearby Andrews Air Force Base.

A crowd of about 300 cheered the Fords on their way from Andrews aboard a presidential jet. A 21-gun salute was fired. A military band played "God Bless America."

And then private citizen Gerald R. Ford was off for Monterey, Calif., to play in a golf tournament.

THE CARTER STYLE: INFORMALITY, FRUGALITY

Even before all the movers' crates had been unpacked, the new occupants had brought their own trademarks to the White House: openness, informality and good humor—with a dash of austerity.

As the Carter administration settled in, the President and his advisers gave priority to energy, the economy and foreign relations. One of Carter's first actions after his swearing-in was to order White House thermostats turned to 65 degrees during the day, lower at night, and to urge all Americans to do the same while the bitter-cold winter depleted the nation's fuel supplies.

A few days later, on Jan. 26, Carter announced an emergency plan to help alleviate the shortages and bring limited relief to the most stricken parts of the country. But, he warned, the legislation he sent to Congress "will not end the shortage, will not improve the weather and will not solve the unemployment problems." He estimated that the energy crisis had caused the shutdown of 4,000 plants and the layoff of 400,000 workers.

The President promised to send his economic stimulus package to Capitol Hill by the end of January. It was expected to total more than $31-billion in 20 months, including a one-shot tax rebate of some $11-billion.

Carter's penchant for frugality extended into his own official household. He ordered his White House aides to give up the chauffeur-driven limousines that had brought their predecessors to and from work. And he told his Cabinet that he would like to see fewer lawyers in the executive agencies.

He sent his Vice President, Walter F. Mondale, on a 10-day trip to Europe and Japan in a gesture of cooperation apparently unprecedented so early in an administration. Other journeys, to the Middle East and Africa, were scheduled soon by Cabinet-level officials.

The first days of the Carter administration were pervaded by an easy-going, occasionally even jocular manner on the part of the President and the people closest to him. For example, when Carter saw Mondale to a helicopter on the south lawn of the White House Jan. 23, he spoke seriously of the importance of limiting nuclear development and of improving U.S. relations with allies.

"Are you sure the helicopter works?" Mondale asked as he prepared to depart for the plane that would fly him to Brussels.

"If it doesn't," replied Carter, "we will all be very disappointed."

First Interview

Carter granted his first interview to reporters on Jan. 23. He met in the White House Oval Office with four reporters for the Associated Press and United Press International.

Much of the interview was devoted to nuclear arms controls. "I am in favor of eliminating the testing of all nuclear devices, instantly and completely," Carter said.

Toward that end, he suggested three steps. The first stage would be a "fairly rapid ratification" of the SALT II (strategic arms limitation talks) agreement with the Soviet Union. "I would like to move very quickly, even prior to the SALT II agreement, toward a much more substantive reduction in atomic weapons as the first step to complete elimination in the future," said Carter.

The next step after the SALT agreement, he said, would be to try to have other atomic nations join in the reduction effort. And the third step would be to prevent the expansion of nuclear capability to nations that do not already have it.

Carter also expressed concern about the reprocessing, for weapons purposes, of radioactive material used for electric power generation. "We would like to have this put under international control, subject ourselves to the restraint along with those who have been processing this material for a number of years, and prohibit completely, within the bounds of our capability, the expansion of the reprocessing plants in the countries that don't have it," he said.

The interview dealt with several other subjects. One was Carter's first executive order, issued Jan. 21, to pardon

President Carter confers with Senate Majority Leader Robert C. Byrd (D W.Va.) and House Speaker Thomas P. O'Neill Jr. (D Mass.)

Vietnam-era draft evaders. The order prompted considerable criticism, including a narrowly defeated Senate resolution of disapproval.

Carter said he had contemplated taking the action for more than two years and drafted the proclamation two weeks before he made it public. "I don't really think there was any surprise about the reaction one way or the other," he said. "It is a proper thing to do. It is one that I feel very much at ease with. It is something that should have been done. I was very grateful to be the one to do it."

One of the interviewers asked Carter about the proportion of women and members of racial minorities appointed to the top levels of his administration. "I am not completely satisfied with what we have done," he answered, "but I am satisfied with the effort we have made." He repeated what he and his spokesmen had said earlier: he would try to compensate for shortages at the top by appointing more women and minorities to sub-Cabinet jobs.

Relaxed Tone

By the end of Carter's first full week in office, all 11 members of his Cabinet had been approved by Congress and sworn in. The biggest swearing-in, however, had been Jan. 23, when eight Cabinet officers and four other Cabinet-level officials assumed office in what Carter called his administration's "first official and completely open ceremony."

In one of the numerous clues to Carter's intention to give the White House a common touch and to reduce the imperial nature of his presidency, Carter announced at the outset of the ceremony that he would forgo the traditional playing of "Ruffles and Flourishes" and "Hail to the Chief" by the Marine Corps band. Guests in the East Room settled for "Georgia on My Mind" after the ceremony.

On a more serious note, the President reaffirmed his belief in "Cabinet government" and promised: "There will never be an instance, while I am President, when the members of the White House staff dominate or actually take a superior position to members of our Cabinet."

The same lack of pretension that had begun with Carter's inauguration was evident Jan. 24 in the casual atmosphere of his first Cabinet meeting. Rex Granum, a deputy press secretary, gave an unusually detailed briefing after the meeting. Cabinet meetings are closed to the press.

The three-hour meeting reportedly was most informal. It gave Carter a chance to spell out some guidelines for the leaders of his administration.

One symbolic guideline was the elimination of chauffeur service for White House staff members, a traditional perquisite for chief aides to Presidents. Jody Powell, Carter's press secretary, said after the meeting that the order would reduce the number of vehicles in the White House motor pool by at least 20 cars, to not more than 36 from 56.

The Ford White House staff used 13 chauffeured limousines and the Nixon and Johnson staffs used 20, said Powell. Carter did not eliminate the service for his Cabinet officers, but he told them it would be a good economy for their staffs.

The new President came down hard at the Cabinet meeting on what he thinks is an excess of government lawyers who churn out "oceans of paperwork" for lack of anything better to do. Carter's irritation is related to his experience with government forms when he was a businessman in Georgia. He suggested, as one way to trim the government's preoccupation with rules and regulations, that his Cabinet officers reduce the numbers of lawyers in their departments.

"I'm determined to stay close to the American people," Carter said. He instructed the Cabinet officers to inform him, in writing, of their plans to do the same.

In another symbolic gesture of their desire to stay close to the people, Carter and his wife, Rosalynn, enrolled their 9-year-old daughter, Amy, in fourth grade at a public school near the White House. She is the first child of a President since Quentin Roosevelt, Theodore's son, to enroll in a public rather than a private school in Washington.

First 'Fireside Chat'

Carter's first report to the American people provided further evidence of his effort to maintain close, informal contact with the public.

In a televised "fireside chat" broadcast from the White House library Feb. 2, he recalled the spirit of World War II, asking the American people for the dedication and sacrifice necessary to achieve national goals. The emphasis of the President's remarks was on the energy crisis that had disrupted social and economic life in many parts of the country. "We must face the fact that the energy shortage is permanent," he said. "There is no way we can solve it quickly."

Carter touched upon many other problems as he delivered his informal remarks, wearing an unbuttoned cardigan sweater and reading from a teleprompter as he sat in a straight-backed chair. He spoke of the economy, of government reorganization, of foreign policy, of his plans for openness in his administration.

Most of the 25-minute talk was a restatement of policies that Carter had expressed earlier. He did, however, make a few new commitments:

● The White House staff, he said, will be reduced by approximately one-third—under President Ford, it numbered approximately 500—and so will the top staffs of his Cabinet officers.

● Carter said he would soon put a ceiling on employment in government agencies, "so we can bring the growth of government under control."

● Government regulations will be reduced and will carry their author's name, said the President. He also said they will be "written in plain English, for a change."

● The strict rules he has imposed on his appointees for financial disclosure and avoidance of conflicts of interest will be made permanent, Carter said. And he pledged to choose his appointees in a way that "will close the revolving door between government regulatory agencies, on the one hand, and the businesses they regulate, on the other."

● Carter spelled out, in greater detail than he had previously in a public statement, his attitude toward frugality at high levels and his plans for reaching out toward ordinary people. "Government officials can't be sensitive to your problems if we are living like royalty here in Washington," he said.

Most of Carter's comments were directed at domestic problems, not foreign policy. He seemed to go out of his way to find praise for Congress. He congratulated Congress for its quick passage, the same day as his talk, of his emergency energy legislation.

Carter's 'People Program': Reaching for the Public

President Carter's televised talk Feb. 2 was only one part of his conscious effort to deliver on his campaign promise to maintain a "direct, intimate relationship" with the American public. He planned to go quite a bit further in the months ahead.

The President's intentions were borne out on March 5 when, in an unprecedented two-hour radio show—later televised—he fielded questions from 42 citizens in 25 states over a special telephone company toll-free network. "I liked it," the President said as the program came to a close, saying he would like to do it again in the future.

Carter also said he was planning a series of "town meetings" around the country. He and members of his Cabinet would participate, bringing their message to voters outside the capital.

While in the capital, according to his advisers, the President may begin issuing invitations to ordinary citizens to have dinner at the White House with him and his family. On occasion, arrangements may be made—as has been done by French President Giscard d'Estaing—for Carter to spend evenings at private homes.

The person in charge of Carter's "people program" was Greg Schneiders, his assistant for special projects. Others directly involved in it included his press secretary, Jody Powell; his special assistant for media and public affairs, Barry Jagoda; and Margaret (Midge) Costanza, his liaison with various interest groups. In one newspaper interview, Schneiders spoke of countering "the institutional forces toward isolation" in the White House.

In another interview, Jagoda said Carter uses symbols "in creative ways of demonstrating his concern. He does have a great understanding of the real content of what may be perceived as purely symbolic."

Some of Carter's actions have origins in his governorship of Georgia from 1971 to 1975. He used the open-line technique, for example, to listen to the complaints of citizens who wanted to talk to him.

He also sometimes flew to the scene of a crisis to take a first-hand look at what was happening. This he did as President on Jan. 30, when he flew by helicopter to make a personal inspection of the storm-besieged area of western Pennsylvania.

The well-publicized symbols of Carter's expressed concern for the public continued to extend to the way he runs his administration. At his first Cabinet meeting, he told his White House aides to forget about riding to work in limousines.

His desire for frugality cut even deeper at the Cabinet meeting Jan. 31. "We're going to cut back drastically," he said. "We're going to cut out the ostentatiousness of things."

Carter urged his Cabinet members to economize in their travels—he himself is no stranger to flying tourist class on commercial airlines, he said pointedly—and to reduce the use of chauffeured limousines in their departments. "I hope you'll go the second mile," he said. "I don't want to be superficial about this."

Vice President Mondale, too, felt the effects of Carter's corner-cutting. The President told his Cabinet that he had instructed the Secret Service not to transport armored limousines to Europe during Mondale's visit. The Vice President rode in cars provided by the host governments.

At the Jan. 31 Cabinet meeting, Carter said he was considering opening future Cabinet meetings to coverage by the press to "let the American public know their government is in good hands." Such coverage probably would be limited to a small number of "pool" reporters. Ground rules, such as barring specific attribution of Cabinet members' remarks, would have to be worked out.

The "fireside" part of the phrase was appropriate Feb. 2 as the sweatered President, appearing relaxed and casual, sat before a fire in the library and asked a shivering nation to turn down its thermostats. But Carter and his advisers were looking for another phrase to describe better the periodic broadcast messages the President planned to deliver.

The "fireside chat" dates back to the occasional radio reports of President Franklin D. Roosevelt, who usually addressed himself to specific problems during a period of prolonged national emergency. Roosevelt reportedly did not like the term either, because some of his talks were made during the heat of summer. And he made most of the talks from the diplomatic reception room of the White House, not from the library.

The casual tone of Carter's first such talk was studied. He and his staff had started planning the talk—they did not call it a speech—weeks earlier.

First News Conferences as President

During his first month in office, Carter fulfilled his intention to hold press conferences twice a month: he held one on Feb. 8 and another on Feb. 23.

At the Feb. 8 meeting with newsmen, Carter placed heavy emphasis on the importance of improving his relations with Congress. He admitted that he had made some mistakes during the first days of his administration.

Questions about defense and nuclear arms dominated the conference. Relaxed and well-briefed, Carter discussed at length his nomination of Paul C. Warnke as director of the Arms Control and Disarmament Agency; Soviet and American nuclear capabilities; and the development of weapons in relation to the strategic arms limitation talks.

At his second news conference, the President said that he thought his relations with Congress were improving. "I think that the progress of the legislation that we consider to be crucial, which seemed to be moving very slowly in the past, is now speeding up," he said. "So I don't believe that we will have nearly the problems with the Congress that has been the case in recent years, and I have to say in summary that I am very pleased with my relationship with the Congress now."

One of the crucial pieces of legislation, referred to by Carter in his opening "progress report to the American people," was a proposed new Energy Department. He predicted quick passage of the bill, which was sent to

(Continued on p. 49)

President Carter's Close-Knit Family at the White House

During President Carter's March 5 radio talk show, a young caller pointedly asked the President whether the American taxpayer was going to foot the bill for the Carter relations who were living at the White House. Specifically, he wanted to know why the President's 26-year old son, Chip (James Earl III), his wife Caron and their infant son, James IV, were living there "on taxpayers' money" and not in "their own house earning a living."

"I want the American people to know that we are not mooching off the American taxpayer," the President responded to his 16-year old questioner. "All of the personal expenses of our family are paid for out of my own pocket or the pocket of my children."

President Carter's need to defend his family's tenancy at the White House was prompted by the fact that the Carters are the first extended First Family to occupy the mansion since President Franklin D. Roosevelt's daughter Anna lived there with her two children after her divorce from Curtis B. Dall.

As of early March, 1976, the following Carter kin were in permanent residence at 1600 Pennsylvania Avenue:
- son James Earl III (Chip), 26, his wife Caron and their infant son James IV;
- son Donnel Jeffrey (Jeff), 24, and his wife Annette;
- the Carter's youngest child and only daughter, nine-year old Amy.

The Carter's oldest son, John William (Jack), age 29, his wife Judy, and 1½-year-old son Jason, chose to return to Calhoun, Ga., where Jack practices law.

Although the Carter children enjoy rent-free lodgings and other amenities such as free rides on Air Force I, none will spend his time loafing while in residence at the White House. Amy, a freckle-faced likeness of her father, attends a District of Columbia public school, Thaddeus Stevens Elementary. Son Jeff is studying geography at nearby George Washington University. And Chip works part-time for the Democratic National Committee, where he is slated to raise funds and find speakers for congressional candidates. Chip also acts as an occasional stand-in for his father, conducting inspection trips and fulfilling other assignments. "Dad can't go everywhere," he said explaining his role during a February inspection of winter-ravaged Buffalo, N.Y.

The Carters have always been a close-knit family. But their togetherness in the White House is in sharp contrast to the life-style they adopted during Carter's long and strenuous fight for the presidency. During both the primary and general election campaigns, Carter family members fanned out across the country to guarantee maximum exposure for their candidate. Carter's wife, Rosalynn, who is one of his most trusted advisers, put in long solo hours on the campaign trail. Campaigning just as doggedly were the three Carter sons and their wives who temporarily put aside their own lives to stump for their father. Carter's brother, Billy, his sister, Ruth Carter Stapleton, and cousin Hugh Carter were among the other Carter relatives who also contributed to the campaign effort.

After Carter's election victory, the family made it clear that they intended to stay close together. On Inauguration Day, when Carter eschewed the traditional limousine ride in favor of a walk down Pennsylvania Avenue to the White House, he did so accompanied by his wife, three sons, their spouses and an occasionally skipping Amy.

Following the inauguration celebrations, as Carter made himself at home in the Oval Office, much of the rest of his family settled into their rooms in the White House's family quarters, which occupies the second and third floors of the mansion. Amy moved her doll house and other possessions into the pink second-floor bedroom that once belonged to Trisha Nixon. Chip and Caron moved into a third-floor three-room suite and Jeff and Annette settled into two rooms across the hall.

Supplementing from time to time the permanent Carter contingent at the White House will be other Carter relatives. Those who can be expected to pay occasional visits are:

- Carter's mother "Miss Lillian," 78, feisty matriarch of the Carter clan, racial liberal, former nurse, dormitory house-mother, nursing home administrator and Peace Corps volunteer. In February, at the end of a two-and-a-half day visit to India as the head of the American delegation to the funeral of President Fakhruddin Ali Ahmed, Miss Lillian paid a nostalgic visit to the clinic and village where she worked as a public health nurse during her 1966-68 Peace Corps service. Carter's father, James Earl Sr., died in 1953.

- Carter's brother Billy, 39, self-proclaimed redneck and "good ol' boy," prodigious beer drinker, gas station proprietor and since February, owner of the controlling interest in the Carter family's peanut warehouse business. Billy, who has been seen sporting a T-shirt incribed "Redneck Power," is also a shrewd businessman who successfully managed the family business while his brother was out on the campaign trail. The younger Carter brother's short-lived political career ended last December, when Billy was defeated in his bid to become the mayor of Plains.

- Carter's sister, Ruth Carter Stapleton, 49, lay minister, faith healer, and author. When not campaigning for her brother, Ruth Stapleton travelled around the country conducting spiritual workshops and healing sessions. Making her home in Fayetteville, N.C., she is the only one of the Jimmy Carter's siblings who does not live in Plains.

- Gloria Carter Spann, 46, Carter's other sister, avid motorcyclist and least well-known of the President's immediate family. A staunch family woman, Mrs. Spann confined her activities during the campaign to handing out leaflets before the Florida primary and writing letters soliciting support for her brother's campaign. Mrs. Spann's son, William Carter Spann, 30, made headlines during the campaign when it was revealed that he was serving a 10-year-to-life sentence for robbery and that he was so impoverished that he was compelled to borrow stamps from fellow inmate, convicted mass-murderer, Charles Manson.

(Continued from p. 47)
Congress March 1. The President said he would meet his deadline of April 20 for drafting a comprehensive energy program, which he planned to present to a joint session of Congress. The program, he said, "is going to be quite profound on its impact on the American consciousness and our society."

On another issue related to Congress, Carter said he favored the public financing of congressional as well as presidential elections.

Carter also said that he continued to oppose wage and price controls as a means of curbing inflation.

'Ask President Carter' Talk-Show

Jimmy Carter's carefully conceived plans for reaching out to the American people moved into full swing March 5 with his two-hour "Ask President Carter" radio program.

The President said: "The questions that come in from people all over the country are the kind that you would never get in a press conference," he commented to moderator Walter Cronkite of CBS at the conclusion of the call-ins. "I think it is very good for me to understand directly from the American people what they are concerned about and questions that have never been asked of me and reported through the news media."

The President said he might do it again, depending partly on the reaction of the people. The reaction was overwhelmingly favorable, Jody Powell, the White House press secretary, said a few days after the show.

More than nine million Americans, it was estimated, tried to call their leader at the toll-free number provided at the expense of CBS.

The calls began with a man from Sterling Heights, Mich., who asked a question about killings in Uganda, and ended with an 11-year-old girl from North Benton, Ohio, who called the President by his first name and asked why he sent his 9-year-old daughter, Amy, to a public school in Washington.

Carter, addressing many of the callers by their first names, answered most of the questions with ease. With the help of an aide, he looked up information and supplied some answers later in the program. He promised to call four persons back, and either he or another administration official did.

Some of the questions were critical, but all the callers were respectful. Some appeared awed. Carter scored obvious points with others, such as the Pennsylvania woman who told him that, "as a registered Republican, I am behind you 100 per cent."

CARTER'S PRIORITIES AND EARLY INITIATIVES

Even before his inauguration, Carter had drawn up a long list of domestic legislative programs that he planned to propose to the 95th Congress. The nucleus of his agenda for domestic legislation was contained in a 100-page draft prepared by Stuart Eizenstat, the 33-year old Atlanta lawyer who was his chief domestic policy adviser during the transition between administrations.

For most domestic programs expiring in 1977, Carter would support a one-year extension while concentrating on a handful of priorities, Eizenstat told a group of reporters Jan. 10. Following are some of Carter's top priorities as outlined by Eizenstat and the President himself in his early news conferences:

Economic Stimulus

Carter revealed the outlines of his economic stimulus package Jan. 7 after a two-day meeting with his economic advisers and congressional leaders. The specifics of the two-year, $31.2-billion proposal were presented during hearings Jan. 27. As outlined by the Carter administration officials, the stimulus package included these elements:

● A one-time rebate on 1976 taxes of $50 per individual that would be paid out 30 to 60 days after Congress completed action. Besides the rebate to each taxpayer and dependents, a $50-payment would go to all Social Security and railroad retirement recipients, to low-income persons receiving the earned income credit and to recipients of supplemental security income (SSI). The aim, said Treasury Secretary W. Michael Blumenthal, was to reach "just about everybody we can find." The total cost of the rebates would be $11.4-billion in fiscal 1977.

● A permanent change in the standard deduction to a flat level of $2,400 for individuals and $2,800 for joint returns,

that would reduce Treasury revenues in fiscal 1977 by $1.5-billion.

● A reduction in corporate taxes, giving businesses a choice between two alternatives for a total loss of revenues in fiscal 1977 of $900-million.

A business could choose to take an income tax credit equal to 4 per cent of its Social Security tax payments. Employers now pay 5.85 per cent of payroll for Social Security. This option would be most advantageous to labor-intensive businesses employing large numbers of persons.

Alternatively, a business could choose to take an increase in the investment tax credit to 12 per cent from the present 10 per cent, which would be advantageous to capital-intensive businesses with large investments in plants and equipment.

● A variety of increases in jobs programs totaling $1.7-billion in fiscal 1977. The number of federally funded public service jobs would be raised to 600,000 from 310,000 in fiscal 1977; an additional $2-billion would be requested for public works jobs in fiscal 1977, but only $200-million would be spent; the countercyclical revenue sharing program for states and local governments would be increased by $500-million over current levels in fiscal 1977; and training and youth programs would be increased by $300-million.

The total of the package for fiscal 1977 would be $15.5-billion, with tax cuts accounting for $13.8-billion.

In the fiscal year starting Oct. 1, 1977, the mix would change, with jobs spending accounting for $7.6-billion, and tax cuts for $8.2-billion, for a total of $15.7-billion. (Totals do not add because of rounding.) The features included:

● Continuation of the permanent changes in the standard deduction, reducing Treasury revenues by $5.5-billion.

● Continuation of the business tax reductions, amounting to $2.7-billion.

● A $600-million increase in countercyclical revenue sharing.

● Increased public service jobs, to 725,000, at a cost of $3.4-billion.

● An additional $2-billion for public works jobs.

● Expanded training and youth programs under the Comprehensive Employment and Training Act, at a cost of $1.6-billion, for a total of 346,000 additional jobs under the act for the two years.

The Carter administration hoped the package would produce real growth in the gross national product (GNP) of about 5.75 to 6 per cent from the fourth quarter of calendar 1977 to the fourth quarter of 1978. Without added stimulus, the growth rate probably would be only about 4.5 per cent, Charles L. Schultze, chairman of the Council of Economic Advisers, said. Unemployment should fall to about 6.7 to 6.9 per cent by the end of 1977 with the stimulus, he continued, and fall further during 1978. Unemployment in December 1976 was 7.8 per cent. He expected "some slight increase" in inflation in 1977, but not because of the stimulus package which would "only minimally" affect the rate of inflation.

If conditions improved by mid-1978 as the Carter administration hoped, then the decline in stimulus in the package would be appropriate, Schultze testified. However, he continued, if the "self-sustaining expansion we envision does not come up to expectations, additional measures can be taken."

Carter's Feb. 22 budget message contained revisions in the initial stimulus figures. The total cost came to $15.7-billion in fiscal 1977 rather than the original estimate of $15.5-billion, and $15.9-billion in fiscal 1978 rather than $15.7-billion, for a total two-year package of $31.6-billion. *(See p. 52)*

Congress acted quickly on the administration's economic proposals and on March 3 gave final approval to new binding budget levels for fiscal 1977. The new spending and deficit levels were large enough to accommodate the full $13.8-billion tax reduction package as outlined by Carter in his Feb. 22 budget message, but provided for a bigger economic shot in the arm than had been requested by the President. The two congressional Budget Committees had assumed a stimulus package totaling $17.5-billion for the remaining seven months of fiscal 1977, compared to $15.7-billion in the Carter program. Congress kept the full tax package and almost doubled the administration's proposed outlays for jobs and local assistance, raising the total to $3.7-billion.

Government Reorganization

Carter gave high priority to legislation restoring presidential authority to reorganize the executive branch, viewing it as necessary to fulfill his campaign pledge to increase government efficiency by whittling down the number of federal agencies. "I hope Congress will act soon on this legislation so our work of reorganization can begin," Carter stated Feb. 4 in a special message to Congress. To reporters at the White House, he added: "This is a commitment that I made in hundreds of speeches around the country during the two-year campaign. It was one of the major reasons I was elected."

Carter sought a four-year renewal of the Reorganization Act of 1949, which expired in April 1973. This law, originally requested by President Truman, gave him and his successors reorganizational authority subject to con-

gressional veto. Truman wanted the authority to be permanent, but Congress first approved it for a period of less than four years. Subsequently it was extended seven times for periods of two years or less.

One of the basic features of the act was the provision granting either the House or Senate veto authority over reorganization plans, with the stipulation that action must be taken within 60 days after a plan's submission. This particular feature was never changed, although Congress made other modifications that tended to limit the executive's reorganization authority.

Faced with those limitations, Carter requested not only a renewal of the reorganization act but a broadening of the executive authority as well. His proposal retained the one-house veto and the 60-day review period in the House and Senate, but added new provisions not included in the act when it expired. Carter asked for a four-year extension of the authority, the power to amend a reorganization plan within 30 days of its submission to Congress, the authority to submit more than one plan every 30 days, elimination of the requirement that each plan deal only with one "logically consistent subject," and an emphasis in each plan on the identification of anticipated management improvements rather than expected cost-saving.

Carter's proposal was introduced in the Senate Feb. 4, where it was passed March 3, 94-0. The bill sailed through the House Government Operations Committee markup March 17 by a vote of 40-3. The overwhelming vote of approval came after a compromise had been reached earlier in the week which mollified committee chairman Jack Brooks (D Texas).

Brooks had been an adamant opponent of the Carter reorganization proposal, objecting to the legislative veto provision which called for a reorganization plan to take effect unless disapproved by either the House or Senate within 60 days. Brooks claimed the legislative veto was unconstitutional, and introduced his own bill, which required each reorganization plan to be approved by an affirmative vote of Congress.

Brooks has remained dubious about the constitutionality of the legislative veto, but faced with widespread support in the House for the President's plan, he agreed to a behind the scenes compromise with administration supporters which retained key features of the Carter plan, including the legislative veto.

The compromise, though, does make it easier for Congress to get a floor vote on reorganization plans. It provided that when the President submits a plan to Congress, a resolution of disapproval is automatically introduced at the same time. If after 45 days the resolution is not discharged by the committees responsible for considering reorganization plans—Senate Governmental Affairs and House Government Operations—the resolution is automatically discharged and can be called up by any member. "That is about as ironclad an assurance as can be written into law," said Brooks, "to guarantee there will be a vote on every plan. It should do away with the possibility that a plan will go into effect without Congress having taken any action."

Energy Reorganization

On March 1, President Carter unveiled his plan to reorganize the federal energy bureaucracy. It was his first step toward creation of a new national energy policy, and at the same time, his first attempt to live up to his oft-repeated campaign promise to streamline the entire federal government if elected.

Carter proposed creation of a new Department of Energy, built mainly by consolidating the Energy Research and Development Administration (ERDA), the Federal Energy Administration (FEA), and the Federal Power Commission (FPC). In addition, the department would absorb energy-related functions from six other agencies.

"Nowhere is the need for reorganization and consolidation greater than in energy policy," Carter said in a message to Congress. "All but two of the executive branch's cabinet departments now have some responsibility for energy policy, but no agency...has the broad authority needed to deal with our energy problems in a comprehensive way."

Immediate Capitol Hill reaction was generally favorable, befitting the administration's careful courting of key legislators before the measure was unveiled publicly. The Democratic leadership in both houses was geared to push for speedy passage, and key committee chairmen appeared willing to go along, some perhaps grudgingly.

There were several possible sticking points, however. The proposal's consolidation of regulatory authority raised fears that the integrity of fair adjudication would be threatened. An unusual arrangement that proposed sharing authority over leasing of public lands for energy development between the Departments of Energy and Interior, a curious co-mingling of authority, was also destined to draw careful review. Critics claimed the plan guaranteed infighting, conflict and confusion.

The consensus of approval could also come unglued if the military bucked at losing control over naval oil reserves, or perhaps if the railroad lobby's fears of coal slurry pipelines led them to fight to keep the pipelines under Interstate Commerce Commission control.

Thus the plan was rife with proposed changes that could threaten special interests, and if they unified in opposition, the proposal could face tough going.

Carter's plan strongly resembled the proposal he outlined Sept. 21 during his presidential campaign, but was beefed up considerably by a call for an Energy Regulatory Administration and the large voice in public lands leasing that his Energy Department would have.

Natural Gas Emergency

Issues related to energy and the environment, apart from reorganization, were likely to occupy a sizable share of the new administration's and Congress' time. In their first major test, the new Democratic President and Congress proved they could work together smoothly—and quickly. Six days after an unrelenting winter forced President Carter on Jan. 26 to request unprecedented powers to meet the nation's energy crisis, he had the powers he sought. Congress passed the Emergency Natural Gas Act of 1977 in less than a week.

The measure gave the President temporary authority to order transfers of interstate natural gas to areas where a merciless cold wave had so depleted fuel supplies that even homes and hospitals were in danger of having no heat. The legislation also gave the President authority through July 31 to approve sales of gas to interstate buyers at unregulated prices, a deviation from federal policies first set in 1938.

Although Congress moved swiftly, few of its members were pleased with the legislation. It was designed only to ensure that homes not go heatless. It did nothing to generate more gas or to send workers back to their jobs. It did not

cure the situation, but was intended only to help people live through it.

Carter had promised to deliver a comprehensive energy program to Capitol Hill by April 20. As debate on the emergency measure flowed, it was apparent that legislators were often only warming up for big debates to follow.

Other Domestic Priorities

These were among the other Carter domestic proposals mentioned by Eizenstat in his Jan. 10 discussion of priorities:

● A bill requiring electors to vote for the presidential candidate who wins a popular plurality in their state.

● Public financing of congressional elections and some sort of "universal voter registration."

● Tighter requirements for registration and disclosure by lobbyists.

● A requirement that officials in the executive branch keep public logs of all their contacts with lobbyists.

● Court appointment of special prosecutors to investigate certain kinds of crimes and scandals.

● An expanded youth employment service corps, to include the Job Corps and other existing programs as well as new ones.

● A mechanism for helping New York and other cities in financial emergencies.

● Legislation dealing with the Amendments to the Clean Air Act of 1970.

● A bill to control stip mining.

● "Rejuvenation" of the rent supplement program as one means of stimulating housing construction as well as additional neighborhood grants and more money for subsidized mortgage interest rates for low-income home-buyers.

● A wiretap bill requiring judicial approval of all or nearly all domestic wiretaps.

● Reform of the welfare system (Carter had made this a major campaign issue).

New Ethics Code

Throughout his campaign for the presidency, Carter had made the issue of political integrity one of his central themes, calling repeatedly for strict conflict-of-interest laws, an all-inclusive federal "sunshine" law, public financing of congressional campaigns and tougher lobbying laws.

On Jan. 4, the President-elect issued a set of strict guidelines that went further than any previous regulations in laying down a code of ethics to be followed by presidential appointees. The guidelines were described by a Carter spokesman as a first step in fulfilling Carter's campaign pledge to "restore the confidence of the American people in their own government."

The guidelines covered three basic areas: public disclosure of financial assets, divestiture of assets that could involve appointees in possible conflicts of interest, and restrictions on the employment of the policy-makers after they have left the government.

The guidelines applied to Carter's staff, his Cabinet officers, the more than 2,000 political appointees to his administration and to tens of thousands of policy-making civil servants.

Plan for Carter. For Carter himself, the plan required:

● Placing most of his financial holdings in a trust.

● Establishing a charitable foundation to finance a future Carter library in his hometown of Plains, Ga. Royalties from

Carter's autobiography and a forthcoming book of his speeches will go to the foundation.

● Leasing for four years, for a fixed amount established this year, the 3,400 acres of farmland he and his family own.

● Leasing for four years under conditions similar to those applying to the land, or selling at the discretion of the trustee, the family's peanut business and warehouse.

Carter explained to reporters that the purpose of the plan was to ensure that "whatever happens here in Plains, based on my decisions concerning agriculture, will not affect my income one way or the other."

But Powell, in briefing the press, said: "There is absolutely no question he can and will receive income from the farm and warehouse operations. But we have tried to remove the possibility that decisions he might make in the White House would affect the amount of that income."

Guidelines for Policy-makers. For policy-making officials in the Carter administration, the guidelines required:

● Filing, at the time of their appointment and annually until two years after they have left the government, public statements of net worth and sources of income for themselves and their immediate families.

● Divesting themselves of investments that could involve conflicts of interest. Exemptions are made for real estate, savings certificates, governmental securities and diversified holdings such as mutual funds.

● Tightening benefits from previous private employers on items such as severance, pensions and stock options.

● Extending to two years the existing one-year restriction on private handling, after they have left government, of matters in which policy-makers are personally involved while they are members of the administration.

● Imposing a one-year restriction on contacts by departed officials with the agency in which they served.

Much of the work of drafting the guidelines was done by John L. Moore, an Atlanta lawyer, part of the Carter transition team. At a briefing when the text of the code was released, Moore said that violations could be reported to the Justice Department. Injunctions could be sought, he said, to prevent top federal employees from taking government-related jobs barred by the guidelines or otherwise violating their "contract" with Carter.

Much of the guidelines' content followed recommendations of Common Cause, the self-described citizens' lobby. John W. Gardner, chairman of Common Cause, called the guidelines "a major breakthrough in the fight to eliminate conflicts of interest in the executive branch."

Revised Budget: Carter Adds $19.4-Billion

President Carter sent his version of the fiscal 1978 budget to Congress Feb. 22, calling for spending $19.4-billion higher than recommended by former President Ford and a deficit almost $11-billion higher.

The revisions were only a partial reflection of the goals and priorities of the new administration. In the month since the Carter administration had taken office, there simply had not been enough time to go through the Ford budget line by line to examine each item, Office of Management and Budget Director Bert Lance told reporters.

Carter made the same point in his message accompanying the budget changes: "The 1978 budget is essentially still President Ford's budget, with only such limited revisions as my administration has had time to make. But these revisions do reflect our careful choices among many possible

options; they are important first steps toward a federal government that is more effective and responsive to our people's needs."

Future budgets, Carter continued, would reflect zero-based reviews of federal spending programs, comprehensive tax reform and government reorganization.

Despite the lack of time, however, Carter did not belittle the changes he was recommending. "Although I have not been able to analyze this budget in depth, these proposals do differ significantly from those of the previous administration," he wrote to Congress.

The changes were across the board and predictably included the restoration of many cuts in domestic assistance programs proposed by Ford. While those restorations were pleasing to members of Congress, Carter proposed other cuts that raised immediate controversy on Capitol Hill.

The revised budget proposed outlays of $459.4-billion and estimated receipts at $401.6-billion, with a deficit of $57.7-billion. The growth in spending was 10 per cent over the latest estimate of fiscal 1977 outlays of $417.4-billion, a revision upward from the Ford estimate. The proposed rate of growth was higher than the 7 per cent requested by Ford and was at the average annual level for the past decade.

The new level of spending requested by Carter was also $12.9-billion higher than the latest estimate of the "current services" level of spending—that is, the cost of continuing current programs and government activities without policy changes. Ford's budget had been $5.4-billion below the current services level as estimated in January.

The Carter budget also presented revised estimates for spending and receipts in fiscal 1977, the year ending Sept. 30. The new estimates were for outlays to rise $6.2-billion over the Ford levels to $417.4-billion; receipts to decrease by $4.7-billion to $349.4-billion, and the deficit to rise by $10.8-billion to $68-billion.

The changes for fiscal 1977 were due largely to re-estimates based on the economy's performance, to Carter's economic stimulus package of tax cuts and increased spending for jobs to prod the nation's economic recovery, and also to the deletion of the package of permanent tax cuts proposed by Ford.

Major Revisions. Lance and other administration officials stressed that while they believed the new budget "corrected the major defects" of the Ford budget, it also did not make all the changes they would have liked.

Almost all the revisions, apart from the economic stimulus package, involved the restoration of Ford's proposed cuts that the Carter administration considered unwarranted, said the budget document. The new figures, it continued, "are on the whole closer to those needed to maintain current programs at their present levels" than were the Ford proposals.

Of a total $12.4-billion in cuts in outlays below current services levels in fiscal 1978 proposed by Ford, the Carter administration recommended restoring $7.8-billion, with the fiscal stimulus accounting for $2.8-billion of that. Ford also had recommended program cuts in fiscal 1977 outlays below current services totaling $1.2-billion, of which the Carter budget would restore $1.6-billion, with the fiscal stimulus accounting for $200-million.

Ford also had included a number of program initiatives, "very few" of which were continued in the Carter document, according to an OMB official.

Program Increases. Carter's proposals for increases over the Ford budget covered the spectrum of government activity, with all functional areas except defense showing gains. But they were concentrated in the areas of employment, health, education, income security and housing.

Substantive increases over Ford levels were included for:

● Security supporting assistance to Middle Eastern areas, and for international financial institutions.

● Higher budget authority for energy conservation programs, petroleum storage and sewage plant construction grants and an increase in employees for the Environmental Protection Agency.

● Highway improvement and construction, mass transit, railroad assistance and subsidies for the Postal Service to cover an extended phase-in of higher rates for certain classes of mail.

● Greater assistance to state and local governments through local public works programs in the stimulus package, restoration of budget cuts for the Economic Development Administration, an increase in the budget authority for the community development block grant program to fund a new urban development grant aimed at neighborhood preservation, and restoration of funding for the Community Services Administration.

● Increases in employment and training, including funding for public service jobs, as part of the stimulus package, and also for other jobs programs aimed at youth and Vietnam-era veterans.

● General increases for lower and higher education, particularly for disadvantaged and handicapped children; the dropping of the Ford proposal for an education block grant, and increases for grants to states for social services to provide for child day-care services.

● General increases in health programs. The bulk of the increased outlays in the health category were accounted for by the dropping of the Ford administration's Medicare proposals. Also, proposed consolidations and block grants were dropped.

● The $50 per capita payments included in the stimulus package; withdrawal of Ford's proposed increases in Social Security tax rates beyond those in existing law; extension of federal supplemental unemployment benefits to provide 13 weeks of supplemental payments in addition to 39 weeks available under other programs; withdrawal of Ford's proposed child nutrition block grant and food stamp revisions; continuation of the earned income credit in 1978; and an increase in subsidized housing programs to increase units to 400,000 from 235,800.

● Proposed cost-of-living increases in 1978 compensation and pension benefits for veterans, and withdrawal of Ford's proposed eight-year limit on the period of eligibility for GI bill education benefits.

● Proposed extension and expansion of anti-recession fiscal assistance to states and local governments as part of the stimulus package.

● Higher costs for interest on the public debt because of a higher deficit and higher interest rates than assumed in the Ford budget.

Controversial Cuts. While Carter restored many of the cuts proposed by Ford which Congress had either ignored or opposed, he also showed no reluctance to risk congressional ire with some of his own proposals.

The only functional area to show a decline in budget authority and outlays was defense, in which Carter proposed to reduce budget authority by $2.7-billion. The revisions, said the budget document, were designed to begin an improvement in the efficiency of military programs. The results of a major review of U.S. defense policy and programs would be reflected in the fiscal 1979 budget, it added. Most of the revisions, explained the document, result from slowing down or postponing various procurement and operations and maintenance programs, along with some production cancellations.

Proposed fiscal 1978 outlays for national defense were down slightly, $300-million. The budget authority figure was more important because it reflected future commitments.

During his campaign Carter had pledged much larger defense reductions, and at the press briefing Lance defended the fiscal 1978 cuts, saying that "significant progress" had been made toward the larger goal.

Carter also proposed to save nearly $300-million in budget authority by eliminating fiscal 1978 appropriations for 19 water resources development projects, a proposal that raised immediate controversy in Congress and some of the states affected.

Another controversy was certain over one of the few Ford recommendations that Carter sustained—reforms in the impact aid program that would limit federal aid to school districts where federal activities placed a heavy economic burden on them, at an estimated savings of $447-million.

Other major reductions included cuts in nuclear research and development, and proposed legislation to limit increases in reimbursements to hospitals paid by Medicare, Medicaid, state and local governments, insurance companies and private individuals.

Pardon for Draft Evaders

Fulfilling a campaign promise in his first executive order as President, Jimmy Carter Jan. 21 granted a blanket pardon to all Vietnam draft evaders who had not been involved in a violent act.

Jody Powell, the White House press secretary, said he had no estimates of the number of people affected by the pardon. But he added that the figure might be in the hundreds of thousands, including those who failed to register for the draft.

Carter's order provoked immediate, strong criticism from leaders of veterans' organizations and from some members of Congress. But it came as no surprise. A blanket pardon had been one of Carter's pledges through much of his presidential campaign. At the national American Legion convention Aug. 24 in Seattle, he was booed when he discussed the proposal in one of his first speeches after receiving the Democratic nomination.

The Senate Jan. 25 narrowly defeated an attempt to put it on record in opposition to President Carter's pardon of Vietnam-era draft resisters.

Killed by a two-vote margin (48-46) was a resolution (S Res 18), introduced by James B. Allen (D Ala.), expressing the sense of the Senate that Carter should not have issued his unconditional pardon to persons who violated the draft laws in the 1960s and early 1970s.

Supporters of the resolution conceded that they could not legally restrict the President's pardon power, which is granted by the Constitution. According to Allen, the purpose of the resolution was to express what he termed the "overwhelming public opinion" against the pardon as well as to discourage Carter from pardoning military deserters.

Carter's pardon proclamation contained the following provisions:

- Granted "full, complete and unconditional pardon" to all persons convicted of violating the draft laws during the Vietnam era (Aug. 4, 1964—March 28, 1973), and to all those who might have violated the draft laws but had not been convicted.
- Permitted Americans who had become citizens of another country, after fleeing the United States to avoid the draft, to visit the U.S. freely and reapply for citizenship.
- Granted "full measure of relief" to persons who had participated in former President Ford's clemency program, which required alternative service for draft evaders.

Excluded from the pardon were the following categories:

- Persons violating the draft laws through force or violence.
- Employees of the Selective Service System who violated the draft laws.
- Military deserters.

Carter promised to study the possibility of upgrading the discharges of deserters who had not received dishonorable or bad conduct discharges.

Election Reform Proposals

On March 22, Carter sent Congress a five-part packet of election reform proposals. The package included a new federal voter registration plan, provisions for public financing of congressional elections, a proposal to increase grassroots participation in presidential election campaigns, revision of the Hatch Act which prohibits federal employees from participating in political campaigns, and recommendations for the elimination of the electoral college.

Under the voter registration proposal, which appeared to have broad backing on Capitol Hill, the states would be required to sign up voters when they went to the polls for a federal election, as long as a voter could produce proof of identity and residence.

In emphasizing increased grass-roots participation in presidential campaigns, Carter suggested allowing candidates to have state committees that could spend limited amounts of money for them.

Regarding campaign financing, Carter urged Congress to act soon on public financing both for primaries and general elections for the House and Senate, so that the new law could be in effect before the 1978 congressional elections.

Carter also gave his support to a constitutional amendment providing for the elimination of the electoral college and the direct election of Presidents. Previously Carter had advocated an automatic vote by presidential electors in order to prevent the "faithless elector" problem. But administration spokespersons explained that the President, in formulating the reform package, had simply become convinced that direct election was the route to take. The proposed amendment was expected to face stiff opposition in the Senate.

Finally, Carter proposed to remove existing political restrictions on the more than 2.8 million federal Civil Service employees. The move, which is expected to receive wide support in Congress, would remove all restrictions on political activity by federal employees.

Foreign Policy Initiatives

The first weeks of the new administration saw a whirlwind of diplomatic activity by President Carter and his foreign-policy team as well as sharp debate in Congress over the administration's defense policies.

Controversy surrounded Carter's proposed reduction of defense budget authority by $2.7-billion. Debate was also heated over Carter's nomination of Paul C. Warnke to head the U.S. SALT delegation and to direct the Arms Control and Disarmament Agency (ACDA). *(For Budget proposal, see p. 53; for Warnke nomination, see p. 21)*

Mondale's Visit to Europe and Japan

The day after the inauguration, Vice President Mondale was dispatched on a 10-day goodwill mission to Western Europe and Japan. Returning to Washington Feb. 1, Mondale reported that "our relations with our friends are on the firmest possible, most hopeful basis." Among the leaders with whom Mondale conferred were West German Chancellor Helmut Schmidt, Italian Premier Giulio Andreotti, British Prime Minister James Callaghan and French President Valery Giscard d'Estaing.

Shortly after Mondale's return, other Carter administration officials embarked on a series of separate overseas fact-finding missions. First to depart was U.S. Ambassador to the United Nations Andrew Young, who toured the African countries of Tanzania, Nigeria and Kenya Feb. 3-10. Immediately preceding and during his trip, Young made several controversial policy statements which seemed to be at variance with stated Carter administration policy. On Jan. 25 Young said that the presence of Cuban troops in Angola brought "a certain stability and order" to that country. At a Jan. 31 news conference, Secretary of State Cyrus Vance rejected Young's statement, asserting that the presence of any outside forces in Angola was "not helpful to a peaceful solution" there.

On Feb. 15, Secretary of State Vance left for a week-long fact-finding tour of the Middle East. Vance's trip, during which he conferred with Israeli, Egyptian and other Middle Eastern leaders, was part of the continuing American effort to seek a comprehensive settlement in the area. The Secretary's immediate aim was to pave the way for reconvening the Geneva peace conference. But Vance said on his departure for the United States Feb. 21 that he foresaw "a very hard and difficult road ahead" in the search for a Middle East peace agreement.

Taking part in efforts to defuse another international hot spot was presidential envoy Clark Clifford, who flew to Cyprus Feb. 17 in an effort to seek ways to resolve the dispute between the Greek and Turkish factions dividing the island nation in half. The trip, which ended Feb. 22, was also an attempt to ease the tensions between Greece and Turkey, and to improve strained relations between each of the two countries and the United States.

'Human Rights'

One focus of the new President's foreign policy was his repeated statements expressing concern over violations of human rights in the Soviet Union, Cuba, Uganda, South Korea and other nations. On Feb. 17, the President took the unprecedented step of addressing a letter of support directly to a Soviet dissident, Andrei Sakharov, writing: "You may rest assured that the American people and our government will continue our firm commitment to promote respect for human rights not only in our own country but also abroad."

And on Feb. 24, the administration announced aid cutbacks for Ethiopia, Argentina and Uruguay because they had allegedly violated internationally recognized human rights standards. On March 2, Secretary of State Vance said the list of countries designated for such cutbacks might be expanded.

Carter's continuing criticism of human rights violations by the Soviet Union and other countries provoked a sharp response from Soviet Communist Party leader Leonid I. Brezhnev, who in a March 21 speech accused the United States of using the issue of human rights to interfere in Soviet internal affairs. He added that it was "unthinkable" that Soviet-American relations could develop normally as long as Carter continued his campaign in support of Soviet dissidents. At a breakfast meeting with some members of Congress the next day, President Carter said that he was not discouraged by Brezhnev's warning. The President said he would not back down on human rights, adding "Some people are concerned every time Brezhnev sneezes."

In other early foreign policy initiatives, the Carter administration welcomed its first state visitors, made cautious overtures to Cuba and Vietnam, sent aid to an African country beset by rebel invaders and made seemingly contradictory statements regarding the Middle East.

On Feb. 14, Carter welcomed to the White House his first state visitor, Mexican President Jose Lopez Portillo. He was followed Feb. 21 by Canadian Prime Minister Pierre Elliott Trudeau. The timing of both of these visits so early in his administration indicated that Carter intended to give top priority to improving relations between the United States and its neighbors. On March 7, Carter welcomed Israeli Prime Minister Yitzhak Rabin to Washington. On March 21, Japanese Prime Minister Takeo Fukuda arrived in Washington for talks on the American military presence in the Western Pacific and in South Korea.

A major source of controversy in the early months of the new administration was the President's statements regarding United States policy in the Middle East. On March 7, Carter caused a stir by using the term "defensible borders," in apparent support of Israel's policy of refusing to return all the Arab land it had seized in the 1967 war. On March 9, Carter backed away from the earlier statement, saying that Israel would have to withdraw from Arab lands occupied since the 1967 war and accept only "minor adjustments" in the prewar borders. He then softened his statement somewhat, adding that Israel could have "defense lines," that might "be extensions of Israeli defense capability beyond the permanent and recognized borders."

Regarding relations with Cuba, Carter linked improved diplomatic relations with the Castro government to the ending of Cuban interference in other countries, particularly Angola, and to a restoration of human rights in Cuba itself.

Carter also said that he would accept an invitation from Vietnam to begin a new round of negotiations in Paris aimed at a normalization of relations. The statement came in the wake of the return of a presidential commission sent to Vietnam to seek an accounting of American servicemen listed as missing in action (MIA). The Vietnam government released to the commission the remains of several American pilots killed during the Vietnam War, and promised to make further efforts to account for the remaining MIAs.

And, in its first involvement in a foreign war, the administration sent nearly $2-million in military supplies, but no arms or ammunition, to the African country of Zaire to help it repel rebel forces attacking across the border from Angola.

Carter Wins Close Race With President Ford

The American electorate called for an end to eight years of divided government Nov. 2, 1976, selecting Democrat Jimmy Carter of Georgia as the 39th President and maintaining lopsided Democratic majorities in both houses of Congress.

Carter's victory over President Ford was narrow, achieved by a popular plurality of fewer than two million and an electoral count of only 297-240. The congressional decision was overwhelming, with Democrats keeping their 2-1 advantage in the House and their 62-38 margin over Republicans in the Senate.

But the combined result was Democratic control at both ends of Pennsylvania Avenue, the first such restoration since John F. Kennedy's election in 1960 and only the party's fourth in the 20th century. Despite the obvious differences between Kennedy and Carter, there were many similarities between the political climates of 1961 and 1977.

As in 1961, the nation inaugurated a President who campaigned on the promise of an aggressive and imaginative new government, but who had offered few specifics about what he would do. Carter's victory, like Kennedy's, was a triumph of party and region, with the nation's majority party drawing just what it had to draw, winning most of the South and losing most of the West.

The Solid South returned in 1976 for the first time since 1944. Oklahoma and Virginia were the only two of the 13 southern states that Carter failed to carry, and he came within a percentage point in both. The South gave Carter 115 of his 297 electoral votes.

The South not only voted for Carter; it voted for him in large numbers. Turnout was up virtually everywhere in the South, and Carter reaped the benefits. He won 11 of the 12 southern states which showed a higher percentage turnout in 1976 than in 1972.

But the Democratic successes would not have been possible without a strong party-line vote in New York and Pennsylvania, states that had shown no discernible fondness for Carter but that went heavily Democratic in 1960 and 1968—and did so again this time. A reversal in New York alone would have given Ford the election; but, as in Pennsylvania, labor unions worked hard to keep their constituency in line, and the majority eventually fell into place.

Even though Carter's national popular vote margin was more than 10 times greater than Kennedy's in 1960 and more than twice as great as Richard M. Nixon's in 1968, the electoral college system came closer to misfiring than it did in either of those two years. Carter's southern strength gave him millions of extra popular votes that were of no electoral value.

The election ended a lackluster campaign that saw Carter's lead in the polls drop from 33 points after the Democratic convention to the point where the race was considered too close to call. The campaign was notable for the first presidential debates since 1960. Carter's poor performance in the first debate was considered of major impor-

tance in Ford's rise in the polls; his improved showing in the remaining two debates may have saved the election for him.

The Long Primary Road

There were three distinct phases to the presidential primary season that lifted Jimmy Carter from obscurity to the Democratic nomination.

The first began in New Hampshire Feb. 24, and extended through Carter's landslide win in Pennsylvania April 27. During this period, Carter established himself as the clear front-runner with a broad national base, and effectively eliminated opposing candidates Jackson, Bayh, Shriver, Harris, Shapp and Wallace. He also managed to survive the brief but worrisome "ethnic purity" controversy.

Then came a brief transition period in late April and early May, in which Humphrey decided not to run, and Udall appeared to offer the only active opposition to a Carter sweep.

This phase ended with Church's surprising win over Carter in Nebraska May 11. The Nebraska result marked the start of a new period, in which Carter faced more intense public scrutiny, and a second line of primary challengers—Church and Brown—probed for his weaknesses.

Between May 11 and June 8, Carter's momentum faded visibly with defeats in Maryland, Idaho, Nevada, Oregon, Montana, Rhode Island, California and New Jersey, and a near-loss to Udall in Michigan. But Carter continued to gain delegates, until victory in Ohio unleashed a stampede of party elders into his camp, destroying the credibility of Brown and Church overnight despite impressive primary victories for each.

Carter was not seriously hurt by his poor showing in the late primaries for two reasons. First, his regional base in the South provided a cushion strong enough to absorb the cascade of defeats elsewhere. He had victories May 25 in Arkansas, Kentucky and Tennessee to counterbalance simultaneous losses to Church and Brown in small western states.

Second, the proportional division of delegates in most primaries allowed Carter to continue accumulating them even in states where he was beaten.

Momentum lost by defeat in the popular vote in these states was more than compensated for by a delegate count that rose steadily toward the 1,505 required for the nomination. In most southern states Carter lost little in the proportional division because his popular majorities were overwhelming enough to garner almost all of the delegates.

Carter's losses thus had minimal impact. Brown's Maryland triumph did not prevent Carter from receiving a majority of that state's delegates, and Church's near-sweep in the Pacific Northwest did not produce enough delegates to make him look like a contender nationally. Ohio, which led to the slew of Carter endorsements, appeared decisive not so much for the size of his victory—which was impressive—but because it was the last primary and guaranteed that there would be no more opportunities to damage him.

The Democratic Convention

Jimmy Carter, whose brilliantly executed presidential primary campaign flouted Democratic Party regulars, brought the party's diverse elements together again July 12-15 in a show of unaccustomed unity at the party's 37th quadrennial convention.

The 51-year old former Georgia governor July 15 accepted his party's nomination and picked Sen. Walter F. Mondale (D Minn.), 48, as his vice-presidential running mate.

The four-day Democratic National Convention in New York City was the most harmonious in 12 years and a stark contrast to the bitter and divisive conventions of 1972 and 1968 in Miami Beach and Chicago. To a large degree the convergence of unity and good feelings was planned and executed by Texan Robert S. Strauss, the pragmatic party chairman.

At times, the emphasis on unity all but eclipsed the attention paid to Carter himself—as it did after the nominee's acceptance speech, when Strauss called dozens of party leaders to the podium to celebrate—and Carter and his family found themselves lost in the crowd.

Much of the oratory celebrated not only unity but renewal. There was the return of the South to good grace and party loyalty, a point made by Mondale in his statement that "we stand together as a nation, reunited at long last, Georgia and Minnesota, one." There was the optimism of Democrats from New York State and New York City, congratulating themselves for being good hosts and offering the peace and harmony of the convention as evidence that better days might be ahead for them.

The general spirit of harmony prevailed from the early period of the convention—which saw no credentials fights or challenges and only one minority platform report—to the end. The convention closed with a fiery benediction delivered by the Rev. Martin Luther King Sr. which led delegates to join hands in an emotional finale, singing "We Shall Overcome."

Credentials, Rules, Platform

For the preceding 12 years, credentials contests had been a focal point of Democratic conventions. There were disputes over civil rights in 1964 and 1968 and over party reforms in 1972.

But in 1976 the spirit of harmony that prevailed in the rest of the convention extended to credentials as well. With no minority reports filed, the report of the Credentials Committee was adopted July 13 by voice vote.

The lack of a spirited competition for the presidential nomination was an important factor in the absence of credentials challenges. However, the groundwork for the harmonious atmosphere had been established months earlier when the Democratic National Committee adopted 1976 delegate selection and convention rules.

The delegate selection rules adopted by the National Committee abolished the controversial implicit quota system that had been the basis of most credentials challenges in 1972.

In 1976, the only basis for a challenge was the violation of a state's delegate selection plan or affirmative action plan to assure the fair representation of minorities. Since all

Carter in the Primaries

These are the results of Jimmy Carter's campaigns in the 1976 presidential preference primary contests. It does not include delegate selection primaries in New York, Texas or Alabama.

Primary	Carter's vote	Percentage	Place
New Hampshire (Feb. 24)	23,373	28.4%	1
Massachusetts (March 2)	101,948	13.9	4
Vermont (March 2)	16,335	42.2	1
Florida (March 9)	448,844	34.5	1
Illinois (March 16)	630,915	48.1	1
North Carolina (March 23)	324,437	53.6	1
Wisconsin (April 6)	271,220	36.6	1
Pennsylvania (April 27)	511,905	37.0	1
Dist. of Columbia (May 4)	9,759	39.7	1
Georgia (May 4)	419,172	83.4	1
Indiana (May 4)	417,463	68.0	1
Nebraska (May 11)	65,833	37.6	2
Maryland (May 18)	219,404	37.1	2
Michigan (May 18)	307,559	43.4	1
Arkansas (May 25)	314,306	62.6	1
Idaho (May 25)	8,818	11.9	1
Kentucky (May 25)	181,690	59.4	1
Nevada (May 25)	17,567	23.3	2
Oregon (May 25)	115,310	26.7	2
Tennessee (May 25)	259,243	77.6	1
Montana (June 1)	26,329	24.6	2
Rhode Island (June 1)	18,237	30.2	2
South Dakota (June 1)	24,186	41.2	1
California (June 8)	690,171	20.5	2
New Jersey (June 8)	210,655	58.4	1
Ohio (June 8)	593,130	52.3	1
Totals:	6,227,809	39.0	

states had their plans approved by the Compliance Review Commission of the Democratic National Committee, the Credentials Committee was not weighing the fairness of the plan, but merely whether the state party had implemented it. Unlike 1972, the burden of proof was on the challenging individual or group, not on the state parties.

The task of challengers was further impeded by the action of the National Committee in October 1975, raising the petition requirement for convention minority reports from 10 per cent to 25 per cent of Credentials Committee members. The change was opposed by party reformers but was strongly backed by party Chairman Robert S. Strauss, who warned: "Let's preserve prime television time for gut issues...those of you who saw George McGovern accept the nomination at 4 a.m. know what I'm talking about."

1976 Rules

The first roll call of the convention was initiated by party liberals who urged adoption of a Rules Committee minority report that would have permitted debate on the platform. With nearly solid opposition from Carter delegates, who did not want the proceedings lengthened, the liberal minority report was defeated, 1,957 to 735.

Debate on this minority report dominated the July 13 Rules Committee action, in which discussion focused on procedural rules for the convention. Debate on minority reports relating to the 1980 convention was deferred until the last afternoon of the convention.

The July 13 minority report was introduced by Michael Bleicher, head of the Fred Harris presidential campaign in Wisconsin. He urged platform debate on a maximum of three issues for a total of one hour, if at least 300 delegates from 10 states signed a petition for such issues. The proposal called for debate only. No votes would have been taken.

Arguing for the minority report, Bleicher claimed that open discussion was in the Democratic Party tradition and would promote delegate participation.

Richard Celeste, Ohio lieutenant governor and leader of the Carter campaign in that state, led the opposition to the report. He implied that adoption of the Bleicher proposal could lead to a situation similar to one in 1972, when the discussion of controversial measures concerning the platform proved embarrassing to the party. "There is no measure in the Bleicher proposal," Celeste said, "to eliminate frivolous proposals. Debate without decision-making can too easily lead to posturing just for the television cameras."

In the event that the Bleicher proposal passed, petitions were circulated among the delegates to debate such issues as tax reform, the divestiture of oil interests and corporate power, amnesty and abortion. Recalling the controversy stirred at the 1972 convention by the discussion of homosexual rights, abortion and welfare reform, the Carter forces were nearly unanimous in their opposition to the minority report.

Future Rules

In a long afternoon session July 15, the convention approved the portion of its Rules Committee report dealing with future party procedures. After debate, the convention rejected four minority reports.

They involved a wide range of topics—the 1978 midterm conference, the "loophole" primary, the presentation of minority reports and the party's new Judicial Council.

After considering these issues, the convention approved by a voice vote the entire Rules Committee report, which included compromise language on the "female quota" issue worked out earlier in the week by Carter and representatives of the women's caucus.

The quota issue was potentially the most explosive of the rules questions. At the Rules Committee meeting in Washington, D.C., in late June the women's caucus had demanded equal representation with men in state delegations at future conventions. The Carter forces balked at this. Carter's views prevailed in the Rules Committee, which urged each state to promote equal division between the sexes but left the implementation of the rule to each state party. The women's caucus filed a minority report.

But both sides expressed a willingness to compromise, and in New York City July 11 and 12, Carter met with representatives of the women's caucus. They reached a compromise that encouraged—but did not require—equal representation for women at the party's midterm conference and at future conventions. Language was inserted calling for the national committee to "encourage and assist" state parties in achieving equal division.

The compromise also included agreements between Carter and the women on other questions. Carter promised to establish an independent women's division in the party outside the realm of the chairman and pledged full party representation for women.

The candidate promised to work for the ratification of the Equal Rights Amendment and pledged high government positions for women.

In an often stormy session on July 13, the women's caucus debated and finally accepted the complete compromise. However, there was substantial dissent that sometimes seemed to threaten disruption of the meeting.

Karen DeCrow, president of the National Organization for Women, set the tone for opponents of the compromise. "A compromise has not been reached on women's issues," she began. "The word 'promote' is not enough. The word 'encourage' is not enough. The only thing that works is requiring equality.... It's nothing to applaud that we have been talked to like human beings. We owe it to women everywhere not to compromise with anyone just because he has a majority of delegates to the Democratic National Convention."

Leaders of the women's caucus backed the compromise, although several of them coupled their support with a warning that Carter should not take them lightly. "I don't want 50 per cent women because there are biologically 50 per cent women," said Betty Friedan. "Our power is that Jimmy Carter and the Democratic Party cannot win this election without women."

With acceptance of this compromise by the women's caucus, the minority report was withdrawn and the compromise language on equal division was worked into the majority report.

Three other minority reports were debated, but only one—on the "loophole" primary—clearly carried Carter's stamp. A loophole primary is one that permits election of delegates on a winner-take-all basis at the congressional district level.

Both Carter and National Democratic Chairman Robert S. Strauss favored the minority position, which called simply for review of the loophole primary by the newly established Commission on the Role and Future of Presidential Primaries, headed by Michigan State Chairman Morley Winograd.

The majority position outlawed these primaries entirely. It had passed the Rules Committee by the scant margin of one-quarter vote, 58½ to 58¼.

Supporters of the majority report argued that the loophole primary violated the party charter, which required proportional representation.

Opponents of the loophole ban countered that the issue should not be prejudged before being considered by the Winograd commission. Rules Committee member Bernard Winograd, brother of the commission chairman, sponsored the minority report and noted that the loophole ban would force the states using that type of primary to change their laws. He predicted that many of the states might simply drop the primary altogether rather than revise it. Thirteen of the 30 primaries in 1976 were of the loophole variety, and it was employed in six of the largest states—Illinois, New Jersey, New York, Ohio, Pennsylvania and Texas.

On a different level, some observers saw the move toward complete proportional representation as a potential embarrassment to an incumbent President, assuring a challenger some delegates that he would have been less likely to win through the loophole system. Alan Baron, a liberal Democratic strategist, said: "Even if somebody ran and got 15 or 20 per cent of the vote, that would be a lot of headlines and a lot of network TV."

Sandy Maisel of Maine, who made the principal speech for the majority report, talked of the possible impact of the loophole ban in 1980 and 1984. "It would not be anti-Carter," he said. "He'll clearly get a huge majority [of delegates in 1980]. It deals with 1984 and takes votes away from huge blocs—from [the] Mayor Daleys and Pat Cunninghams," a reference to the Chicago mayor and the New York Democratic chairman.

Two other issues debated on the floor produced roll-call votes. The first was on a minority report presented by Joseph Gebhardt of Maryland to mandate a midterm conference of at least 2,000 delegates, with at least two-thirds of the delegates elected from units no larger than congressional districts.

The amendment also called for the conference to have a prescribed agenda, including the discussion of policy matters. The majority report was indefinite about the size and scope of the midterm conference, leaving such matters to the Democratic National Committee.

Proponents of the Gebhardt amendment stressed the importance of having elected rather than appointed delegates. Opponents argued that the party should not be tied to a midterm conference of arbitrary size and shape.

On the roll call, the Gebhardt amendment ran ahead, 1,240 to 1,128, but failed because of convention rules requiring 1,505 votes, a majority of the full convention.

The second roll call came on an unsuccessful attempt by liberal delegates to have the minority report requirement at future conventions lowered to 15 from 25 per cent of convention committee members.

Backers of the minority report argued that the 25 per cent requirement was difficult to attain and stifled debate. Supporters of the 25 per cent figure countered that the opportunity for free debate existed in 1976 and cited the minority reports on rules as an example. They added that the lower figure would allow issues to reach the floor that had no chance of passage. By a vote of 1,249 to 1,354½, the minority report failed.

The final minority report advocated limiting the powers of the party's new Judicial Council. It was defeated by a voice vote.

Supporters of the minority report wanted the role of the Judicial Council restricted to reviewing state delegate selection plans and deciding challenges that resulted. Proponents of the majority report, led by Minnesota Rep. Donald M. Fraser, argued for a stronger judicial council, one that could serve as a "Supreme Court" for the party. They noted that no one currently had the power to interpret party rules.

Platform

The 1976 Democratic platform, written with unusual party agreement a month before the convention, was approved early in the morning of July 14 by delegates who appeared to be only mildly interested in the document.

Adoption by voice vote came at 12:21 a.m. after four hours of discussion by 23 speakers. The platform was merely discussed, not contested. There was debate on just one minority plank, calling for revision of the Hatch Act. It was approved with the blessings of Jimmy Carter's supporters, who had shaped the platform from the beginning.

For the most part, the platform gave party leaders and congressional candidates a chance to address supporters in the convention hall and to appear on network television while praising Democratic goals for the election year. It contrasted with the scene four years earlier in Miami Beach when the Democrats had sharp, divisive debate on 20 minority planks and did not recess until dawn.

Minnesota Gov. Wendell R. Anderson, chairman of the Platform Committee, opened the four-hour general discussion by claiming that careful preparation made the 1976 platform "more open to more people" than any other such document. Anderson's committee held 13 public hearings and heard more than 500 witnesses. The platform was divided into six sections: the economy, government reform, human needs, state, counties and cities, natural resources and international relations.

The single minority report called for revision of the 1939 Hatch Act "so as to extend to federal workers the same political rights enjoyed by other Americans as a birthright, while still protecting the Civil Service from political abuse." It was designed to allow federal employees to run for federal office and to participate in partisan election campaigns. President Ford on April 12 vetoed a bill (HR 8617) that would have permitted such activity.

Delegate Carl Oldham of Oklahoma, a member of the Platform Committee, originally sponsored a minority plank calling for repeal of the Hatch Act. But the language was changed and softened, Oldham said, at the request of the committee staff in order to please the Carter forces. The report was adopted by voice vote after 20 minutes of debate.

Nomination

July 15 was the day the Democrats did what they had come to New York to do—they ratified the decision that the primaries had actually made more than a month before. They nominated Jimmy Carter, 51, of Plains, Ga., a former governor, peanut farmer and nuclear engineer, as the Democratic candidate for President.

There were no surprises and little drama in the three-hour process, and the atmosphere in Madison Square Garden ranged from casual to frivolous. As on the convention's other nights, most of the delegates gave the speakers sporadic attention, listening closely only to the roll call itself and to the nomination and withdrawal of Arizona Rep.

Morris K. Udall, Carter's most persistent primary challenger.

The job of placing Carter's name in nomination went to Rep. Peter W. Rodino Jr. of New Jersey, who became a celebrity as chairman of the House Judiciary Committee during the 1974 impeachment debate and semi-finalist for Carter's ticket until he himself dropped out earlier in the week for health reasons.

"I have watched him carefully," Rodino said in the high-pitched New Jersey accent he had made famous on television two years earlier. "I have talked with him at length about his vision of America and its future. And I say to you, his heart is honest, and the people will believe him. His purpose is right, and the people will follow him."

Next came Margaret Costanza, vice mayor of Rochester, N.Y., an early supporter of the Carter campaign. "He's not only good on the issues," Costanza said, "he's good on the job."

The other seconding speech was made by Rep. Andrew Young of Georgia, Carter's most prominent black supporter and the man who pleaded successfully with other blacks not to abandon Carter during the "ethnic purity" controversy in April. Young talked about the special meaning of nominating a candidate from the South. "I'm ready to lay down the burden of race," Young told the delegates, "and Jimmy Carter comes from a part of the country which, whether you know it or not, has done just that."

Udall, Brown, McCormack

Three other names were placed in nomination: those of Udall, California Gov. Edmund G. Brown Jr. and anti-abortion crusader Ellen McCormack.

The Udall nomination was made by Archibald Cox, a Harvard law professor and the former Watergate special prosecutor. It was designed as part of a sequence in which Udall was to be given a chance to address the convention. After Cox delivered the nominating speech, asserting that Udall had "dissipated the despair and raised the spirits of millions of young men and women," Udall came to the platform to release his delegates.

The debate between Udall and Carter had not been friendly in the later primaries; Udall ran critical commercials in both the Ohio and Michigan contests, accusing Carter of taking deliberately vague and contradictory positions on major issues. But Udall's speech was as effusive in its praise as anything a Carter loyalist could have hoped for.

"When Jimmy Carter says he'll beat you, he'll beat you," Udall said, "and he beat us fair and square.... As I leave the convention hall tonight, I'm going to have one of those green buttons that dogged me all over America. Tomorrow I'm enlisting as a soldier in the Carter campaign, and I'm going to do everything I can."

Udall's address delighted his supporters in the hall, most of whom voted for him on the roll call even though he had freed them to do otherwise.

The speeches for Brown were more routine. The governor's name was placed in nomination by Cesar Chavez, leader of the United Farm Workers, but Chavez used his time to argue for social justice and equal rights, mentioning Brown's name only once and leaving out any discussion of his views or his record.

The McCormack nominating speech was given by James Killilea of Massachusetts, but the crowd was so noisy and restless while it was being delivered that even those who tried to pay attention seemed unable to hear. It was an angry speech; Killilea denounced Carter and his followers because he said they would not pay sufficient attention to McCormack or her views.

Color Without Excitement

The roll call itself had none of the excitement of roll calls at past conventions, but it had all the color and a few moments of fun.

The early votes produced noisy cheers from Udall partisans, as the representative's home state gave him a 19-6 majority and the Arkansas chairman described him as the "gallant Congressman from Arizona." California's vote gave Brown 205 delegates and a momentary lead, but the District of Columbia put Carter ahead to stay, and it was merely a matter of waiting until a majority was on the scoreboard.

New Jersey cast an unexpected unanimous vote for Carter, who finished a weak second behind an uncommitted/Brown/Humphrey slate in the state's delegate selection primary June 8. But Carter had met with the delegation early July 14, and Minnesota Sen. Hubert H. Humphrey also had addressed them, urging them to vote for Carter.

That left Ohio and Pennsylvania as possibilities for the vote that would give Carter a majority. The state that did so turned out to be the same state where he won his crucial primary victory June 8—Ohio. The delegation leader announced the vote in an authoritative voice that seemed to be speaking for history.

A Restrained Demonstration

The formal achievement of Carter's nomination brought another placard-waving, balloon-tossing demonstration, although a relatively restrained one by past convention standards. It caught the orchestra off guard. When the crowd began to make noise, bandleader Peter Duchin had to race for his baton and for the earphones that connected him to convention officials on the podium. Finally the band struck up "Happy Days Are Here Again," the song that had become a Democratic trademark but one given new relevance by the party's conspicuous unity.

The response to Carter's nomination was less than frenzied. Delegates clapped and cheered, but there were few tears of joy, few displays of emotion. The visitor's galleries, nearly full for one of the few times in the convention, were quiet.

The nomination belonged to Carter at that point, but the roll call was not over. Brown appeared in the California delegation and moved to make the state's vote for Carter unanimous. "I was down at the hotel," Brown said casually, "and I thought I'd come down and see what was going on."

The governor finally gave the endorsement he had refused to give throughout the pre-convention weeks. He predicted an overwhelming victory for the Democrats in November. He also said that for him, the campaign had only been a beginning—that he would continue to press the "lowered expectation" issues he had been talking about in his primary campaign. "It's going to be a long, difficult struggle to live within our environment," Brown warned. "It won't be done in the first thousand days."

Soon after that, George Busbee, Carter's successor as governor of Georgia, moved to make the entire convention vote unanimous, and the delegates happily agreed by voice vote.

(Continued on p. 62)

Vote on Democratic Presidential Nomination

(Before switches)

State	Delegate Votes	Carter	Udall	Brown	McCormack	Others[1]
Alabama	35	30				5
Alaska	10	10				
Arizona	25	6	19			
Arkansas	26	25	1			
California	280	73	2	205		
Colorado	35	15	6	11		3
Connecticut	51	35	16			
Delaware	12	10.50		1.50		
Florida	81	70		1		10
Georgia	50	50				
Hawaii	17	17				
Idaho	16	16				
Illinois	169	164	1	2	1	1
Indiana	75	72				3
Iowa	47	25	20	1		1
Kansas	34	32	2			
Kentucky	46	39	2			5
Louisiana	41	18		18		5
Maine	20	15	5			
Maryland	53	44	6	3		
Massachusetts[2]	104	65	21		2	16
Michigan	133	75	58			
Minnesota	65	37	2	1	11	14
Mississippi[3]	24	23				
Missouri	71	58	4	2	7	
Montana	17	11	2			4
Nebraska	23	20		3		
Nevada	11	3		6.50		1.50
New Hampshire	17	15	2			
New Jersey	108	108				
New Mexico	18	14	4			
New York	274	209.50	56.50	4		4
North Carolina[4]	61	56				3
North Dakota	13	13				
Ohio	152	132	20			
Oklahoma	37	32	1			4
Oregon	34	16		10		8
Pennsylvania	178	151	21	6		
Rhode Island	22	14		8		
South Carolina	31	28		1		2
South Dakota	17	11	5			1
Tennessee	46	45				1
Texas	130	124		4		2
Utah	18	10		5		3
Vermont	12	5	4	3		
Virginia	54	48	6			
Washington	53	36	11	3		3
West Virginia	33	30	1			2
Wisconsin	68	29	25		1	13
Wyoming	10	8	1	1		
District of Columbia	17	12	5			
Puerto Rico	22	22				
Canal Zone	3	3				
Guam	3	3				
Virgin Islands	3	3				
Democrats Abroad	3	2.50		0.50		
TOTAL	3,008	2,238.50	329.50	300.50	22.00	114.50

1. Other votes follow:
   Wallace 57—Ala. 5; Fla. 10; Ill. 1; Ind. 3; Ky. 5; La. 5; Mass. 11; N.C. 3; S.C. 2; Tenn. 1; Texas 1; Wis. 10.
   Church 19—Colo. 3; Mont. 4; Nev. 1; Ore. 8; Utah 1; Wash. 2.
   Humphrey 10—Minn. 9; S.D. 1.
   Jackson 10—Mass. 2; N.Y. 4; Wash. 1; Wis. 3.
   Harris 9—Mass. 2; Minn. 4; Okla. 3.
   Shapp 2—Mass. 1; Utah 1.
   Receiving one vote each: Robert C. Byrd—W.Va.; Cesar Chavez—Utah; Leon Jaworski—Texas; Barbara C. Jordan—Oklahoma; Edward M. Kennedy—Iowa; Jennings Randolph—W.Va.; Fred Stover—Minn.
   In addition, a Nevada delegate cast one-half vote for "nobody."

2. Massachusetts passed when it was first called and cast its votes at the end of the ballot.

3. One abstention.

4. Two abstentions.

Vice Presidential Balloting

Carter announced the choice of Mondale to the country at 10 a.m. July 15. The fact that Carter had clinched the nomination early gave him an unusual opportunity to select a running mate at leisure. Mondale had been one of seven members of Congress to be carefully scrutinized for the job. At one point, Sen. John Glenn (D Ohio) had been thought to have the edge. A lackluster keynote speech on the opening night of the convention, when he was overshadowed by a rousing followup by co-keynoter, Rep. Barbara C. Jordan (D Texas), was thought to have dimmed Glenn's chances.

The balloting for Mondale's nomination July 15 was even more one-sided than the balloting for Carter the night before. Mondale won 2,817 votes, leaving fewer than 200 for one declared opponent, Gary Benoit of Massachusetts, two who were nominated but withdrew—Rep. Ronald V. Dellums of California and war resister Fritz Efaw of Oklahoma—and an assortment of political personalities who each won a scattering of votes.

The Democrats had tightened up the requirements for introducing minority reports on platform and rules since 1972, and this left some who wanted to address the convention with only one way—a spurious nomination for President or Vice President. The requirements for placing names in nomination were relatively light, and three names were introduced to the convention. The best-known was that of Dellums, the militant black legislator from Berkeley, who was nominated by Rep. John Conyers Jr. of Michigan and who then went to the podium himself to plead with Carter to pay attention to the needs of minorities at home and the third-world aspirations abroad.

The other two nominating speeches were given in behalf of two men who were not old enough to serve in the office. Efaw, 29, was an alternate delegate representing Democrats living overseas and was a fugitive from U.S. draft-evasion laws. His name was placed in nomination by Louise Ransom, a woman whose son was killed in Vietnam, and seconded by Ron Kovic, a Vietnam veteran paralyzed from the chest down...

Benoit, a Massachusetts college student, was nominated by Wallace supporters in that state's delegation. The nominating and seconding speeches for him stressed opposition to busing and to federal gun control.

The names were placed in nomination in an order chosen by lot, and Mondale's followed those of Benoit and Dellums. The crowd came to life when Mondale's Minnesota colleague, Sen. Hubert H. Humphrey nominated him, calling him "my colleague in the Senate, my personal friend and a truly good and great American."

Acceptance Speeches

Carter began his address before 11 p.m., in the prime television time slot that Strauss had promised as a contrast to George McGovern's nearly unheard 3 a.m. acceptance speech in 1972.

Like less-heralded Carter addresses earlier in the campaign, the acceptance speech ranged across a variety of issues and featured at least a few lines for those at different ends of the political spectrum. For the right, there were criticisms of wasteful federal bureaucracy, a call for a balanced budget and praise for business competition with "minimal intrusion of government in our free economic system."

For the left, there were endorsements of national health insurance, reform of the tax structure and further efforts to end discrimination by race and sex.

There was populism, with partisan overtones: "I see no reason why big-shot crooks should go free and the poor ones go to jail."

There were appeals to humanism: "We should make major investments in people, not in buildings and weapons. The poor, the aged, the weak and the afflicted must be treated with respect and with compassion and with love."

Throughout the speech was Carter's familiar emphasis on competence—a competent American people, a need for competence in the federal bureaucracy and derision for an incompetent Republican administration. "We can have an American government," Carter said, "that has turned away from scandal and corruption and official cynicism and is once again as decent and competent as our people."

"Love must be translated into simple justice," Carter said at one point, dropping his voice almost to a velvety whisper and holding the attention of the audience. A few moments later, he called for "full involvement by those who know what it is to suffer from discrimination," raising his voice almost to a shout and drawing loud applause. Then he added quietly, "and they'll be in the government if I'm elected."

It was not a rousing speech, in the traditional sense. Mondale's, which preceded, was. Known in the Senate for his quiet, restrained arguments on complicated issues, he surprised many in the audience with a series of strident assaults on the Republican administrations of the past eight years.

In some respects, Mondale's oratorical style was reminiscent of his Minnesota mentor, Hubert H. Humphrey.

"We have just lived through the worst scandal in American history," Mondale said, "and are now led by a President who pardoned the person who did it." His reference to the Watergate affair and to the Nixon pardon brought the delegates to their feet.

"They have asked us to accept high unemployment," Mondale said of the Republicans, "and cruel inflation, high interest rates, a housing depression and a massive increase in welfare...they have used the power and prestige of the White House to try to persuade America to abandon its most cherished objective: That special American notion of fairness and compassion."

The Fall Campaign

With the summer preliminaries behind them, President Ford and Jimmy Carter moved into the final, eight-week phase of their campaigns for the presidency.

The contrast in the ways they moved could hardly have been more distinct. Carter, the Democratic challenger, stuck with tradition and gave a rousing, emotional Labor Day speech on Sept. 6. Then he headed into a strenuous week of travels to industrial cities of the Northeast and Midwest.

Ford, the Republican incumbent, attempted to capitalize on the prestige of the presidency. He remained at the White House and left the travel up to his running mate, Kansas Sen. Robert Dole. But he still found time to use the Rose Garden and the press briefing room to score some partisan points against his opponent.

Neither side was without its problems. Carter ran into some unexpectedly vehement opposition from anti-abortion groups in North Philadelphia and Scranton, Pa. Dole was pushed onto the defensive by reports of oil-company contributions to past campaigns.

Even as the campaign was hitting its stride, a sense of expectancy prevailed as plans continued for the first of four televised debates. Philadelphia was chosen as the site of the first debate between Ford and Carter, to be sponsored by the League of Women Voters and held at 9:30 p.m. Sept. 23.

Carter went on the attack immediately in his speech from the steps of the house in Warm Springs, Ga., where President Franklin D. Roosevelt had died in 1945.

Playing the Roosevelt theme for all it was worth, Carter compared Ford with the Republican President, Herbert Hoover, in 1932. "This year, as in 1932, our nation is divided, our people are out of work and our national leaders do not lead," said Carter. "Our nation is drifting without inspiration, without vision and without purpose."

The former Georgia governor took his hardest slap at Ford in a comparison with Harry Truman. "When Truman was in the White House, there was never any doubt who was captain of the ship," he said. "Now, every time another ship runs aground—CIA, FBI, Panama, unemployment, deficits, welfare, inflation, Medicaid—the captain hides in his stateroom and the crew argues about who is to blame."

Carter also invoked the memory of President Kennedy, who had spoken at Warm Springs during his 1960 campaign. Slightly modifying the Kennedy slogan of 16 years earlier, Carter said that it was time "to get our country on the move again."

His biggest applause from the crowd on the lawn of Roosevelt's "little White House" came from this statement: "As a political candidate, I owe nothing to special interests. I owe everything to the people."

President Ford finally left the White House Sept. 15 to launch his election campaign at his alma mater, the University of Michigan. He combined proposals to increase home ownership with a strong attack on his Democratic opponent, Jimmy Carter.

Speaking to a generally enthusiastic crowd—there were boos mixed with the applause—at the school in Ann Arbor where he starred at football four decades ago, the President promised "specifics, not smiles; performance, not promises." He stressed Republican claims that Carter flip-flops on issues and lacks experience.

"Trust is not having to guess what a candidate means," said Ford. "Trust is leveling with the people before the election about what you're going to do after the election. Trust is not being all things to all people, but being the same thing to all people. Trust is not cleverly shading words so that each separate audience can hear what it wants to hear, but saying plainly and simply what you mean, and meaning what you say."

Ford, whose previous campaigning had been done only in Washington, as he attempted to project an image of a hard-working and competent Chief Executive, told the largely student crowd: "The question in this campaign of 1976 is not who has the better vision of America. The question is who will act to make that vision a reality."

The President did not mention Carter by name. Nor did he mention his own predecessor, Richard M. Nixon, when he said the country had been "betrayed by corruption at the highest levels of government." He continued, to loud cheers: "Fortunately, the skies are far brighter. My administration has restored trust in the White House."

Trust in government, or lack of it, was the subject of a Carter speech in nearby Dearborn, Mich., the same day.

Speaking to a Michigan AFL-CIO dinner, Carter said: "Because of a war our people did not want, because of scandals our people did not want, because of economic mismanagement our people did not want, millions of Americans have lost faith in our government."

The Democratic nominee said he was glad to see Ford's "final and reluctant emergence from the Rose Garden, but I think in a larger sense the presidential campaign began a long time ago. My opponent and I, and the two parties we represent, do not exist in isolation, but are part of the currents of history."

In this campaign, said Carter, "the lines are drawn with special clarity, for my opponent, in his long career in Congress, has distinguished himself not with legislation that bears his name but with tireless opposition to all the great legislation that bears the names of Democrats who cared for people and were not controlled by special interests."

As Carter was assailing him from elsewhere in his home state, however, Ford was not only returning the favor but proposing some new legislation. Although he had indicated that his kickoff speech would contain some surprises, his dual proposal to spur home ownership was the only initiative.

Carter's Rightward Drift

As the President was launching his campaign, Carter continued to pursue the conservative themes that he had threaded through the speeches of his campaign's first week. Assessing that week—he thought he was "off to a good start"—he offered this explanation for his emphasis:

"When the Republican convention was devoted to describing me as a spendthrift, irresponsible, ultraliberal candidate, I thought it was good to re-emphasize my basic themes of balanced budget, strengthened local government, a maximum of personal privacy and a minimum of governmental secrecy."

In his speech to the Michigan AFL-CIO, Carter touched on this line when he said: "We feel we have lost control of our government, that it has become our master instead of our servant, that we are being ruled by special interests and by politicians who don't care about us. To a tragic degree, that is exactly what has happened."

Carter was more outspoken earlier that day in a speech to a "Farm Fest 1976" audience in Lake Crystal, Minn. The farmers were attentive but undemonstrative as he told them:

"I never met a farmer who wanted a handout. I never met a farmer who wanted to go on welfare. I never met a farmer who wanted the government to guarantee him a profit. But we do want to be treated fairly. In rural America, where I grew up and live and where you grew up and where you live, we have maintained the basic values of our country."

On a swing through his native South on Sept. 13, he told an audience of businessmen in Birmingham, Ala.: "Business is basically honest—more so than they're given credit for. One thing a President can do is to help restore the stature, approval and the public support and confidence in the business community. It's a cheap shot when elected officials blame the business community for the economic, social and political problems of our country."

Later that day, at the University of Oklahoma at Norman, Carter said: "The best way to guarantee peace is to eliminate waste at the Pentagon and have a tough, supple, well-organized, muscular fighting force."

(Continued on p. 66)

Carter's Team: Young, Southern and Loyal...

The campaign strategy used by Carter to win the Democratic nomination relied heavily on smooth and orderly operations, with Carter wielding ultimate control. His strategy to secure the presidency appeared to follow the same organizational lines.

The people that made up Carter's organization chart were for the most part southerners, and most of them were young. Many worked with Carter in his previous campaigns for public office. Several worked with other liberal Democratic presidential contenders.

Farter's emphasis on efficiency in government was reflected in the clear-cut lines of responsibility for his own staff. Personality conflicts were minimal, and the organizational structure remained intact.

Following is a list of the people that formed the Carter hierarchy:

Rosalynn Carter

The candidate's wife for more than 30 years, Rosalynn Carter was probably her husband's most influential adviser. As indefatigable a campaigner as her husband, she crossed the primary and caucus states, preaching the virtues of a Carter administration. Although she reportedly found campaigning painful when Carter first ran for the Georgia Senate in 1962, in 1976 she appeared confident in her role.

Like her husband, Mrs. Carter has a soft southern drawl and a smile that masks a great deal of discipline, self-confidence and ambition. She would be an active first lady—as Georgia's first lady she supervised mental health centers. This campaign year she has already spoken of her support for community day-care centers and the Equal Rights Amendment.

Mrs. Carter attended junior college in Americus, Ga., nine miles from Plains. Before reaching her nineteenth birthday, she married Carter, who was three years older and had been at the U.S. Naval Academy in Annapolis. The Navy was her first chance to see the world and she argued against returning to Plains and the peanut business when Carter's father died in 1953. She lost and the couple expanded the business to its estimated current market value of more than $500,000.

Joseph L. (Jody) Powell, Jr.

As Carter's press secretary, Powell, 32, was also one of his closest advisers. He played a key role in speechwriting and strategy planning for the campaign.

Powell comes from southern Georgia Baptist roots, the same as Carter. He was expelled from the Air Force Academy for cheating on a history exam, and later began work on his doctorate in political science at Atlanta's Emory University. In 1969 Powell wrote Carter a long letter outlining his political thinking and offering his help. Just three months before his graduation from Emory, Powell joined Carter's 1970 gubernatorial campaign as his driver.

In the Carter administration in Atlanta, Powell not only served as press spokesman but also ran the legal office, drafting and keeping progress of legislation, lobbying and working on appointments as Carter's right-hand man.

Powell has proven himself adroit at media manipulation. When *Harper's* magazine prepared a highly critical piece on Carter early in 1976, Powell managed to get a copy beforehand. He immediately issued an effective rebuttal, which received about as much attention as the story itself.

Powell brought a light personal touch and considerable humor to the Carter camp. But unlike the man he served with great loyalty, Powell was outgoing and irreverent. His sense of humor made him a favorite of reporters.

Hamilton Jordan

An easy-going southerner, Jordan (he uses the southern pronunciation JER-dun) was Carter's national campaign director. He mainly confined himself to administrative details, leaving issues and political strategy to Carter and other aides.

A native of Albany, near Carter's home in Plains, Jordan first met Carter in 1966 while still a student at the University of Georgia. Impressed with Carter, he joined the campaign as state youth coordinator. When Carter lost the race, Jordan left for a two-year tour in Vietnam with the International Voluntary Service.

In 1970 Jordan returned home to manage Carter's second gubernatorial attempt, this one successful. He served as Carter's executive secretary in 1971-1972, and drafted a master plan for a national Carter campaign. In 1973-74, he became Carter's aide at the Democratic National Committee when Carter headed the congressional election campaign effort.

Despite Jordan's casual appearance, he was a sharp political operative and analyst. At 31, he worked almost full-time in one Carter effort or another since he left college.

Gerald Rafshoon

One of the non-Georgia natives among Carter's upper echelons, Rafshoon, born in New York City was the campaign's advertising director. He was a member of Carter's inner circle of advisers.

The only mod dresser on the Carter team, Rafshoon, 42, went to the University of Texas where he majored in journalism. After graduation he did a three-month stint for a TV station owned by former President Lyndon B. Johnson, then spent three years in the Navy.

Upon leaving the Navy, Rafshoon joined 20th Century Fox pictures and later became its national advertising manager in New York. In 1963 he resigned and moved to Atlanta to open his own advertising agency, now the fifth largest in Atlanta.

Rafshoon handled Carter's political advertising since 1966.

Stuart Eizenstat

An intense Atlanta lawyer, Eizenstat, 33, served as Carter's issues coordinator. He played a major role

...A Close Group during the Fall Campaign

representing Carter's views during the final drafting stages of the Democratic platform.

Born in Chicago, Eizenstat has lived in Atlanta since he was an infant. He went to the University of North Carolina and graduated from Harvard Law School in 1967. After a brief time as a speech writer in the Johnson White House, he became national issues director for Humphrey in the 1968 presidential campaign. Later he returned to Atlanta to work as a law clerk in the U.S. District Court, and to join a law firm. During that time he served as issues coordinator for the 1970 Carter campaign, and Rep. Andrew Young's (D Ga.) campaign for Congress (1972).

Eizenstat was in charge of 16 advisory task forces that developed detailed position papers for Carter.

Patrick Caddell

Caddell was Carter's chief public opinion analyst and adviser. A native of Rock Hill, South Carolina, Caddell is 26.

A Harvard graduate, Caddell was an adviser to Sen. George McGovern in his 1972 presidential campaign. He was president of Cambridge Survey Research Inc., which he co-founded in 1971, and Cambridge Research Inc., which he co-founded in 1974. He did polling work for Carter on a contract basis through the Florida primary, and handled polling operations full-time for the campaign.

Charles Kirbo

A conservative southerner who likes to work behind the scenes, Kirbo at 59 called himself the "old man of the Carter campaign.

Born into poverty in a small southwest Georgia town near the Florida and Alabama state lines, Kirbo attended the University of Georgia, where he earned a law degree. He began as a country lawyer in southwest Georgia, but later joined an Atlanta law firm.

Carter ran for the Georgia Senate in 1962 and was declared the loser. The victim of obvious ballot-box stuffing, Carter retained Kirbo to prove election fraud. Kirbo did, the election results were reversed, and the Kirbo-Carter friendship grew.

Kirbo's counsel and judgment were trusted and valued by Carter, who in 1971 offered Kirbo the unexpired term of the late U.S. Sen. Richard Russell (D Ga.). Kirbo declined.

He served as Georgia Democratic chairman briefly during the Carter regime, and as talent scout for Carter when he staffed his administration. Kirbo helped Carter during the selection process of a vice presidential candidate.

Landon Butler

A part of the original campaign planning group, Butler was the Campaign's political director. He holds an English degree from Washington and Lee University and graduated from Harvard Business School in 1968. He worked in the 1972 presidential campaign of Sen. Edmund S. Muskie (D Maine).

He met Carter in 1970 while working to establish the Cumberland Island National Seashore in Georgia. He later worked as part of Carter's gubernatorial staff on the "Goals for Georgia" program that collected and assessed industrial and economic data.

Butler, 34, owns a development company that rehabilitates subsidized housing.

Morris S. Dees

A millionaire southerner and a widely known civil rights lawyer, Dees was Carter's finance chairman. Dees, a former direct-mail magnate from Montgomery, Alabama, was national fund-raising director for McGovern's 1972 presidential campaign.

A 39-year-old native of Shorter, Alabama, Dees was a defense attorney in the North Carolina trial of Joan Little, who was acquitted of murder charges after fatally stabbing a jailer she claimed was making a sexual assault. Dees was removed from the case by the trial judge after he allegedly tried to get a witness to change her testimony to make it favorable to Miss Little.

Robert J. Lipshutz

An Atlanta lawyer and leader in the city's Jewish community, Lipshutz was the Carter campaign treasurer. He served on the state human relations board under Carter and was a major policy adviser.

A graduate of the University of Georgia and Georgia Law School, Lipshutz, 54, worked for Carter in his unsuccessful gubernatorial campaign in 1966. When Carter became governor, Lipshutz helped in the reorganization of the state government.

A quiet, soft-spoken man, Lipshutz raised funds for Carter's travel when Carter headed the Democratic National Committee's congressional campaign effort in 1974.

Andrew Young

A Democratic representative from Atlanta who was executive director of the Southern Christian Leadership Conference under Dr. Martin Luther King, Young occupied a special role within the Carter campaign. He was the leading adviser on black issues and reportedly was responsible for persuading Carter to apologize for his use of the term "ethnic purity" during the primaries.

Young, 44, was consulted in 1972 about Carter's national possibilities. His support of the Georgian helped in establishing Carter's credentials among wary liberals.

Jack H. Watson, Jr.

A Harvard-trained antitrust specialist who had quietly assisted Carter campaigns since 1970, Watson headed Carter's White House transition team. He was a partner in the Atlanta-based King and Spalding law firm (along with senior Carter adviser Charles Kirbo).

Watson, 37, was expected to rely on a close-knit group of budget experts, including some staffers of the House and Senate Budget Committees, to turn position papers into legislative programs. Watson was also responsible for compiling a list of potential Carter administration officials.

To a group of local officials on a bus ride between Norman and Oklahoma City, he said: "I do favor a shifting back toward the removal of technicalities which obviously prevent the conviction and punishment of those who are guilty. I believe the Burger court is moving back in the proper direction."

Carter's comments on the Nixon-appointed Supreme Court caused some liberals to flinch. Even Minnesota Sen. Walter F. Mondale, his running made, said the next day that he and Carter might have "a difference of emphasis" on the matter.

The conservative thrust of the Carter-Mondale campaign was nothing new. In an apparent shift of economic emphasis on Sept. 3, Carter seemed to assign more importance to inflation than to unemployment when he said: "There will be no programs implemented under my administration unless we can be sure that the cost of those programs is compatible with my goal of having a balanced budget before the end of that term."

"To be able to work and refuse to work is, in my opinion, un-American," Mondale told a Labor Day crowd at Barberton, Ohio. Nothing is more indispensable to the country, he said, than the "millions of decent, able-bodied Americans who work, who pay their taxes and who stay off welfare."

With Alabama Gov. George C. Wallace at his side in Birmingham Sept. 13, Carter told a cheering shopping-center crowd: "We southerners believe in work, not welfare."

First Debate: Many Barbs, No Clear Winner

Gerald R. Ford and Jimmy Carter met in their first debate Sept. 23, exchanging charges that the challenger was inconsistent and a spendthrift and that the incumbent was insensitive and a week leader.

Most of what was said during the 90-minute confrontation repeated themes both men had stressed in their earlier campaigning. But their quiet demeanor masked rhetoric—laced with an almost numbing assortment of details and statistics—that often was stinging.

The candidates' face-to-face meeting in Philadelphia's historic Walnut Street Theater was the first in 16 years between two presidential candidates and the first ever to include an incumbent President.

Neither candidate appeared to have triumphed, and neither was embarrassed. Ford supporters were able to claim that the incumbent appeared "presidential," in command of his job.

Carter's backers could argue that the challenger demonstrated a grasp of specifics his detractors had insisted he did not have.

Most of the debate fit into traditional Republican and Democratic patterns. The two men reargued the issues of inflation and unemployment, with Carter sticking to New Deal advocacy of federal jobs for the unemployed, and Ford brandishing orthodox fiscal conservatism.

The only real surprise came when, for some reason not explainable at the time, the sound was abruptly cut off just before the candidates were about to make their summary statements. The audio finally was restored 28 awkward minutes later.

For the first half of the debate, it was the President who appeared to be on the offensive, frequently taking advantage of the short time allotted for rebuttal to attack his opponent for being hazy on issues, for adding more employees

to the payroll in Georgia when he reorganized the state government and for indicating "he would raise the taxes on those in the medium- or middle-income brackets or higher."

Carter, hesitant and nervous in the early part of the debate, appeared to gain confidence as time went on. He charged that Ford "takes the same attitude that the Republicans always take. In the last three months before an election they're always for the programs that they always fight the other 3½ years."

The former governor also accused the President of being insensitive to people out of work. "This affects human beings," Carter said in one of the rare emotional exchanges of the debate. "And his insensitivity in providing those people a chance to work has made this a welfare administration and not a work administration."

Responses to First Debate

Preliminary ratings by the A.C. Nielsen Co. indicated that between 85 million and 90 million Americans tuned into the first debate. Sixteen years earlier, an estimated 77 million watched the first Kennedy-Nixon debate.

Early surveys produced mixed results of varying reliability on the relative performances of Carter and Ford. The most immediate, conducted by Burns Roper as the first debate ended, gave Ford a lead of 39 per cent to Carter's 31 per cent, with 30 per cent of the viewers interviewed calling it a tossup.

The Roper survey measured the responses of only 336 people who watched the debate. Roper said the margin of error in such a survey was plus or minus 5 or 6 per cent. His poll was sponsored by two public television stations.

A second poll, conducted by Chilton Research Associates for the Associated Press, was less conclusive. The Chilton poll found that Ford won the debate with 34.4 per cent of those who watched, while Carter had 31.8 per cent. The remaining 33.8 per cent said neither had won or they had no opinion.

Chilton's telephone survey was taken within 90 minutes after the debate had ended, and 1,065 registered voters were called nationwide. Ford's margin, the pollster said, was too small to be considered precise, because the sample could have erred by nearly 3 per cent.

A nationwide telephone poll by *The New York Times* and CBS News showed that 37 per cent of the respondents thought Ford won the first debate; 24 per cent thought Carter won; 35 per cent considered the debate a draw

The Times-CBS poll of 1,167 persons offered further encouragement to Ford and gloom to Carter. The post-debate survey found that Ford had cut Carter's national lead in half, had overtaken him among independent voters and had gained the lead in the West.

A special telephone poll of 1,516 persons by the Harris Survey just after the debate gave Ford a victory of 40 to 31 per cent in the debate. But Carter held a lead of 50 to 41 per cent over Ford in the presidential contest.

Four of the five members of a panel of college debate coaches who scored the first debate for the Associated Press thought Ford led narrowly. The fifth thought Carter won by two points. The total points of all five: Ford 108, Carter 101.

Second Debate: Tough Carter, Angry Ford

Jimmy Carter went on the offensive in the foreign policy debate with Gerald R. Ford Oct. 6, peppering the President and the administration with charges of weak leadership, secretive style and absence of moral principles.

Ford was generally specific and vehement in his responses to Carter, but the dynamics of the debate—an incumbent with a record to defend and a challenger without one—left Ford on the defensive for most of the 90 minutes. The President was visibly irritated at much of what Carter was saying, and often glowered while listening.

It was this difference in style that separated the two men most. On the substance of foreign policy, they agreed on many issues. Both men were blunt in their insistence on preserving American military strength, their concern for U.S. influence over the Panama Canal and their unwillingness to sacrifice Taiwan in the quest for detente with the People's Republic of China.

The sharpest areas of disagreement were in the international arms field. Carter criticized the Ford administration for what he said was an excessive level of weapons sales and argued that the most recent U.S.-Soviet arms negotiations had been unsuccessful.

Ford was vigorous and precise in his defense of both the arms limitation talks (SALT) and the arms export policy. The only remark that appeared likely to cause serious repercussions was Ford's statement that the nations of Eastern Europe do not live under Soviet domination. Carter was quick to insist that they do.

Most of the arguments went back over ground the candidates had already covered in previous campaign speeches and interviews, but there were two new statements of policy. Carter came out against any future U.S. trade embargoes on food alone. He said that if Arab nations do deny oil shipments to the United States in the future, he would respond with an embargo on trade in all commodities

Ford announced a retaliatory measure against Arab boycotts of American firms doing business with Israel. He announced that the Commerce Department would publish a list the following day of U.S. firms that had complied with Arab demands that they cease to trade with Israel. The next morning, however, Commerce Secretary Elliot L. Richardson said the list would only include those firms that comply with the demands in the future. He said it would not be retroactive.

What was most obvious to the nationwide television audience, however, was the difference between the atmosphere of this debate and the first one, held 13 days earlier.

Carter's hesitancy in the first confrontation was totally absent in the second one. He no longer was deferential toward the President, and he aggressively criticized Ford and his policies.

Carter's performance paid off in public-opinion surveys conducted during or immediately after the debate. In a reversal of the reception to the first debate, when Ford led Carter by a few percentage points in most surveys, Carter led Ford this time.

A telephone survey of 300 viewers, taken by Burns Roper for the Public Broadcasting System as the second debate was ending, gave Carter a 40-30 edge over Ford. An Associated Press telephone survey of 1,071 registered voters conducted by Chilton Research Services was closer: 38.2 per cent for Carter, 34.6 per cent for Ford.

The 90-minute debate was held in the Palace of Fine Arts Theater in San Francisco, where the United Nations Charter had been signed 31 years earlier. Moderator of the panel of journalists was Pauline Frederick of National Public Radio. The panelists were Max Frankel of *The New York Times*, Henry Trewhitt of *The Baltimore Sun* and Richard Valeriani of NBC.

Both candidates occasionally gave answers that were unresponsive to the questions, either for the purpose of rebutting a point made previously by their opponent or simply of making a point they had planned in advance to make. This prompted Ron Nessen, the White House press secretary, to suggest to an interviewer after the debate that the rules be changed for the next one to require answers to be responsive.

The third and final debate between Ford and Carter will be Oct. 22 at the College of William and Mary in Williamsburg, Va. The vice presidential nominees will be featured in the third debate of the series, to be held Oct. 15 in Houston. The debates are sponsored by the League of Women Voters.

The Last Debate

Heading into the final 10 days of the presidential election campaign, President Ford and Jimmy Carter planned to go where the votes were, in the big industrial states.

Democrat Carter entered the last stage of the campaign with a modest lead over the Republican President in most public-opinion polls. But there were unusually high numbers of uncommitted voters, and knowledgeable observers felt the decision could go to either man.

Both sides placed a great deal of emphasis on their showing in the last of four televised debates, held Oct. 22 in Williamsburg, Va. Each candidate had been declared the unofficial "winner" of one of the first two debates. Both had been out-debated, in a livelier confrontation than their own, by vice presidential nominees Robert Dole and Walter F. Mondale Oct. 15.

The viewing public gleaned few new facts from the third and last televised confrontation between Ford and Carter, held at the College of William and Mary in Williamsburg. Nearly all the positions stated by both men had been stated earlier in the campaign.

But the last debate gave voters their best opportunity to compare the approaches of the competing candidates to a wide range of issues, starting with a question on the economy and ending with one on election prospects.

Ford concluded by talking about a "new spirit in America." The people, he said, "are healed, are working together." He asked the voters to support him on election day and say, "Jerry Ford, you've done a good job. Keep on doing it."

Carter, acknowledging that Ford is "a good and decent man," asked his listeners to consider what had been accomplished during the President's two years in office. "A lot remains to be done," he said, listing his opponent's failures. "I believe the American people are ready for a change in Washington."

Restored to the debate, in marked contrast to their second meeting on Oct. 6 in San Francisco, was an atmosphere of civility. Missing, for the most part, were the personal jibes and cutting comments.

The outcome, as measured by public-opinion pollsters, was more mixed than it had been in the first two presidential debates or in the Oct. 15 debate between the vice presidential candidates.

A television survey of 353 persons by Burns Roper as the debate was ending gave the advantage to Carter over Ford, 40 to 29 per cent, with 31 per cent calling it a draw. But a telephone poll of 1,027 viewers by the Associated Press found Ford ahead of Carter, 35.5 to 33.1 per cent, with 31.4 per cent undecided or calling it a draw.

Electoral College Votes

(270 Electoral Votes Needed to Win)

State	VOTES Carter	VOTES Ford
Alabama	9	
Alaska		3
Arizona		6
Arkansas	6	
California		45
Colorado		7
Connecticut		8
Delaware	3	
District of Columbia	3	
Florida	17	
Georgia	12	
Hawaii	4	
Idaho		4
Illinois		26
Indiana		13
Iowa		8
Kansas		7
Kentucky	9	
Louisiana	10	
Maine		4
Maryland	10	
Massachusetts	14	
Michigan		21
Minnesota	10	
Mississippi	7	
Missouri	12	
Montana		4
Nebraska		5
Nevada		3
New Hampshire		4
New Jersey		17
New Mexico		4
New York	41	
North Carolina	13	
North Dakota		3
Ohio	25	
Oklahoma		8
Oregon		6
Pennsylvania	27	
Rhode Island	4	
South Carolina	8	
South Dakota		4
Tennessee	10	
Texas	26	
Utah		4
Vermont		3
Virginia		12
Washington*		8
West Virginia	6	
Wisconsin	11	
Wyoming		3
TOTALS	**297**	**240**

* Even though Ford carried the state of Washington by more than 60,000 votes, one Republican elector who was pledged to Ford refused to vote for him. The elector cast his ballot instead for Ronald Reagan.

The questions were more pointed and less general than they had been in earlier debates. The answers tended to be more direct and less discursive. But Carter laid himself open to exploitation by Ford in his answer to the one question about foreign policy.

When asked about his assertion a few days earlier concerning the sending of U.S. troops to Yugoslavia, he replied that "I would never go to war, become militarily involved, in the internal affairs of another country unless our own security was directly threatened. And I don't believe that our security would be directly threatened if the Soviet Union went into Yugoslavia. I don't believe it will happen. I certainly hope it won't. I would take the strongest possible measures, short of actual military action there by our own troops, but I doubt that that would be an eventuality."

No President, said Ford, "should signal in advance to a prospective enemy what his decision might be or what option he might exercise."

Only in a couple of instances did the answers of the candidates take on a personal edge. Ford predicted a decline in unemployment and inflation and an increase in jobs. "I think this is a record the American people will understand and appreciate," he said.

Carter replied that Ford "ought to be ashamed of mentioning that statement, because we have the highest unemployment rate now than we had at any time between the Great Depression caused by Herbert Hoover and the time President Ford took office."

A few minutes later it was Ford's turn. Assessing his chances on Nov. 2, he said they were improving because Carter "is inconsistent in many of the positions that he takes. He tends to distort on a number of occasions."

But on the whole, the final debate stayed on the high road. Carter expressed regret for his *Playboy* magazine interview and pledged—in an indirect slap at the Ford organization—not to use ads personally attacking his opponent. The President admitted guilt for sometimes using "rather graphic language" in the campaign and suggested "that we do together what we can to stimulate voter participation."

Campaign's End: A Photo Finish

Jimmy Carter just missed being the sixth president in this century and the third since 1960 to be elected with less than half of the popular vote. Carter collected a bare majority, 50.1 per cent, in a compilation of the presidential vote by Congressional Quarterly based on official returns from the states.

Carter registered a comfortable plurality of nearly 1.7 million votes, but his percentage was reduced slightly from his 51-48 edge in the election night tally as third-party and write-in votes were tabulated.

Carter's strength was concentrated in his native South and the traditionally Democratic East. He carried 11 of 13 states in his home region and rolled up a plurality of nearly 1.8 million votes there. President Gerald R. Ford ran ahead of Carter in the rest of the nation, although the Democrat took seven of the 12 states in the East (plus the District of Columbia) and swept that region by nearly one million votes.

Of the 10 states Carter won with more than 55 per cent of the vote, all were in the South and East. He rolled up his best percentages in the District of Columbia (81.6 per cent), Georgia (66.7 per cent) and Arkansas (65.0 per cent).

The regional nature of the election was further shown by Ford's dominance in the Midwest and West. Although

(Continued on p. 70)

Official 1976 Presidential Vote

Total Popular Votes: 81,551,948
Carter's Plurality: 1,680,974

State	JIMMY CARTER (Democrat) Votes	%	GERALD R. FORD (Republican) Votes	%	OTHER Votes	%		Plurality
Alabama	659,170	55.7	504,070	42.6	19,610	1.7	C	155,100
Alaska	44,055	35.7	71,555	57.9	7,935	6.4	F	27,500
Arizona	295,602	39.8	418,642	56.4	28,475	3.8	F	123,040
Arkansas	498,604	65.0	267,903	34.9	1,028	0.1	C	230,701
California	3,742,284	47.6	3,882,244	49.3	242,515	3.1	F	139,960
Colorado	460,801	42.5	584,456	54.0	37,709	3.5	F	123,655
Connecticut	647,895	46.9	719,261	52.1	14,370	1.0	F	71,366
Delaware	122,559	52.0	109,780	46.6	3,403	1.4	C	12,779
Dist. of Columbia	137,818	81.6	27,873	16.5	3,139	1.9	C	109,945
Florida	1,636,000	51.9	1,469,531	46.6	45,100	1.4	C	166,469
Georgia	979,409	66.7	483,743	33.0	4,306	0.3	C	495,666
Hawaii	147,375	50.6	140,003	48.1	3,923	1.3	C	7,372
Idaho	126,549	36.8	204,151	59.3	13,387	3.9	F	77,602
Illinois	2,271,295	48.1	2,364,269	50.1	83,269	1.8	F	92,974
Indiana	1,014,714	45.7	1,185,958	53.4	21,690	1.0	F	171,244
Iowa	619,931	48.5	632,863	49.5	26,512	2.1	F	12,932
Kansas	430,421	44.9	502,752	52.5	24,672	2.6	F	72,331
Kentucky	615,717	52.8	531,852	45.6	19,573	1.7	C	83,865
Louisiana	661,365	51.7	587,446	46.0	29,628	2.3	C	73,919
Maine	232,279	48.1	236,320	48.9	14,610	3.0	F	4,041
Maryland	759,612	52.8	672,661	46.7	7,624	0.5	C	86,951
Massachusetts	1,429,475	56.1	1,030,276	40.4	87,807	3.4	C	399,199
Michigan	1,696,714	46.4	1,893,742	51.8	63,293	1.7	F	197,028
Minnesota	1,070,440	54.9	819,395	42.0	59,754	3.1	C	251,045
Mississippi	381,329	49.6	366,846	47.7	21,205	2.8	C	14,483
Missouri	998,387	51.1	927,443	47.5	27,770	1.4	C	70,944
Montana	149,259	45.4	173,703	52.8	5,772	1.8	F	24,444
Nebraska	233,293	38.4	359,219	59.2	14,237	2.3	F	125,926
Nevada	92,479	45.8	101,273	50.2	8,124	4.0	F	8,794
New Hampshire	147,645	43.5	185,935	54.7	6,047	1.8	F	38,290
New Jersey	1,444,653	47.9	1,509,688	50.1	60,131	2.0	F	65,035
New Mexico	201,148	48.3	211,419	50.7	4,023	1.0	F	10,271
New York	3,389,558	51.9	3,100,791	47.5	43,851	0.7	C	288,767
North Carolina	927,365	55.2	741,960	44.2	9,589	0.6	C	185,405
North Dakota	136,078	45.8	153,470	51.7	7,545	2.5	F	17,392
Ohio	2,011,621	48.9	2,000,505	48.7	99,747	2.4	C	11,116
Oklahoma	532,442	48.7	545,708	50.0	14,101	1.3	F	13,266
Oregon	490,407		492,120	47.8	47,306	4.6	F	1,713
Pennsylvania	2,328,677	50.4	2,205,604	47.7	86,506	1.9	C	123,073
Rhode Island	227,636	55.4	181,249	44.1	2,285	0.6	C	46,387
South Carolina	450,807	56.2	346,149	43.1	5,627	0.7	C	104,658
South Dakota	147,068	48.9	151,505	50.4	2,105	0.7	F	4,437
Tennessee	825,879	55.9	633,969	42.9	16,498	1.1	C	191,910
Texas	2,082,319	51.1	1,953,300	48.0	36,265	0.9	C	129,019
Utah	182,110	33.6	337,908	62.4	21,200	3.9	F	155,798
Vermont	78,789	42.8	100,387	54.6	4,726	2.6	F	21,598
Virginia	813,896	48.0	836,554	49.3	46,644	2.7	F	22,658
Washington	717,323	46.1	777,732	50.0	60,479	3.9	F	60,409
West Virginia	435,864	58.0	314,726	41.9	290	0.0	C	121,138
Wisconsin	1,040,232	49.4	1,004,987	47.8	58,956	2.8	C	35,245
Wyoming	62,239	39.8	92,717	59.3	1,387	0.9	F	30,478
Totals	40,828,587	50.1	39,147,613	48.0	1,575,748	1.9	C	1,680,974

NOTE: This chart is based on official results obtained from the states in December 1976. The "other" vote listed after Carter and Ford is a combination of third party and scattered write-in votes.

The Presidential Election: Vote by Regions

The following chart is based on official presidential results obtained from the states. A breakdown of the states within each region is found in the voter turnout chart, page 63. All candidates are listed who were on the ballot in at least two states. A dash (—) indicates candidate received less than one-tenth of one per cent of the vote.

	East	South	Midwest	West	National Vote	National Per Cent
Jimmy Carter (D)	51.5%	53.7%	48.3%	45.7%	40,828,587	50.1%
Gerald R. Ford (R)	47.0	45.0	49.7	51.0	39,147,613	48.0
Eugene J. McCarthy (Ind.)	0.8	0.4	1.3	1.3	755,358	0.9
Roger MacBride (Lib.)	0.1	0.1	0.2	0.6	172,765	0.2
Lester G. Maddox (AIP)	0.2	0.2	0.1	0.5	170,887	0.2
Thomas Anderson (Amer.)	—	0.4	0.2	0.2	161,047	0.2
Peter Camejo (SWP)	0.1	0.1	0.1	0.2	91,228	0.1
Gus Hall (Communist)	0.1	0.1	0.1	0.1	59,119	0.1
Margaret Wright (People's)	—	—	—	0.3	49,025	0.1
Lyndon H. LaRouche (U.S. Labor)	0.1	—	—	—	40,046	—
Benjamin C. Bubar (Proh.)	—	—	—	—	15,898	—
Jules Levin (SLP)	—	—	—	—	9,610	—
Frank P. Zeidler (Soc.)	—	—	—	—	6,036	—

Carter made inroads in the Farm Belt, holding Ford's advantage in the Midwest to 325,000 votes, the Republican ticket carried eight of the 12 states in the region. Ford's lead in the West was more one-sided, as he swept all but one state (Hawaii) and produced a plurality in the region of nearly 800,000 votes.

Ford carried six states with more than 55 per cent of the vote, five in the West and the other (Nebraska) in the Midwest. The President's best showing was in Utah, where he received 62.4 per cent.

Although there were efforts by the U.S. Labor Party to overturn Carter's election by challenging his narrow victories in several states, such as Ohio and Wisconsin, Ford actually won more states by close margins than did Carter. There were 11 states in which the difference between Carter and Ford was two percentage points or less—and Ford carried eight of them.

Carter is only the third presidential candidate to ever receive more than 40 million votes in a general election. Richard M. Nixon, with 47.2 million votes in 1972, and Lyndon B. Johnson, with 43.1 million votes in 1964, were the others. Ford's 39.1 million votes is the most ever received by a losing candidate, easily eclipsing Nixon's old mark of 34.1 million set in 1960.

Turnout Rate. Carter is only the third presidential candidate to ever receive more than 40 million votes in a general election. Richard M. Nixon, with 47.2 million votes in 1972, and Lyndon B. Johnson, with 43.1 million votes in 1964, were the others. Ford's 39.1 million votes is the most ever received by a losing candidate, easily eclipsing Nixon's old mark of 34.1 million set in 1960.

More than 81.5 million Americans voted in the 1976 presidential election, a figure that can be deceptive. On one hand, it was a record turnout, nearly four million more voters than 1972. The turnout was up over four years ago in more than half the states and nearly 30 million more voters

participated in this election than in the 1974 congressional election.

On the other hand, the turnout rate was only 54.4 per cent, a full percentage point below 1972 and the lowest rate of voter participation since the Dewey-Truman contest in 1948, which drew only 53 per cent of the voters to the polls. The turnout rate was down from 1972 in eight of the 10 largest states, with only Texas (up 2.6 per cent) and Florida (up .5 per cent) showing increases. *(Box, this page)*

The turnout rate also dropped in three of the four regions, increasing only in the South. Ironically, while the rate in the South jumped from 45.3 per cent in 1972 to 48.1 per cent this year, the region's voter participation rate remained lower than any other region.

As in 1972 the turnout rate was highest in the Midwest, although there was a slight decline from 60.8 per cent four years ago to 60.4 per cent this year. In the other two regions the decline was more precipitous.

The turnout in the East dropped from 57.7 per cent to 55.0 per cent, with the fall off due primarily to a decrease in the turnout rate in the major industrial states—New York, Pennsylvania and New Jersey. In spite of relaxed registration requirements, the rate declined most sharply in New York, with the turnout dropping six percentage points to 50.6 per cent. Outside the South, only three other states had a lower turnout rate than New York.

The decline in the turnout rate was even sharper in California—7.7 per cent below 1972. California's fall off was the largest of any state in the nation and contributed to a massive decline in the voter participation rate in the entire western region. The turnout dropped from 59.9 per cent of the eligible western voters in 1972 to 54.4 per cent.

The states compiling the best turnout rates were in the upper Midwest and the Rocky Mountains. The top state was Minnesota with 71.6 per cent followed by Utah, North Dakota, Wisconsin and Maine.

Carter on the Issues: 1976-1977

The following excerpts from Jimmy Carter's statements on various issues were made during the primary campaign, the general election campaign and the first month and one-half of his administration. The excerpts were compiled from Carter's presentation to the Platform Committee of the Democratic Party, released June 12, 1976; from the three presidential election debates and from Carter's statements and speeches during the period between June 12, 1976 and March 1, 1977.

Domestic Policy

Agriculture and Rural America

Presentation to the Platform Committee, June 12, 1976:

It is time that we developed a coherent, predictable, stable, coordinated food and fiber policy. This policy should...increase opportunities in the world market for our agricultural commodities through an innovative, aggressive foreign sales program;...reduce the tremendous increase in the price of farm goods from the farm to the consumer (which is not passed along to the farmer in the form of profit) by studying ways to avoid excessive profits often made by middlemen and processors;...insure coordination of the policies of the many federal agencies and bureaus, in addition to the Department of Agriculture, which affect the farmer; close the revolving door that now exists between the boards of the grain inspection companies and the processors that supply them with their grain, since both the farmer and the consumer pay when regulatory agencies fail to do their job; guarantee adequate price supports and a parity level that assures farmers a reasonable return on their investment....

Remarks at the Iowa State Fair in Des Moines, Aug. 25, 1976:

...There aren't going to be any more [grain] embargoes if I'm elected President....

...[We will take] agricultural leadership in Washington out of the hands of the corporate interests and the grain speculators [and close] the revolving door that exists between the Agriculture Department and the large special interests....

Second Election Debate, Oct. 6, 1976:

And the last thing I'd like to say is this. This grain deal with the Soviet Union in '72 was terrible, and Mr. Ford made up for it with three embargoes, one against our own ally Japan. That's not the way to run our foreign policy, including international trade....

Budget Reform

Presentation to the Platform Committee, June 12, 1976:

...[T]he federal government should be committed to requiring zero-base budgeting by all federal agencies. Each program, other than income support programs such as Social Security, should be required to justify both their continued existence and their level of funding....

Congressional Quarterly interview with Carter, Aug. 24, 1976:

I've tried to be very conservative and assess different opinions that I get from my economic advisers, and I would say that before I finish my term, in the year 1980, we will have a balanced budget. And that's based on relatively careful projections of unemployment, inflation, and average increase in our gross national product per year. It also, by the way, meets every commitment that I have made to the American people on services to them.

News Conference, Dec. 14, 1976:

I intend to keep my commitment of a balanced budget at the end of four years and so I'll be very cautious about implanting new spending programs until I am convinced that they can be accommodated within that commitment....

Cities

Presentation to the Platform Committee, June 12, 1976:

...There is no meaningful Republican policy that addresses the growing urban revenue expenditure imbalance. There is no Republican policy to arrest the steady deterioration of the inner cities. In fact, the Republican policy has been nothing short of conscious, willful indifference to the plight of urban America....

...To make dramatic improvement in the unacceptably high [urban] unemployment rate, I propose a creative, joint program of incentives to private employers and a public needs employment program funded by the federal government....

...To alleviate the suffering our cities are being put through by high inflation and continued recession, I propose the following: counter-cyclical assistance to deal with the fiscal needs of cities particularly hard hit by recession;...extension of the Revenue Sharing program for five years, with an increase in the annual funding level to compensate for inflation, and with stricter enforcement of the civil rights provisions of the bill to guarantee against discriminatory use of the funds....

First Election Debate, Sept. 23, 1976:

Another thing is to deal with our needs in the central cities where the unemployment rate is extremely high—sometimes among minority groups, or those who don't speak English, or who are black, or young people—are 40 per cent unemployment. Here a CCC [Civilian Conservation Corps] type program would be appropriate to...employ young people who are now out of work.

Third Election Debate, Oct. 22, 1976:

...[T]his [Ford] administration has no urban policy....

...I remember the headline in the *Daily News* that said, "Ford to New York: Drop Dead." I think it's very important that our cities know that they have a partner in the federal government....

...I favor all revenue-sharing money being used for local governments and also to remove prohibitions on the use of revenue-sharing money so that it can be used to improve education and health care....

The last point is that the major thrust has got to be to put people back to work. We've got an extraordinarily high unemployment rate among downtown urban ghetto areas, particularly among the very poor and particularly among minority groups—sometimes 50 or 60 per cent. And the concentration of employment opportunities in those areas would help greatly not only to reestablish the tax base, but also to reduce the extraordinary welfare cost....

Consumer Protection

Presentation to the Platform Committee, June 12, 1976:

Major reforms are necessary to protect the consumers of this country.

First, we must institutionalize the consumer's role through the creation of a Consumer Protection Agency. This agency...could insure that the consumer's interest is considered....

Second, we should establish a strong nationwide program of consumer education to give the consumer the knowledge to protect himself in the market place....

...[T]o guarantee further protection to the consumer, we should work toward: quality standards, where feasible, for food and manufactured items; warranty standards,...full product labelling....

...[C]onsumers must achieve greater protection against dangerous products.... I recommend strong enforcement of existing laws; enforcement of stringent flammability standards for clothing;...expanded pre-market testing for all new chemicals to elicit their general characteristics and environmental and health effects.

Crime and Gun Control

Presentation to the Platform Committee, June 12, 1976:

...[W]e should reform our judicial system to ensure that swift, firm and predictable punishment follows a criminal conviction. I believe that crime is best deterred by the certainty of swift justice.

...[T]he federal government can provide a model for the states by revising our system of sentencing, eliminating much of the discretion given to judges and probation officers, insuring greater certainty in sentencing and confinement, and insuring a higher percentage of serious criminals being imprisoned....

...[W]e should place reasonable restrictions on the purchase of handguns, including the prohibition of ownership by persons with certain criminal backgrounds....

...[T]here is a need for a coordinated, concerted attack on drug traffic and organized criminal activity....

First Election Debate, Sept. 23, 1976:

...We have got a sharp distinction drawn between "white-collar crime," the big shots who are rich, who are influential very seldom go to jail. Those who are poor and who have no influence quite often are the ones who are punished. And the whole subject of crime is one that concerns our people very much, and I believe the fairness of it is what is a major problem....

Third Election Debate, Oct. 22, 1976:

...I have been a hunter all my life and happen to own both shotguns, rifles and a handgun. The only purpose I would see in registering handguns and not long guns of any kind would be to prohibit the ownership of those guns by those who have used them in the commission of a crime, who have been proven to be mentally incompetent to own a gun. I believe that limited approach to the question would be advisable and, I think, adequate. But that's as far as I would go with it.

Civil Rights and Women's Rights

Presentation to the Platform Committee, June 12, 1976:

I have long advocated eliminating discrimination against blacks, other minorities, and women.

I believe that the various Civil Rights Acts, including the Voting Rights Act, have had a tremendously positive effect on the South and the nation....

...I believe that our platform should reflect a strong commitment to enforcement of the Open Housing Act of 1968 and the Community Development Act of 1974. Moreover, we should enable the Equal Employment Opportunity Commission to function more effectively and expeditiously in employment discrimination complaints....

I am a strong supporter of the Equal Rights Amendment (ERA).... I support actions necessary to close [the earning] gap [between men and women]. I also support the need for flexible hours for full-time employees and additional employment of part-time persons....

...We need to provide high quality, accessible child-care facilities so that mothers who wish to work can do so....

Moreover, it is time that women were appointed to high level positions in American education, and to the boards of important agencies and heads of important government departments.

In addition we must assure that laws prohibiting sex discrimination in credit, employment, advancement, education, housing and other endeavors are strengthened and strictly enforced; [and that] women have equal access to health care systems and voluntary family planning programs....

Third Election Debate, Oct. 22, 1976:

I think the greatest thing that ever happened to the South was the passage of the Civil Rights Act and the opening up of opportunities to black people—the chance to vote, to hold a job, to buy a house, to go to school and to participate in public affairs, and not only liberate our black people but it also liberated the whites....

We've got a 30 per cent or 40 per cent unemployment rate among minority young people, and there has been no concerted effort given to the needs of those who are both poor and black, or who are poor and speak a foreign language. And that's where there has been a great generation of despair and ill health and lack of education, lack of purposefulness and lack of hope for the future. But it doesn't take just a quiet or minimum enforcement of the law. It requires an aggressive searching out and reaching out to help people who especially need it....

News Conference, Dec. 18, 1976:

...I think in the past, there's no doubt that women have been excluded from adequate consideration for the Cabinet and sub-Cabinet posts. And another factor that I think apparent is that when a woman has become pre-eminent in the business or professional world, either in law or in education or in the business world, she can demand and receive superb salaries.... [T]his has made it difficult for some of them to decide to come into government....

[I]'ve had several women who've expressed some concern that they would like to serve in the government but that their husbands were either professors in college, or headed up a business, and they just couldn't split their families, and the husband was not willing to move. So I've done the best I could and still the best I can to get well-qualified women and men, black and white, others to serve in the Cabinet. And I'm going to make a special effort at the under secretary, deputy and assistant secretary level to bring into the administration those who are now in the process of being trained for a higher position....

...The members of the Congressional Black Caucus, or the representatives of the Congressional Black Caucus, each had a presentation to make to me about different aspects of government life. One of the presentations made to me, very briefly, was the need to recruit black leaders to be in the government. The position that we talked about most was someone within the White House itself who would serve a useful purpose, not a position of tokenism, but he would be a connecting link between the black community as such and my own constant decision-making process. But there was no discussion made, no commitments made, about a specific number of blacks who might serve in the Cabinet....

...I think it's a good guess to say that there will be at least a woman or more than one woman. There will be a black or more than one black in the Cabinet....

News Conference, Dec. 20, 1976:

...I am applying the same criteria in the selection of all Cabinet members, without regard to their race or sex; and that is, the highest possible competence, and complete confidence of myself in their ability to perform well. I don't think it would be fair to either minority citizens nor women to lower the standards just to increase the number who would serve in the Cabinet. And I think when the Cabinet is completed that there will be a favorable comparison that can be drawn between my own Cabinet as far as minority groups and women compared to the previous ones.

Education

Presentation to the Platform Committee, June 12, 1976:

...If existing inequalities [in education] are to be eliminated and American teachers provided with a decent standard of living, this federal portion [of public education costs] must be increased.

The following steps are necessary: the creation of a separate Department of Education; ...expanded vocational and career education opportunities; ...expansion of educational rights of the handicapped must be assured; ...imaginative reforms to strengthen colleges and universities in times of financial difficulties....

Third Election Debate, Oct. 22, 1976:

...[W]e have now, for instance, only 7 per cent of the total education cost being financed by the federal government. When the Nixon-Ford administration started, it was 10 per cent. That's a 30 per cent reduction in the portion that the federal government contributes to education in just eight years....

Energy

Presentation to the Platform Committee, June 12, 1976:

...Our national policy for energy must include a combination of energy conservation and energy development, together with price protection for the consumer.

The price of all domestic oil should be kept below that of OPEC [Organization of Petroleum Exporting Countries] oil. There is no need to, and I oppose efforts to, deregulate the price of old oil. For natural gas, we should deregulate the price of only that natural gas not currently under existing contract (less than 5%), for a period of 5 years. At the end of that period of time, we should evaluate this program to see if it increases production and keeps gas-related products at prices the American people can afford.

Imports of oil from foreign countries should be kept at manageable levels. Increasing amounts of oil from remaining domestic and foreign sources should then be channeled into permanent storage facilities until we have accumulated at least an additional 30-day reserve supply. We should place the importation of oil under government authority, to allow strict control of purchases and the auctioning of purchase orders.

...[O]ur anti-trust laws must be effectively and rigidly enforced. Moreover, maximum disclosure of data on reserve supplies and production must be required.

I support restrictions on the right of a single company to own all phases of production and distribution of oil....

I support legal prohibitions against ownership of competing types of energy, such as oil and coal....

It is time that we had a nationwide program of energy conservation....

We need to encourage mass transit as a means of energy conservation; strict fuel efficiency standards and ratings must be established for motor vehicles....

To help conserve our dwindling energy supplies, unnecessary electrical power plant construction should be stopped....

We must substantially shift our efforts to increase our production of coal, ...without at the same time destroying the surface of our lands through uncontrolled strip mining. At the same time, make a major research and development thrust to greatly increase the use of solar energy.

While it is unrealistic given present administration policies to become energy independent by 1986, we should attempt to be free from possible blackmail or economic disaster which might be caused by another boycott. Our reserves should be developed, imports set at manageable levels, standby rationing procedures evolved and authorized, and aggressive economic reprisals available to any boycotting oil supplier.

First Election Debate, Sept. 23, 1976:

We have just advocated this past week consolidation of the responsibilities for energy. Our country now has no comprehensive energy program or policy. We have 20 different agencies in the federal government responsible for the production, the regulation, the information about energy, the conservation of energy, spread all over government. This is a gross waste of money....

...[S]hift from oil to coal, emphasize research and development of coal use and also on solar power, strict conservation measures—not yield every time that the special interest groups put pressure on the President, like this administration has done—and use atomic energy only as the last resort, with the strictest possible safety precautions. That's the best overall energy policy....

Second Election Debate, Oct. 6, 1976:

...[I]f the Arab countries ever again declare an embargo against our nation on oil, I would consider that not a military but an economic declaration of war. And I would respond instantly and in kind. I would not ship that Arab country anything—no weapons, no spare parts for weapons, no oil drilling rigs, no oil pipe, no nothing....

News Conference, Dec. 14, 1976:

...I believe that there's a general realization now on the part of the OPEC nations—most of them in fact—that a raising of the price of oil might be counterproductive to their own welfare and benefit.

The profound impact that it will have on the economic strength of the developing nations of the world and on other nations that are not quite so well off as we are—nations like Italy or England or Mexico—is much more serious than it is on us....

News Conference, Dec. 16, 1976:

...I think in the long run that a temporary deregulation of natural gas prices is probably advisable. Leaving in effect the existing contracts which extend in many instances beyond the year 2000. But I think it would be to some degree inflationary. But I think at the same time, we've got to have a continued exploration for natural gas....

News Conference, Dec. 23, 1976:

...[W]e need to reduce the dependence that presently exists on an overuse of oil and natural gas and shift toward enhanced uses of coal, and then use atomic energy to make up the difference between what those supplies will create for us and the total demand....

"Fireside Chat," Feb. 2, 1977:

One of our most urgent projects is to develop a national energy policy....

We will also stress development of our rich coal reserves in an environmentally sound way; we'll emphasize research on solar energy and other renewable energy sources; and we'll maintain strict safeguards on necessary atomic energy production.

The responsibility for setting energy policy is not split among more than 50 different agencies, departments and bureaus in the federal government. Later this month, I will ask the Congress for its help in combining many of these agencies in a new Energy Department to bring order out of chaos....

...The Congress has made great progress toward responsible strip-mining legislation, so that we can produce more energy without unnecessary destruction of our beautiful lands. My administration will support these efforts this year. We will also ask Congress for its help with legislation which will reduce the risk of future oil-tanker spills and help deal with those that do occur.

Environmental Protection

Presentation to the Platform Committee, June 12, 1976:

...We should not be diverted from our cause by false claims that the protection of our ecology and wildlife means an end to growth and a decline in jobs. This is not the case.

The Democratic Party should: ensure that the Army Corps of Engineers stops building unnecessary dams and public works projects harmful to the environment, and that the Soil Conservation Service ends uncalled for channellization of our country's rivers and streams; hold fast against efforts to lower clean air requirements of the Clean Air Act. I support strict enforcement of the non-degradation clause of the Clean Air Act; ...insist on strict enforcement of anti-water pollution laws to protect our oceans, lakes, rivers, and streams from unneeded and harmful commercial pollution, and oppose efforts to weaken the federal Water Pollution Control Act; protect against the noise pollution which our advanced technology challenges us. I opposed development of the SST on this basis, and I also opposed granting landing rights to the Concorde; ...support the need for better land-use planning; ...support efforts to place reasonable limits on strip mining....

Third Election Debate, Oct. 22, 1976:

I think it's accurate to say that the strip-mining law which was passed twice by the Congress...would have been good for the country. The claim that it would have put 140,000 miners out of work is hard to believe when at the time Mr. Ford vetoed it, the United Mine Workers was supporting the bill....

There has been a consistent policy on the part of this [Ford] administration to lower or to delay enforcement of air pollution standards and water pollution standards. And under both President Nixon and Ford, moneys have been impounded that would have gone to cities and others to control water pollution....

We need a heritage trust program, similar to the one we had in Georgia, to set aside additional lands that have geological and archeological importance, natural areas for enjoyment....

Federal Reserve System

Presentation to the Platform Committee, June 12, 1976:

Better coordination between fiscal and monetary policy should be assured by: giving the President the power to appoint the Chairman of the Federal Reserve for a term coterminous with the President's; ...requiring the Secretary of the Treasury, the Director of the Office of Management and Budget and the Chairman of the Federal Reserve Board to show in a consolidated report that their policies are mutually consistent or explain the reasons they are not consistent.

First Election Debate, Sept. 23, 1976:

...[T]he President ought to have a chance to appoint a chairman of the Federal Reserve Board to have a co-terminous term: in other words, both of them serve the same four years. The Congress can modify the supply of money by modifying the income tax laws. The President can modify the economic structure of our country by public statements and general attitudes on the budget that he proposes. The Federal Reserve has an independent status that ought to be preserved. I think that Mr. Burns did take a typical erroneous Republican attitude in the 1973 year when inflation was so high. They assume that the inflation rate was because of excessive demand, and therefore put into effect tight constraint on the economy, very high interest rates, which is typical also of a Republican administration, tried to increase the tax payments by individuals, cut the tax payments by corporations.

I would have done the opposite. I think the problem should have been addressed by increasing productivity, by putting people back to work so they could purchase more goods; lower income taxes on individuals, perhaps raise them if necessary on corporations in comparison. But Mr. Burns, in that respect, made a very serious mistake....

News Conference, Nov. 15, 1976:

I've had communications from Mr. Burns, who pledges cooperation with me during the next administration. I understand the autonomy of the Federal Reserve System and would not like to eliminate that autonomy....

...[Arthur Burns has] announced that he's not going to step down and my first inclination, of course, would be to work with him harmoniously and to let him stay on as chairman. I have said in the past that I prefer to have the chairmanship of the Federal Reserve Board coterminus with the term of the President; I still feel that way

and will seek legislation to that degree. But I would guess that I can work well with Mr. Burns if he should stay on as chairman, which I think is the most likely prospect.

Government Reorganization

Presentation to the Platform Committee, June 12, 1976:

...We must give top priority to a drastic and thorough revision and reorganization of the federal bureaucracy, to its budgeting system and to the procedures for analyzing the effectiveness of its services....

...What is at fault is the unwieldy structure and frequently inefficient operation of the government: the layers of administration, the plethora of agencies, the proliferation of paperwork....

...[T]he Democratic Party should commit itself to undertaking the basic structural reforms necessary to streamline federal operations and make the government efficient once again. The number of federal agencies should be reduced to no more than 200....

First Election Debate, Sept. 23, 1976:

...The present bureaucratic structure of the federal government is a mess. And if I am elected President, that is going to be a top priority of mine: to completely revise the structure of the federal government to make it economical, efficient, purposeful and manageable for a change....

...We now have a greatly expanded White House staff. When Mr. Nixon went in office, for instance, we had three and a half million dollars spent on the White House and the staff. That has escalated, now, to sixteen and a half million dollars in the last Republican administration. This needs to be changed. We need to put the responsibilities back on the Cabinet members....

News Conference, Nov. 15, 1976:

I believe in the tightest possible control over the government process, a simple and comprehensive management entity where the President, through his representatives, can manage the affairs of the government. I believe in giving Cabinet members maximum authority. I don't intend to run the individual departments out of the White House, especially staff members....

"Fireside Chat," Feb. 2, 1977:

I am reducing the size of the White House staff by nearly one-third, and I have asked the members of the Cabinet to do the same at the top staff level. Soon I will put a ceiling on the number of people employed by federal government agencies, so we can bring the growth of government under control.

We are now reviewing the government's 1,250 advisory committees and commissions, to see how many could be abolished without harm to the public.

We have eliminated expensive and unnecessary luxuries, such as door-to-door limousine service for many top officials, including all members of the White House staff. Government officials can't be sensitive to your problems if we are living like royalty here in Washington....

The Office of Management and Budget is now working on this [reorganization] plan, which will include zero-based budgeting, removal of unnecessary government regulations, sunset laws to cancel programs that have outlived their purpose and elimination of overlap and duplication among government services....

Health

Presentation to the Platform Committee, June 12, 1976:

Our present health care system is in need of drastic reorganization....

First, we need a national health insurance program, financed by general tax revenues and employer-employee shared payroll taxes, which is universal and mandatory....

We must shift our emphasis in both private and public health care away from hospitalization and acute-care services to preventive medicine....

Another major problem is to better utilize the health personnel available to us....

A third major thrust should be to improve the delivery of health care and to bring care within the reach—as well as the means—of all our people.... Our national needs require redirecting medical education toward primary care as one means to correct the geographic and professional maldistribution of services and personnel....

We must also reorganize the physical plant of our health care delivery system....

...We must shift our emphasis away from limited-application, technology-intensive programs to broad-based delivery of primary care for every citizen....

I believe the basic concept behind OSHA [Occupational Safety and Health Administration] is excellent. We should continue to clarify and expand the state role in the implementation of Health and Safety. OSHA must be strengthened to ensure that those who earn their living by personal labor can work in safe and healthy environments....

We should seek strong and effective legislation to promote mine safety and to protect mine workers against the black lung disease....

Third Election Debate, Oct. 22, 1976:

We spend $600 per person in the country, every man, woman and child, for health care. We still rank 15th among all the nations of the world in infant mortality. And our cancer rate is higher than any country in the world. We don't have good health care. We could have it.

"Fireside Chat," Feb. 2, 1977:

...I will support the Congress in its efforts to deal with the widespread fraud and waste and abuse of our Medicaid system.

Housing

Presentation to the Platform Committee, June 12, 1976:

The following agenda on housing is aimed at putting to work hundreds of thousands of unemployed construction workers and fulfilling our national commitment to build 2 million housing units per year: direct federal subsidies and low interest loans to encourage the construction of low and middle class housing; expansion of the highly successful Section 202 housing program for the elderly, which utilizes direct federal subsidies; greatly increased emphasis on the rehabilitation of existing housing to rebuild our neighborhoods; ....greater effort to direct mortgage money into the financing of private housing; ....prohibiting the practice of red-lining by federally sponsored savings and loan institutions and the FHA, which has had the effect of depriving certain areas of the necessary mortgage funds to upgrade themselves; providing for a steady source of credit at low interest rates to stabilize the housing industry.

First Election Debate, Sept. 23, 1976:

...[W]e need to have a commitment in the private sector to cooperate with government in matters like housing. Here, a very small investment of taxpayers money in the housing field can bring large numbers of extra jobs and the guarantee of mortgage loans and the putting forward of "202" programs for housing for older people, and so forth, to cut down the roughly 20 per cent unemployment now existing in the construction industry.

Third Election Debate, Oct. 22, 1976:

...[I]n 1975 we had fewer housing starts in this country, fewer homes built, than any year since 1940. That's 35 years. And we've got a 35 per cent unemployment rate in many areas of this country among construction workers. Now Mr. Ford hasn't done anything about it, and I think this shows a callous indifference to the families that have suffered so much....

Third Election Debate, Oct. 22, 1976:

FHA [Federal Housing Administration], which used to be a very responsible agency, who everyone looked to to help on a home, lost $600-million last year.... And now the federal government has become the world's largest slum landlord.

Inflation and Wage and Price Controls

Presentation to the Platform Committee, June 12, 1976:

There are more humane and economically sound solutions to inflation than the Republican program of forced recessions and high unemployment. We must battle inflation through: steady flow of jobs and output; ...strict anti-trust and consumer protection enforcement; increased emphasis on productivity; lower interest rates; effective monitoring of inflationary trends and forces; standby wage and price controls, which the President could apply selectively. There is no present need for the use of such standby authority.

First Election Debate, Sept. 23, 1976:

...[W]e now have such a low utilization of productive capacity, about 73 per cent—I think it is about the lowest since the Great Depression years—and such a high unemployment rate, now 7.9 per cent, that we have a long way to go in getting people to work before we have the inflationary pressures; and I think this would be easy to accomplish, to get jobs down without having the strong inflationary pressures that would be necessary....

News Conference, Dec. 3, 1976:

...I have no intention of asking the Congress to give me standby wage and price controls and have no intention of imposing wage and price controls in the next four years. If some national emergency should arise, and I think that's a very remote possibility, that would be the only indication I can see for a need for wage and price controls. I believe that the primary threat in these next four years is with continued unemployment, and I believe that with strong leadership, with my appealing to both industry and business on the one hand, and labor on the other, to show constraints, that an adequate mutual responsibility will be assumed and unnecessary increases of prices and wages can be avoided. So I don't see any possibility or advisability of my having or asking for wage and price control authority.

I think [voluntary wage-price guidelines are] a good option....

...I would say that..., if I use it, it would be done in close consultation with business, industry and labor leaders.

Mondale's Role in the Administration

Third Election Debate, Oct. 22, 1976:

The one major decision that I have made since acquiring the nomination...is the choice of a Vice President. I think this should be indicative of the kind of leaders I would choose to help me if I am elected. I chose Senator Walter Mondale. And the only criterion I ever put forward in my own mind was who among the several million people in this country would be the best person qualified to be President if something should happen to me and to join me in being Vice President if I should win that in return. And I'm convinced now,

more than I was when I got the nomination, that Walter Mondale was the right choice....

News Conference, Dec. 23, 1976:

...[Sen. Mondale] will play a role within my administration that's unprecedented in American history for a Vice President. I look on Sen. Mondale as my top staff person. His office, I believe, will be within the White House itself, very near to mine, and he will get all CIA briefings and other security briefings, FBI reports, international messages concerning foreign policy, that I get. He will be kept completely conversant with all the problems that I face and will help me as a very close and intimate adviser. I also have asked him, and he has agreed, to make trips abroad, representing me directly, and I think the extent to which he will be actively identified as being very close to me and involved in the decision-making process will make his functions within our own country and abroad much more effective....

Open Government

Presentation to the Platform Committee, June 12, 1976:

The Attorney General of this nation must be removed from politics; ...an all-inclusive "Sunshine Law"...should be implemented in Washington. With narrowly defined exceptions, meetings of federal boards, commissions and regulatory agencies must be opened to the public, along with those of congressional committees; broad public access, consonant with the right of personal privacy, should be provided to government files. Maximum security declassification must be implemented; ...the sweetheart arrangement between regulatory agencies and the regulated industries must be broken up and the revolving door between them should be closed. Federal legislation should restrict the employment of any member of a regulatory agency by the industry being regulated for a set period of time.

Annual disclosure of all financial involvements of all major federal officials should be required by statute. Involvements creating conflicts should be discontinued....

Second Election Debate, Oct. 6, 1976:

I would restore the concept of the fireside chat, which was an integral part of the administration of Franklin Roosevelt....

"Fireside Chat," Feb. 2, 1977:

Reforming the government also means making the government as open and honest as it can be....

I have asked the people appointed by me to high positions in government to abide by strict rules of financial disclosure and to avoid all conflicts of interest. I intend to make those rules permanent, and I will select my appointees in such a way which will close the revolving door between government regulatory agencies on the one hand and the businesses they regulate on the other.

My Cabinet members and I will conduct an open administration, with frequent press conferences and reports to the people and with "town hall" meetings all across the nation, where you can criticize, make suggestions and ask questions.

We are also planning with some of the radio networks live call-in sessions in the Oval Office during which I can accept your phone calls and answer the questions that are on your mind. I have asked the members of the Cabinet to travel regularly around the country to stay in close touch with you out in your communities, where government services are delivered....

Senior Citizens

Presentation to the Platform Committee, June 12, 1976:

Senior citizens need adequate income, housing, health care and transportation....

I have proposed that the Social Security system be strengthened through an increase in benefits in proportion to earnings before retirement. I likewise favor strengthening and broadening the laws against age discrimination and discouraging the trend by employers toward early forced retirement.

To make the elderly less subject to the financial burden caused by illness, I support a comprehensive, universal national health care program, with interim relief until the system is fully implemented through expansion of Medicare coverage....

...We need strict enforcement of the laws that guarantee the financial integrity of pension funds, and strict accountability for those who administer those funds....

Tax Reform

Presentation to the Platform Committee, June 12, 1976:

Our national tax system is a disgrace.... Carefully contrived loopholes have created a regressive system which lets the total tax burden shift more and more toward the average wage earner. Some of our largest corporations with extremely high profits pay virtually no tax at all....

...Basically, I favor a simplified tax system which treats all income the same, taxes all income only once, and makes our system of taxation more progressive.

First Election Debate, Sept. 23, 1976:

...The present tax structure is a disgrace to this country. It is just a welfare program for the rich....

A few things that can be done: we have now a default system so that the multinational corporations who invest overseas, if they make a million dollars in profits overseas, they don't have to pay any of their taxes unless they bring their money back into this country. When they don't take

their taxes, the average American pays their taxes for them....

Another thing is the system called "DISC," which was originally designed, proposed by Mr. Nixon to encourage exports. This permits a company to create a dummy corporation to export their products and then not to pay the full amount of taxes only. This costs our government about $1.4-billion a year....

...I wouldn't do away with all business deductions.... But if you could just do away with the ones that are unfair, you could lower taxes from everyone.

...[W]hat I want to do is not to raise taxes but to eliminate loopholes.

"Fireside Chat," Feb. 2, 1977:

We will...move quickly to reform our tax system....

I said in the campaign that our income tax system was a disgrace, because it is so arbitrary, complicated and unfair. I made a commitment to a total overhaul of the income tax laws.

The economic program that I have already mentioned earlier will, by enabling more taxpayers to use the standard deduction, be just a first step toward a much better tax system.

My advisers have already started working with Congress on a study of a more complete tax reform, which will give us a fairer, simpler system. We will outline the study procedures very soon, and, after consultation with many American citizens and with the Congress, we will present a comprehensive tax reform package before the end of this year.

Transportation

Presentation to the Platform Committee, June 12, 1976:

...Priority now needs to be given not to developing massive new national transportation systems, except in the case of public transportation, but rather to achieving more effective utilization of the existing rail, highway and airport networks....

...Arresting [the] deterioration [of highway, street and railroad systems] and completing needed work on new urban transit systems, must become the nation's first transportation priority.

...[T]he task of rebuilding the existing transportation system is so massive, so important and so urgent that private investment will have to be supplemented with substantial direct public investment....

We must substantially increase the amount of money available from the Highway Trust Fund for public mass transportation, study the feasibility of creating a total transportation fund for all modes of transportation, and change the current restrictive limits on the use of mass transit funds by localities so that greater amounts can be used as operating subsidies....

Priority attention should also be given to restructuring the nation's antiquated system of regulating transportation. The present patch-work scheme or rail, truck

and airline regulation at the federal level needlessly costs consumers billions of dollars every year. However valid the original purpose of promoting a fledgling industry and protecting the public from the tyranny of monopoly or the chaos or predatory competition, the present system has, more often than not, tended to discourage desirable competition.

Unemployment

Presentation to the Platform Committee, June 12, 1976:

...The first [economic] priority must be a rapid reduction of unemployment and the achievement of full employment with price stability. For the near future, economic policy should be expansionary. By 1979, we can achieve a balanced budget within the context of full employment.

To reach full employment we must assure...an expansionary fiscal and monetary policy for the coming fiscal year to stimulate demand, production and jobs; stimulation and incentives for the private sector to hire the unemployed and to retain workers already employed even during periods of economic downturn. To provide an additional incentive, the unemployment compensation tax paid by employers should be provided for business[es] which hire persons previously unemployed; an increased commitment by the federal government to fund the cost of on-the-job training by business;...improved manpower training programs; creation of meaningful and productive public needs jobs as a supplement to the private sector, including jobs for unmet needs in areas such as housing rehabilitation and repairing our railroad roadbeds; we should provide 800,000 summer youth jobs and double the CETA [Comprehensive Employment and Training Act] program from 300,000 to 600,000 jobs.

First Election Debate, Sept. 23, 1976:

[A] very important aspect of our economy would be to increase production every way possible; to hold down taxes on individuals; and to shift the tax burdens onto those who have avoided paying taxes in the past. These are kind of specific things, none of which are being done now, and would be a great help in reducing unemployment.

There is an additional factor that needs to be done and covered very succinctly, and that is to make sure that we have a good relationship with management; business on the one hand, and labor on the other. In a lot of places where unemployment is very high, we might channel specific targeted job opportunities by paying part of the salary of unemployed people, and also sharing with local governments the payment of salaries, which would let us cut down the unemployment rate much lower before we get to [an] inflationary level. But I believe that by the end of the first four years of the next term, we could have the unemployment rate down to three per cent adult unemployment, which is about four—four and a half per cent overall; control the inflation rate, and have a balanced growth of about four to six per cent, around five per cent, which would give us a balanced budget.

News Conference, Dec. 3, 1976:

...As I've said many times, the principle of the Humphrey-Hawkins [full employment] bill is one that I think is admirable—to cut down unemployment with a heavy dependence on the private sector of employment, with reasonable goals for achievement, for a degree of unemployment, I think now, 4.5 per cent at the end of four years; and as the Humphrey-Hawkins bill has been amended many, many times in the last two years, it's become closer and closer in consonance with my own beliefs. So as far as the exact form of the Humphrey-Hawkins bill now, I can't say whether I favor it or not, I don't know it. But I'll do everything I can to reduce unemployment.

"Fireside Chat," Feb. 2, 1977:

...[M]y primary concern is still jobs, and these one-time tax rebates are the only quick, effective way to get money into the economy and create those jobs....

We will also provide tax incentives to business firms, to encourage them to fight inflation by expanding output and to hire more of our people who are eager for work. I think it makes more sense for the government to help workers stay on the payroll than to force them onto unemployment benefits or welfare payments....

Now because unemployment is the most severe among special groups of our people—the young, the disabled, minority groups—we will focus our training programs on them.

The top priority in our job-training programs will go to young veterans of the Vietnam War. Unemployment is much higher among veterans than among others of the same age who did not serve in the military. I hope that putting many thousands of veterans back to work will be one more step toward binding up the wounds of the war years and toward helping those who have helped our country in the past....

Vietnam War Draft Resisters

Address Before the American Legion Convention Seattle, Wash., Aug. 24, 1976:

...Amnesty means what you did is right. Pardon means that what you did—right or wrong—is forgiven....

...I could never equate what they [Vietnam veterans] have done with those who left this country to avoid the draft. But I think it is time for the damage, hatred and divisiveness of the Vietnam War to be over....

...I do not favor a blanket amnesty, but for those who violated Selective Service laws, I intend to grant a blanket pardon....

First Election Debate, Sept. 23, 1976:

...I don't advocate amnesty. I advocate pardon. There is a difference, in my opinion.... Amnesty means that what you did was right. Pardon means that what you did—whether it was right or wrong—you are forgiven for it. And I do advocate a pardon for draft evaders.

Pardon for Draft Resisters, Jan. 21, 1977:

Acting pursuant to the grant of authority in Article II, Section 2, of the Constitution of the United States, I, Jimmy Carter, President of the United States, do hereby grant a full, complete and unconditional pardon to: (1) all persons who may have committed any offense between August 4, 1964 and March 28, 1973 in violation of the Military Selective Service Act or any rule or regulation promulgated thereunder; and (2) all persons heretofore convicted, irrespective of the date of conviction, of any offense committed between August 4, 1964 and March 28, 1973 in violation of the Military Selective Service Act, or any rule or regulation promulgated thereunder, restoring to them full political, civil and other rights....

Welfare Reform

Presentation to the Platform Committee, June 12, 1976:

Our welfare system is a crazy quilt of regulations administered by a bloated bureaucracy. It is wasteful to the taxpayers of America, demeaning to the recipients, discourages work, and encourages the breakup of families. The system lumps together dissimilar categories of poor people, and differs greatly in its benefits and regulations from state to state....

...[W]e must recognize there are three distinct categories of poor people—the unemployable poor, the 1.3 million employable but jobless poor, and the working poor; no person on welfare should receive more than the working poor can earn at their jobs; strong work incentives, job creation and job training should be provided for those on welfare able to work; family stability should be encouraged by assuring that no family's financial situation will be harmed by the bread-winner remaining with his dependents; efforts should be made to have fathers who abandon their family be forced to continue support; the welfare system should be streamlined and simplified....

To achieve these goals, I propose one fairly uniform, nationwide payment, varying according to cost of living differences between communities. It should be funded in substantial part by the federal government with strong work and job incentives for the poor who are employable and with income supplementation for the working poor....

First Election Debate, Sept. 23, 1976:

...I would not favor the payment of a given fixed income to people unless they are not able to work. But with tax incentives for the low income groups, we could build up their income levels above the poverty level, and not rate welfare more profitable than work.

Third Election Debate, Oct. 22, 1976:

...I favor a shifting of the welfare cost away from the local governments altogether, and over a longer period of time, let the federal government begin to absorb part of it that's now paid by the state governments....

"Fireside Chat," Feb. 2, 1977:

The welfare system also needs a complete overhaul....

The Secretary of Labor and the Secretary of Health, Education and Welfare, and others, have already begun a review of the entire welfare system. They will of course work with the Congress to develop proposals for a new system which will minimize abuse, strengthen the family and emphasize adequate support for those who cannot work and training and jobs for those who can work....

Foreign Policy and Defense

Arms Control and Nuclear Proliferation

Presentation to the Platform Committee, June 12, 1976:

We must get about the business of arms control. The Vladivostok Agreement set too high a ceiling on a strategic nuclear weapons. The [SALT] talks must get off of dead center. The core of our dealings with the Soviet Union must be the mutual reduction in arms. We should negotiate to reduce the present SALT ceilings in offensive weapons before both sides start a new arms race to reach the current maximums, and before new missile systems are tested or committed for production....

...[W]e need firm and imaginative international action to limit the proliferation of nuclear weapons and to place greater safeguards on the use of nuclear energy. The Democratic Party should put itself squarely on record as favoring a comprehensive test ban treaty prohibiting all nuclear explosives for a period of five years....

[B]y asking other nations to forego nuclear weapons, through the Non-Proliferation Treaty, we are asking for a form of self-denial that we have not been able to accept ourselves. I believe we have little right to ask others to deny themselves such weapons for the indefinite future unless we demonstrate meaningful progress toward the goal of control, then reduction, and ultimately, elimination of nuclear arsenals....

Second Election Debate, Oct. 6, 1976:

...I advocated last May in a speech at the United Nations that we move immediately as a nation to declare a complete moratorium on the testing of all nuclear devices, both weapons and peaceful devices—that we not ship any more atomic fuel to a country which refuses to comply with strict controls over the waste, which can be reprocessed into explosives. I've also advocated that we stop the sale by Germany and France of reprocessing plants to Pakistan and Brazil, and Mr. Ford hasn't moved on them. We also need to provide an adequate supply of enriched uranium. Mr. Ford again, under pressure from the atomic energy lobby, has insisted that this reprocessing or rather re-enrichment be done be done by private industry and not by the existing government plants....

Inaugural Address, Jan. 20, 1977:

...We pledge perseverance and wisdom in our efforts to limit the world's armaments to those necessary for each nation's own domestic safety. And we will move this year a step toward our ultimate goal—the elimination of all nuclear weapons from the earth.

Interview with AP and UPI reporters, Jan. 22, 1977:

As far as nuclear arms limitations are concerned, I would like to proceed quickly and aggressively with a comprehensive test ban treaty. I am in favor of eliminating the testing of all nuclear devices, instantly and completely.... On the SALT negotiations.... I would guess there would be a two-stage evolution. One is a fairly rapid ratification of the SALT II agreement.

...I would like to move very quickly, even prior to the SALT II agreement, toward a much more substantive reduction in atomic weapons as the first step to complete elimination in the future.

If we can reach an agreement with the Soviet Union for major reductions on atomic weapons, of course the next step would be to get other atomic nations to try to join in this effort, including, of course, France and England and the People's Republic of China.

...The third item is the nonproliferation effort where we constrain with every means available to us in all diplomatic means the expanding of a nuclear arms capability on weapons to nations that don't presently have this capacity.

We are quite concerned about the reprocessing of spent fuel where you change normal radioactive materials which have been used for the production of electric power into weapon quality.

We would like to have this put under international control, subject ourselves to the restraint along with those who have been processing this material for a number of years, and prohibit completely, within the bounds of our capability, the expansion of the reprocessing plants in the countries that don't have it.

Arms Sales Abroad

Second Election Debate, Oct. 6, 1976:

...[I]n our international trade...we have become the arms merchant of the world. When this Republican administration came into office we were shipping about $1-billion worth of arms overseas. Now, $10- to $12-billion worth of arms overseas to countries, which quite often use these arms to fight each other. This shift in emphasis has been very disturbing to me....

Interview with AP and UPI Reporters, Jan. 22, 1977:

...[I]n our first National Security Council meeting we discussed, in I think unanimity, the necessity for reducing arms sales or having very tight restraints on future commitments to minimize the efforts by arms manufacturers to initiate sales early in the process.

The Secretary of State will be much more hesitant in the future to recommend to the Defense Department the culmination of arms sales agreements. I have asked that all approval of arms sales, for a change, be submitted to me directly before the recommendations go to Congress. We also have asked Vice President Mondale in his early trip among our own allies and friends, some of whom are heavy arms exporters, to join with us on a multilateral basis.

We will also be talking to some of the primary arms purchasers, particularly the Middle East, when Secretary Vance goes there very shortly, to hold down their own purchases of arms from us and other countries. This will be a continuing effort on my part.

China

Presentation to the Platform Committee, June 12, 1976:

Our relations with China are important to world peace and they directly affect the world balance. The United States has a great stake in a nationally independent, secure, and friendly China. I believe that we should explore more actively the possibility of widening American-Chinese trade relations and of further consolidating our political relationships.

Second Election Debate, Oct. 6, 1976:

In the Far East I think we need to continue to be strong and I would certainly pursue the normalization of relationships with the People's Republic of China. We opened up a great opportunity in 1972, which pretty well has been frittered away under Mr. Ford, that ought to be a constant inclination towards friendship. But I would never let that friendship with the People's Republic of China stand in the way of the preservation of the independence and freedom of the people of Taiwan.

CIA and Secrecy in Foreign Policy

Presentation to the Platform Committee, June 12, 1976:

...[W]e must not use the CIA or other covert means to effect violent change in any government or government policy....

...We cannot buy friends, and it is obvious that other nations resent it if we try....

...[E]very time we have made a serious mistake in recent years in our dealings with other nations, such as Cambodia, Vietnam, and Chile, the American people have been excluded from the process of evolving and consummating our foreign policy....

Second Election Debate, Oct. 6, 1976:

Every time we've had a serious mistake in foreign affairs, it's been because the American people have been excluded from the process. If we can just tap the intelligence and ability, the sound common sense and the good judgment of the American people, we can once again have a foreign policy to make us proud instead of ashamed, and I'm not going to exclude the American people from that process in the future as Mr. Ford and Kissinger have done.

This is what it takes to have a sound foreign policy—strong at home, strong defense, permanent commitments, not betray the principles of our country, and involve the American people and the Congress in the shaping of our foreign policy....

News Conference, Nov. 4, 1976:

...[I would] open up the policy-making decision process to the Congress and to the American people and then...deal with these [foreign policy] problems in an open fashion so the American people would understand them.

News Conference, Feb. 23, 1977:

I have not found anything illegal or improper [about CIA payments to King Hussein and other foreign leaders]. If in the figure...I discover such an impropriety or illegality I will not only take immediate action to correct it but also will let the American people know about it.

I might say this: This is a very serious problem of how in a democracy to have adequate intelligence gathered, assessed and used to guarantee the security of our country. It is not part of the American nature to do things in secret. Obviously, historically and still at this modern time, there is a necessity to protect sources of information from other nations.

...I will try to be sure and so will Stan Turner, who will be the next Director of the intelligence community,...that everything we do is not only proper and legal, but also compatible with the attitudes of the American people.

One other point I would like to make is this: It can be extremely damaging to our relationship with other nations to the potential security of our country even in peacetime for these kinds of operations, which are legitimate and proper, to be revealed. It makes it hard for us to lay a groundwork on which we might predicate a successful meeting of a threat to us in time of war if we don't have some degree of secrecy.

I am quite concerned about the number of people now who have access to this kind of information and I have been working very closely with the congressional leaders yesterday and today to try to reduce the overall number of people who have access to the sources of information.... I am also assuming on a continuing basis a direct personal responsibility for the operation of all the intelligence agencies in our government to make sure that they are meeting these standards.

Defense Spending

Presentation to the Platform Committee, June 12, 1976:

Without endangering the defense of our nation or commitments to our allies, we can reduce present defense expenditures by about $5 to $7 billion annually.... Exotic weapons which serve no real function do not contribute to the defense of this country. The B-1 bomber is an example of a proposed system which should not be funded and would be wasteful of taxpayers' dollars....

The Pentagon bureaucracy is wasteful and bloated. We have more generals and admirals today than we did during World War II....

Second Election Debate, Oct. 6, 1976:

...Our country is not strong anymore. We're not respected anymore. We can only be strong overseas if we're strong at home. And when I become President, we'll not only be strong in those areas but also in defense. A defense capability second to none....

...We've got to be a nation blessed with a defense capability—efficient, tough, capable, well organized, narrowly focused fighting capability. The ability to fight, if necessary, is the best way to avoid the chance for or the requirement to fight....

...I've never advocated any cut of $15-billion in our defense budget. As a matter of fact, Mr. Ford has made a political football out of the defense budget. About a year ago, he cut the Pentagon budget $6.8-billion. After he fired James Schlesinger, the political heat got so great that he added back about $3-billion. When Ronald Reagan won the Texas primary election, Mr. Ford added back another $1.5-billion. Immediately before the Kansas City convention he added back another $1.8-billion in the defense budget.

And his own Office of Management and Budget testified that he had a $3-billion cut insurance added to the defense budget under pressure from the Pentagon. Obviously this is another indication of trying to use the defense budget for political purposes, like he's trying to do tonight.

News Conference, Feb. 23, 1977:

...In the short time that we had available to work on the previous administration's budget...we were able to reduce the suggested [defense] expenditures by almost $3-billion. I think about $2.75-billion. This was done...without weakening our defense capability.

The substantial savings in defense spending that will still leave us some muscle will be in such things as the sanitization of weapons, long-range planning, a more businesslike allocation of defense contracting, an assessment of the defense contracts for construction and repair already outstanding, a reassessment of priorities of the evolution of new weapons which in the future can become enormously expensive, a longer assignment of military personnel to a base before they are transferred, some emphasis on the correction of inequities and unfairnesses in the retirement system....

...The analysis that I made of the defense budget so far...indicates that that [a $5- to $7-billion savings in future defense budgets] is a goal that will be reached.

News Conference, Feb. 23, 1977:

...I have serious questions about whether or not the B-1 [bomber] ought to be in the future the center of our airborne defense capability. I have several more months before I have to make a decision on that matter....

I don't know whether we will decide to go on with it or not and I don't know whether we will expedite production of it or not at this time. Part of the factor to be assessed is the attitude of the Soviet Union. If we can have a general lessening of tension, a demonstrated commitment on their part toward disarmament, it would certainly make it less likely that we would go ahead with the B-1.

Détente

Presentation to the Platform Committee, June 12, 1976:

The policy of East-West détente is under attack today because of the way it has been exploited by the Soviet Union.... [I]n places like Syria or Angola, in activities like offensive missile development, the Soviets seem to be taking advantage of the new relationship to expand their power and influence, and increase the risk of conflict....

The relationship of détente is one of both cooperation and competition, of new kinds of contacts in some areas along with continued hostility in others. In the troubled history of our relationships with the Soviet Union, this is where we have arrived. The benefits of détente must accrue to both sides, or they are worthless....

But while détente must become more reciprocal, I reject the strident and bellicose return to the days of the cold war with the Soviet Union....

Second Election Debate, Oct. 6, 1976:

...[W]e've become fearful to compete with the Soviet Union on an equal basis. We talk about détente. The Soviet Union knows what they want in détente, and they've been getting it. We have not known what we've wanted and we've been out-traded in almost every instance.

Developing Countries

Presentation to the Platform Committee, June 12, 1976:

Our policies toward the developing countries need revision. For years, we have either ignored them or treated them as pawns in the big power chess game. Both approaches were deeply offensive to their people. Our program of international aid to these nations should be redirected so that it meets the human needs of the greatest number of people. This means an emphasis on food, jobs, education, and public health—including access to family planning. In our trade relations with these nations, we should join commodity agreements in such items as tin, coffee and sugar.

Eastern Europe

Presentation to the Platform Committee, June 12, 1976:

We should remember that Eastern Europe is not an area of stability and it will not become such until the Eastern European countries regain their independence and become part of a larger cooperative European framework. I am concerned over the long-range prospects for Rumanian and Yugoslavian independence, and I deplore the recent infliction upon Poland of a constitution that ratifies its status as a Soviet Satellite. We must reiterate to the Soviets that an enduring American-Soviet détente cannot ignore the legitimate aspirations of other nations.

Second Election Debate, Oct. 6, 1976:

...We have...seen a very serious problem with the so-called Sonnenfeldt document—which apparently Mr. Ford has just endorsed—which says there is an organic linkage between the Eastern European countries and the Soviet Union. And I would like to see Mr. Ford convince the Polish Americans and the Czech Americans and the Hungarian Americans in this country that those countries don't live under the domination and the supervision of the Soviet Union behind the Iron Curtain.

Third Election Debate, Oct. 22, 1976:

I have maintained from the very beginning of my campaign, and this was a standard answer that I made in response to the Yugoslavian question, that I would never go to war, become militarily involved, in the internal affairs of another country unless our own security was directly threatened. And I don't believe that our security would be directly threatened if the Soviet Union went into Yugoslavia. I don't believe it will happen. I certainly hope it won't. I would take the strongest possible measures, short of actual military action there by our own troops, but I doubt that that would be an eventuality.

News Conference, Nov. 4, 1976:

...I have made my position on Yugoslavia clear: that if the Soviet Union should invade Yugoslavia, that this would be an extremely serious breach of peace. It would be a threat to the entire world, as far as a peaceful world is concerned. It would make it almost impossible for us to continue under the broad generic sense of détente. And whether or not we actually committed troops to Yugoslavia, with the—the conjecture of my opinion is that that would be unlikely—but I would have to make a decision on a final basis at that point. I might add that my information from Yugoslavia has been that the nation is strong militarily, very highly united, very deeply committed to independence and that the chance for a Soviet invasion would be extremely unlikely.

Human Rights and Morality

Presentation to the Platform Committee, June 12, 1976:

[Détente to the Soviets] is having the benefits of the Helsinki Accords without the requirement of living up to the human rights provisions which form an integral part of it....

...We must...insist that the Soviet Union and other countries recognize the human rights of all citizens who live within their boundaries, whether they be blacks in Rhodesia, Asians in Uganda, or Jews in the Soviet Union....

...I think there are certain basic principles which should guide whatever is done in foreign lands in the name of this country. Our policies should be open and honest, shaped with the participation of Congress from the outset. Our policies should treat the people of other nations as individuals with the same dignity and respect we demand for ourselves. It must be the responsibility of the President to restore the moral authority of this country in its conduct of foreign policy. We should work for peace and the control of arms in everything we do. We should support the humanitarian aspirations of the world's peoples....

Second Election Debate, Oct. 6, 1976:

In the case of the Helsinki agreement—it may have been a good agreement at the beginning, but we have failed to enforce the so-called basket three part, which ensures the right of people to migrate, to join their families, to be free, to

speak out. The Soviet Union is still jamming Radio Free Europe....

...I think that militarily we are as strong as any nation on earth. I think we've got to stay that way and to continue to increase our capabilities to meet any potential treat. But as far as strength derived from commitment to principle; as far as strength derived from the unity within our country, as far as strength derived from the people, the Congress, the Secretary of State, the President, sharing in the evolution and carrying out of our foreign policy, as far as strength derived from the respect of our own allies and friends—so they're assured that we will be staunch in our commitment and will not deviate and will give them adequate attention—as far as strength derived from doing what is right, caring for the poor, providing food and becoming the breadbasket of the world instead of the arms merchant of the world, in those respects we're not strong....

News Conference, Nov. 15, 1976:

...I think the allocation of foreign aid and the normal friendship of our country would be determined or affected certainly by the attitude of those countries toward human rights....

News Conference, Feb. 8, 1977:

...I think we come out better in dealing with the Soviet Union if I am consistently and completely dedicated to the enhancement of human rights, not only as it deals with the Soviet Union, but all other countries. I think this can legitimately be severed from our inclination to work with the Soviet Union, for instance, in reducing dependence upon atomic weapons and also seeking mutually balanced force reductions in Europe.

I don't want the two to be tied together. I think the previous administration, under Secretary Kissinger, thought there ought to be linkage and if you mentioned human rights or if you failed to invite Mr. Solzhenitsyn to the White House that you might endanger the progress of the SALT talks. I don't feel that way....

News Conference, Feb. 23, 1977:

I think, without my tring to take credit for it, there has been a substantial move to a concern about human rights throughout the world. I think this has taken place in probably a dozen or more different countries....

...We have, I think, a responsibility and a legal right to express our disapproval of violations of human rights. The Helsinki agreement, so-called Basket III provision, insures that some of these human rights shall be preserved. We are signatory to the Helsinki agreement. We are, ourselves, culpable in some ways for not giving people adequate right to more around our country, or restricting unnecessarily in my opinion visitation to this country by those who disagree with us politically.

So I think we all ought to take a position in our country and among our friends

and allies, among our potential adversaries that human rights is something on which we should bear a major responsibility for leadership. And I have made it clear to the Soviet Union and to others in the Eastern European Community that I am not trying to launch a unilateral criticism of them; that I am trying to set a standard in our own country and make my concerns expressed throughout the world and not singled out against any particular country.

Israel and the Middle East

Presentation to the Platform Committee, June 12, 1976:

...I believe deeply that the foundation of our Middle East [policy] must be insuring the safety and security of Israel. This country should never attempt to impose a settlement in Israel, nor should we force Israel to make territorial concessions which are detrimental to her security. We should attempt to promote direct negotiations between Israel and her Arab neighbors. Israel must be allowed to live within defensible borders. As President, I would never force Israel to give up control of the Golan Heights to the Syrians nor would I recognize the Palestinean Liberation Organization or any other group purporting to represent the Palestines when those organizations refuse to recognize Israel's right to exist in peace. The negotiations that will lead to permanent peace can only proceed on the basis of a clear and absolute American commitment to insure Israel's security and survival as a Jewish State.

Second Election Debate, Oct. 6, 1976:

...[U]nder the last Democratic administration, 60 per cent of all weapons that went into the Middle East were for Israel, Nowadays—75 per cent went for Israel before—now, 60 per cent go to the Arab countries, and this does not include Iran. If you include Iran, our present shipment of weapons to the Middle East, only 20 per cent goes to Israel.

There is a deviation from idealism; it's a deviation from our commitment to our major ally in the Middle East, which is Israel; it's a yielding to economic pressure on the part of the Arabs on the oil issue....

...[I]n 1975 we almost brought Israel to their knees, after the Yom Kippur war, by the so-called reassessment of our relationship to Israel. We in effect tried to make Israel the scapegoat for the problems in the Middle East and this weakened our relationship with Israel a great deal and put a cloud on the total commitment that our people feel toward the Israelis. There ought to be a clear, unequivocal commitment, without change, to Israel....

...I believe that the boycott of American businesses by the Arab countries because those businesses trade with Israel or because they have American Jews who are owners or directors in the company is an absolute disgrace. This is the first time that I remember in the history of our country that we've let a foreign country circumvent or change our Bill of Rights. I'll do everything I can as President to stop the boycott of American businesses by the Arab countries.

It's not a matter of diplomacy or trade. It's a matter of morality....

Interview with AP and UPI reporters, Jan. 22, 1977:

I think the [Geneva] conference on the Middle East is very likely this year....

...If the Palestinians should be invited to the meeting as agreed by the other participating nations, along with us, it would probably be as part of one of the Arab delegations. But that is something still to be decided.

NATO, Relations with Allies

Presentation to the Platform Committee, June 12, 1976:

We must more closely coordinate our policy with our friends—countries like the democratic states of Europe, North America and Japan....

We have learned the hard way how important it is during times of international stress to keep close ties with our allies and friends and to strive for multilateral agreements and solutions to critical problems.

Second Election Debate, Oct. 6, 1976:

...We've tried to buy success from our enemies at the same time we've excluded from the process the normal friendship of our allies.

...And we have weakened our position in NATO because the other countries in Europe supported the democratic forces in Portugal long before we did. We stuck to the Portugal dictatorships much longer than other democracies did....

...Our allies feel that we've neglected them. The so-called Nixon shock against Japan has weakened our relationships there. Under this administration, we've also had an inclination to keep separate the European countries, thinking that if they are separate then we can dominate them and proceed with our secret, Lone Ranger type diplomatic efforts.

Another thing that we need to do is re-establish the good relationship that we ought to have between the United States and our natural allies in France. They have felt neglected....

Under this administration we've had a continuation of a so-called balance of power politics where everything is looked on as a struggle between us on the one side and the Soviet Union on the other. Our allies, the smaller countries, get trampled in the rush. What we need is to try to seek individualized bilateral relationships with countries regardless of their size....

News Conference, Nov. 4, 1976:

...One [foreign policy priority] would be to restore good relationships with our own allies and friends, which I think to some degree have been neglected in recent years.

"Fireside Chat," Feb. 2, 1977:

Yesterday, Vice President Mondale returned from his 10-day visit with leaders of Western Europe and Japan. I asked him to make this trip to demonstrate our intention to consult our traditional allies and friends on all important questions....

Vietnam, Missing in Action

Second Election Debate, Oct. 6, 1976:

One of the most embarrassing failures of the Ford administration and one that touches specifically on human rights is his refusal to appoint a presidential commission to go to Vietnam, to go to Laos, to go to Cambodia and try to trade for release of information on those who are missing in action in those wars....

...I also would never normalize relationships with Vietnam nor permit them to join the United Nations until they've taken this action. But that's not enough. We need to have an active and aggressive action on the part of the President, the leader of this country, to seek out every possible way to get that information, which has kept the MIA families in despair and doubt, and Mr. Ford has just not done it.

News Conference, Dec. 16, 1976:

...I've said during the campaign, and I still maintain the position, that until I am personally convinced that there has been the maximum possible accounting for those who are Missing in Action, that I would not favor normalization of relationships with Vietnam....

1974-77 Chronology: From Plains to Washington

1974

Dec. 12. Georgia Gov. Jimmy Carter announces his candidacy in Atlanta for the Democratic presidential nomination. He says he will enter all state primaries and will devote full time to the race. Carter is the second Democrat to announce his candidacy. The first was Rep. Morris K. Udall (Ariz.), who declared Nov. 23.

1975

Jan. 11. Former Oklahoma Sen. Fred R. Harris announces his candidacy for the Democratic presidential nomination.

Feb. 6. Sen. Henry M. Jackson (Wash.) announces his candidacy for the Democratic presidential nomination.

Feb. 17. Sen. Lloyd M. Bentsen (Texas) announces his candidacy for the Democratic presidential nomination.

March 12. Meeting in New York with potential contributors and Democratic party workers, Carter offers himself "as a good southern alternative to [Alabama Gov. George C.] Wallace."

May 17. Carter says he supports President Ford's use of military force to rescue the crew of the merchant ship, *Mayaguez*, seized May 12 in the Gulf of Siam by Cambodian government forces.

May 29. Terry Sanford, president of Duke University and former governor of North Carolina, announces his candidacy for the Democratic presidential nomination.

July 8. President Ford announces his candidacy for the Republican presidential nomination.

Aug. 14. Carter announces he has qualified for federal matching campaign funds by raising the required minimum of $100,000 in small contributions from at least 20 states. He says he has raised $435,000 in seven months of active campaigning, with individual contributions coming from all 50 states.

Aug. 23. Sen. Birch Bayh (Ind.), with 138 votes, leads all other announced and unannounced candidates for the Democratic presidential nomination in a straw poll taken at the Young Democrats of America convention in St. Louis, Mo. Carter places second with 86 votes, Udall is third with 68, and Sen. Hubert H. Humphrey (Minn.) finishes fourth with 53. Wallace, who receives 17 votes, finished ninth among the 10 candidates listed on the ballot.

Sept. 20. R. Sargent Shriver, 1972 Democratic vice presidential candidate, announces his candidacy for the Democratic presidential nomination.

Sept. 25. Pennsylvania Gov. Milton J. Shapp announces his candidacy for the Democratic presidential nomination.

Oct. 21. Sen. Bayh announces his candidacy for the Democratic presidential nomination.

Oct. 25. A straw poll of 1,094 Iowa Democrats taken at a party fundraiser by the *Des Moines Register* shows Carter finishing ahead of the other candidates with 23 per cent of the vote. Iowa is important to Carter because a win in its Jan. 19, 1976, precinct caucuses, where the national selection of delegates begins, will provide a significant boost to his national campaign.

Nov. 1. *The New York Times* reports that Carter has captured broad support among liberal southern Democrats.

Nov. 2. *The New York Times* reports that Carter is making impressive strides in New England primary states.

Nov. 12. Wallace announces his candidacy for the Democratic presidential nomination.

Nov. 16. In a show of strength at the Florida state Democratic convention in Orlando, Carter wins the support of two-thirds of the delegates from all parts of the state. Of a total of 1,049 votes cast, Carter wins 697, Shapp receives 60, and Wallace, Carter's principal rival in the state, wins 57.

Nov. 20. Former California Gov. Ronald Reagan announces his candidacy for the Republican nomination.

Dec. 13. The Gallup Poll reports that Humphrey is the top choice of Democratic voters for the party's 1976 nomination, winning the support of 30 per cent of Democrats polled nationwide. He is followed by Wallace with 20 per cent. Next in the survey are Sen. George McGovern (S.D.) and Sen. Henry Jackson (Wash.), each with 10 per cent, and Sen. Edmund S. Muskie (Maine) with seven per cent. Sen. Birch Bayh is next with five per cent. All other candidates, including Carter, receive less than five per cent.

1976

Jan. 9. West Virginia Sen. Robert C. Byrd announces his candidacy for the Democratic presidential nomination.

Jan. 19. Carter emerges from the crowded field of Democratic contenders to win 29.1 per cent of the vote in the Iowa precinct caucuses. He outdistances his nearest rival, Sen. Birch Bayh, by a margin of more than two-to-one. All the candidates fall far behind the vote for uncommitted delegates, which is 38.5 per cent.

Jan. 23. Former North Carolina Gov. Terry Sanford announces his withdrawal from the presidential race. He says he is too weak nationally to be a viable candidate for the nomination.

Feb. 10. Three days after his third-place finish in the Oklahoma precinct caucuses, Texas Sen. Lloyd Bensen announces his withdrawal from the presidential race. He says his poor showing in the early caucuses forced him to adopt a favorite son candidacy.

Feb. 24. Carter places first in the New Hampshire preference primary with 28.4 per cent of the vote. Udall is second with 22.7 per cent.

March 2. Sen. Henry Jackson places first in the Massachusetts preference primary, polling 22.3 per cent of the vote. Carter, with 13.9 per cent, finishes fourth, behind Udall and Wallace.

Carter wins the Vermont primary with 42.2 per cent of the vote. Sargent Shriver lags far behind in second place with 27.6 per cent. Carter's win in Vermont is considered a psychologically important offset to his defeat in Massachusetts.

March 4. Bayh, who finishes seventh in the Massachusetts primary, suspends his active campaign for the presidency. By suspending, rather than formally closing his campaign, Bayh is able to retain his share of federal matching campaign funds.

March 9. In a serious setback for the Wallace campaign, Carter defeats the Alabama governor 34.5 to 30.5 per cent in the Florida preference primary.

March 12. California Gov. Edmund G. Brown Jr. announces he will run as a favorite son candidate in the California preference primary June 8. He leaves open the question of whether he will launch a national campaign.

Gov. Milton Shapp announces his withdrawal from the presidential race, claiming a lack of campaign funds.

March 15. In its first trial heat pitting Carter against President Ford, the Gallup Poll shows Carter leading 47-42 per cent among nationwide voters surveyed.

March 16. Carter wins a decisive victory in the Illinois preference primary, polling 48.1 per cent of the vote. Wallace's second place finish of 27.6 per cent is another serious blow to his campaign. Sargent Shriver, who had expected to score well in the contest, is a distant third with 16.3 per cent of the vote. He suspends his active campaign after learning the results.

March 18. Idaho Sen. Frank Church announces his candidacy for the Democratic presidential nomination.

March 22. Shriver formally declares an end to his presidential bid, releasing his 11 delegates.

March 23. Jimmy Carter's win over Wallace in the North Carolina preference primary is yet another severe blow to the Alabama governor's national hopes. Carter wins 53.6 per cent of the vote. Wallace polls 34.7 per cent. Carter's win makes him the first Democrat to receive a majority of the vote in any primary.

April 4. In an interview with the *New York Daily News*, Carter says he sees "nothing wrong" with preserving neighborhood "ethnic purity." The statement arouses a storm of controversy. Carter later apologizes for the remark.

April 6. Carter wins a narrow victory in Wisconsin's preference primary, edging Morris Udall 36.6 to 35.6 per cent. The predictions early in the evening of two television networks that Udall is the winner, prompts the Arizona representative to publicly claim the triumph, but late returns prove Carter the victor. Despite the close race, Carter's come-from-behind win lends an air of success to his showing in the state.

Jackson wins a plurality of delegates (38 per cent) in New York's delegate selection primary. Udall places second with 25.5 per cent. Carter is third with 12.8 per cent. Uncommitted delegates receive 23.7 per cent of the vote. Though Jackson wins more delegates than any other candidate, his total falls short of the majority he had anticipated.

April 8. After winning only 1.1 per cent of the vote in the Wisconsin primary and no delegates in the New York contest, Fred Harris ends his active campaign for the presidency. Harris insists that he will still "concentrate on uncommitted delegates and respond to requests from local supporters" to campaign in selected areas. But he says he will not continue to mount primary campaigns "which have no serious prospects of success."

April 13. The Reverend Martin Luther King Sr. endorses Carter for the Democratic presidential nomination.

April 26. Brown announces he will be a candidate in the Maryland preference primary May 18.

April 27. Carter wins a decisive victory in the Pennsylvania preference primary, demonstrating with his 37 per cent win, considerable strength in an industrial state. His principal rival, Sen. Henry Jackson, who has strong backing from the state's Democratic and labor leaders, finishes second with 24.6 per cent of the vote.

April 29. Rejecting the urging of friends who say he is the only man standing between Jimmy Carter and the nomination, Sen. Hubert H. Humphrey (Minn.) declines to enter the Democratic race.

May 1. Carter wins an unexpectedly lopsided victory in the Texas delegate selection primary, defeating favorite son Lloyd Bentsen and Alabama Gov. George Wallace. Carter wins 92 of the state's 98 delegates, while Bentsen takes the remaining six.

Jackson announces he is ending his "active pursuit" of the Democratic presidential nomination. He cites as the reasons for his withdrawal a lack of campaign funds and a disappointing showing in the Pennsylvania primary.

May 3. Birch Bayh endorses Carter for the Democratic presidential nomination.

May 4. Carter wins 68 per cent of the vote in the Indiana preference primary.

He also wins 83.4 per cent of the vote in Georgia's preference primary.

Wallace wins 17 of the 27 delegates chosen in the Alabama state's delegate selection primary. Two uncommitted delegates are also elected. The remaining eight delegates are chosen May 25 in run-off elections in which four Wallace, two Carter and two uncommitted delegates are chosen.

Carter wins the District of Columbia preference primary with 39.7 per cent of the vote. Udall finishes second with 26 per cent. The contest is marred by an unusual number of invalid ballots.

May 6. The Gallup organization releases the results of a survey showing Carter leading seven other Democrats for the party's nomination. Carter leads his closest rival, Hubert Humphrey, by a margin of 39 to 30 per cent.

May 7. Leonard Woodcock, president of the United Auto Workers union, endorses Carter for the Democratic presidential nomination.

May 9. The latest Gallup Poll shows Carter, who had been narrowly ahead of Ford in polls taken in March and early April, pulling ahead of the President by a margin of 52-42 per cent.

May 11. Carter wins 33.2 per cent of the vote in the unofficial Democratic Party-operated Connecticut primary. Udall finishes a close second with 30.8 per cent of the vote.

Church, who conducted an intensive campaign in the state, defeats Carter in the Nebraska preference primary. Church wins 38.5 per cent of the vote to Carter's 37.6 per cent. Carter's loss is not seen as a major disruption in the progress of his campaign.

Favorite son Sen. Robert C. Byrd defeats Wallace in the West Virginia preference primary. Byrd receives 89 per cent of the vote to Wallace's 11 per cent. Carter is not listed on the ballot.

May 18. Carter wins a narrow victory over Udall in the Michigan preference primary, edging the Arizona representative by 43.4 to 43.1 per cent. A small turnout and an intensive Udall television campaign nearly costs the Georgian a victory in a contest he was slated to win easily.

In his first foray into national politics, Jerry Brown outdistances Carter 48.4 to 37.1 per cent in the Maryland preference primary.

May 25. Carter wins primary victories in three states. In Tennessee, he receives 77.6 per cent of the vote to Wallace's second-place finish of 10.9 per cent. In Kentucky, Carter outdistances Wallace 59.4 to 16.8 per cent. Carter captures 62.6 per cent of the vote in the Arkansas preference primary; Wallace places second with 16.5 per cent of the vote.

Brown wins the Nevada preference primary, capturing 52.7 per cent of the vote. Carter places second with 23.3 per cent.

Idaho Sen. Church wins a landslide victory in his home state's preference primary. He receives 78.7 per cent of the vote to Carter's second-place finish of 11.9 per cent.

Church also wins the Oregon preference primary with 33.6 per cent of the vote. Carter finishes second with 26.7 per cent. Brown, who conducted an intensive write-in campaign, places third with 24.7 per cent of the vote.

May 26. New York City Mayor Abraham Beame endorses Carter for the Democratic presidential nomination.

May 30. In its first trial heat pitting Carter against Ronald Reagan, the Gallup Poll shows Carter leading the former California governor by a wide margin of 56-36 per cent.

June 1. An uncommitted slate backed by Brown wins 31.5 per cent of the vote in the Rhode Island preference primary. Carter places second with 30.2 per cent and Church finishes third with 27.2 per cent.

Carter wins the South Dakota preference primary with 41.2 per cent of the vote. Udall is second with 33.3 per cent.

Church wins the Montana preference primary with 59.4 per cent of the vote. Carter finishes second with 24.6 per cent.

June 7. Sen. Abraham A. Ribicoff (Conn.), one of four Jewish Democratic senators, endorses Carter for the Democratic presidential nomination. (Many Jewish voters expressed concern about Carter's Southern Baptist beliefs.)

June 8. Carter's win in the Ohio preference primary wraps up the nomination for the once unknown former Georgia Governor. Carter wins the contest with 52.3 per cent of the vote, while Udall trails far behind in second place with 21.2 per cent.

Brown wins the California preference primary with 59 per cent of the vote. Carter is second with 20.4 per cent.

An uncommitted delegate slate, friendly to Humphrey and Brown, takes 83 of 108 delegates chosen in the New Jersey delegate selection contest. Carter wins the remaining 25. In the non-binding preference primary, Carter wins 58.4 per cent of the vote. Church places second with 13.6 per cent.

June 9. Carter's Ohio victory leads to a parade of endorsements from Democratic leaders. Chicago Mayor Richard Daley, who had said prior to the Ohio primary that a victory there would give Carter the nomination, heads the list of supporters. Sen. Henry Jackson, who indicates he will support Carter, issues a formal endorsement June 16.

June 10. Pennsylvania Gov. Shapp endorses Carter for the Democratic presidential nomination. West Virginia Sen. Byrd releases the 31 delegates pledged to his favorite son candidacy "in the interest of party unity." Texas Sen. Bentsen announces his support for Carter, saying that Carter gives the Democratic party "its best hope of regaining the White House." Mayors Frank L. Rizzo of Philadelphia and Walter Washington of the District of Columbia also endorse Carter.

June 12. New York Gov. Hugh L. Carey endorses Carter for the Democratic presidential nomination.

June 14. Frank Church announces his withdrawal from the presidential race and endorses Carter. Udall announces he is suspending his active campaign for the presidency. He says his delegates are free to support Carter.

June 15. The National Democratic Platform Committee approves the party's 1976 platform. The platform, written in an atmosphere of party unity rare in recent Democratic Party experience, strongly reflects Carter's views.

June 16. Humphrey once again says he will not be a presidential candidate; he appeals for party unity.

June 24. Senate Democrats unanimously endorse Carter for the Democratic presidential nomination.

June 25. Brown says he will "enthusiastically support...[Carter's] candidacy in the fall" if Carter is the party's nominee.

July 6. Twenty-nine of the thirty Democratic governors attending the annual meeting of the National Governors Conference endorse Carter for the Democratic presidential nomination. The lone dissenter is Louisiana Gov. Edwin E. Edwards.

July 12. The 37th quadrennial Democratic National Convention is called to order at 8:15 p.m. by Democratic National Committee Chairman Robert S. Strauss. Sen. John Glenn (Ohio) and Rep. Barbara Jordan (Texas) deliver the keynote addresses.

Carter pledges to appoint women to cabinet, ambassadorial and judicial posts, and to consider them for Supreme Court seats. He gives his full commitment to passage of the equal rights amendment to the U.S. Constitution.

July 14. The Democratic Party Platform is adopted by voice vote. Rep. Peter W. Rodino Jr. (N.J.) nominates Carter for President. Rochester N.Y. Vice Mayor Margaret Constanza and Rep. Andrew Young (Ga.) second the nomination. The convention votes to nominate Carter on the first ballot. Carter receives 2,238½ of the convention's 3,008 votes, the largest percentage of any non-incumbent Democratic candidate since 1908.

July 15. Carter announces his choice of Sen. Walter F. Mondale (Minn.) to be his vice presidential running mate. Humphrey formally nominates Mondale. Gov. David Pryor (Ark.) and Rep. Yvonne Brathwaite Burke (Calif.) second the nomination. Mondale receives 2,817 of the convention's 3,008 votes. Mondale delivers his acceptance speech, which is followed by Carter's address accepting the presidential nomination. The convention adjourns at 11:42 p.m.

July 19. The AFL-CIO Executive Council endorses the Carter-Mondale ticket.

July 26. A Louis Harris Poll conducted immediately after the Democratic Convention shows Carter leading Ford by a margin of 66 to 27 per cent and Reagan by a margin of 68 to 26 per cent. The Harris organization says Carter's lead is "one of the most substantial" it has ever recorded. A Gallup Poll, released Aug. 1, also shows Carter with huge leads over Ford and Reagan. He leads Ford 62-29 per cent and Reagan 63-28 per cent.

Aug. 16-19. The 31st quadrennial Republican National Convention meets in Kansas City, Mo. and votes to nominate incumbent President Gerald R. Ford and Sen. Robert Dole (Kan.) as its presidential and vice presidential candidates. In his Aug. 19 acceptance speech Ford challenges Carter to meet him in a televised "face-to-face" debate. Carter issues a statement Aug. 20 agreeing to Ford's call.

Aug. 25. President Ford registers substantial gains in the Gallup Poll conducted immediately after the Republican Convention. The survey finds 50 per cent of the electorate supporting Carter, 37 per cent backing Ford, 10 per cent undecided, and 3 per cent for other candidates. Ford's standing is a 20 point improvement over his score in the July 26 survey.

Sept. 1. In a survey released by the Gallup organization, Carter regains some of his falloff in the polls with a 54-36 per cent showing against Ford.

Representatives for Ford and Carter reach agreement on the basic format for a series of nationally televised debates between the two candidates. Three presidential and one vice presidential debate are planned. The debates will be sponsored by the non-partisan League of Women Voters.

Sept. 6. Carter officially opens his presidential campaign with a speech delivered from the steps of President Franklin D. Roosevelt's "Little White House" in Warm Springs, Ga.

Sept. 15. President Ford officially opens his presidential campaign with a speech delivered at his alma mater, the University of Michigan in Ann Arbor.

Sept. 20. *Playboy* magazine releases the text of an interview in which Carter gives his views on lust and adultery. He says that he has "looked on a lot of women with lust" and has "committed adultery in [his] heart many times," but that God forgives sinners. During the same interview, Carter makes some remarks critical of former President Lyndon B. Johnson. Carter is quoted as saying that his religious beliefs would prevent him from ever taking on "the same frame of mind that Nixon or Johnson did—lying or cheating and distorting the truth." On Sept. 22 Carter calls Johnson's widow, Lady Bird, to apologize for the remark.

Sept. 23. Ford and Carter meet in their first debate. The encounter over domestic policy is televised nationally from Philadelphia's Walnut Street Theater. The debate is the first in 16 years between two presidential candidates and the first ever to include an incumbent President. A post-debate poll, conducted by the Gallup organization, finds that the public, by a 4-to-3 ratio, thinks Ford has "won" the encounter.

Sept. 30. A Gallup Poll, conducted immediately after the first debate, shows Carter's lead over Ford continuing to evaporate. Carter holds a nine-point lead of 51-40 per cent over Ford, down from his Sept. 1 margin of 54-36 per cent. Another survey conducted Sept. 27-Oct. 4 shows Carter's lead shrinking even further, to a slight edge of 47-45 per cent over Ford.

Oct. 6. Ford and Carter meet in their second debate to discuss foreign policy issues. During the 90-minute debate, held in the Palace of Fine Arts Theater in San Francisco, Calif., Ford says that there has been "no Soviet domination of Eastern Europe" and "there never will be" under a Ford administration. The remark provokes a storm of controversy. After attempting to clarify his assertion, Ford publicly acknowledges his error in a statement issued Oct. 12.

Oct. 14. Carter again widens his margin in the public opinion polls by registering a 48-42 per cent lead over Ford in the latest Gallup Poll. The latest survey, reports Gallup, reflects Carter's "win," by a 5-3 vote, of the second debate.

Oct. 15. Ford and Dole meet in the first debate ever between vice presidential candidates. The debate, televised nationally, is held at the Alley Theater in Houston, Tex.

Oct. 22. Ford and Carter meet in their third and final debate, televised nationally from the College of William and Mary in Williamsburg, Va. Both men respond cautiously to questions posed on a wide range of domestic and foreign topics. Telephone surveys conducted immediately after the debate show public opinion split on the outcome.

Nov. 1. On the eve of the election, public opinion polls show Ford and Carter virtually tied in their race for the presidency. The Gallup Poll, which calls Ford's comeback the "most dramatic in polling history," shows Ford edging Carter 46-47 per cent. Other polls give Carter the advantage. The final *New York Times*/CBS poll shows Carter with a 3 point lead over Ford. The Harris organization has Carter leading Ford by 47-46 per cent.

Nov. 2. Carter is elected the 39th President of the United States. Mondale is elected Vice President. Carter wins 23 states and the District of Columbia for a total of 297 electoral votes—27 more than the required majority of 270. Ford wins 27 states with 241 electoral votes. The popular vote margin is 40,274,975, or 51 per cent for Carter, and 38,530,614, or 48 per cent for Ford. Carter is the first man from the Deep South to be elected President since the Civil War. Ford becomes only the eighth incumbent President in the nation's history to be defeated and the first since Herbert Hoover was beaten decisively by Franklin Roosevelt in 1932.

Nov. 3. Ford concedes defeat in a telephone call to Carter shortly after 11 a.m. At a news conference later in the day, Ford, his voice hoarse from the last strenuous days of campaign, asks his wife, Betty, to read a telegram of concession to Carter. Carter in his statement of reply, says he appreciates Ford's "gracious expression of congratulations and cooperation."

Nov. 4. President-elect Carter holds his first news conference, in his home town of Plains, Ga. He says his narrow popular vote margin does not deny him a "mandate" for vigorous pursuit of his goals as President.

Nov. 5. Representatives of President Ford and President-elect Carter meet at the White House to plan the transition of administrations.

Nov. 17. Carter meets with 16 Democratic congressional leaders at the Georgia home of Sen. Herman E. Talmadge. After the meeting, all the participants exchange pledges of harmony and cooperation.

Carter's transition office officially opens in the Health, Education and Welfare building in Washington, D.C. The transition staff, headed by Atlanta attorney, Jack H. Watson Jr., has been working on transition plans since July.

Nov. 22. Carter and Ford confer at the White House. Both men re-emphasize their desire for cooperation between the incoming and outgoing administrations. Carter also meets at Blair House with key Ford administration officials, among them Defense Secretary Donald H. Rumsfeld and Treasury Secretary, William E. Simon.

Nov. 23. Carter spends the day on Capitol Hill in meetings with congressional leaders of both parties.

Dec. 3. Carter announces his first two cabinet-level appointments. He names Cyrus R. Vance, a Washington veteran, to be his Secretary of State and Thomas B. (Bert) Lance, an Atlanta banker and a long-time political supporter, to be his director of the Office of Management and Budget.

Dec. 23. Carter fulfills his promise to complete his cabinet-level appointments before Christmas with the announcement that he has chosen Joseph A. Califano Jr. as Secretary of Health, Education and Welfare, Theodore C. Sorensen as director of the Central Intelligence Agency and James R. Schlesinger as presidential assistant in charge of coordinating energy policy. At news conferences earlier in the month Carter announced the appointment of W. Michael Blumenthal as Secretary of the Treasury, Rep. Brock Adams (D Wash.) as Secretary of Transportation, Zbigniew Brzezinski as national security affairs adviser, Charles Schultze as chairman of the Council of Economic Advisers, Rep. Andrew Young (D Ga.) as ambassador to the United Nations, Cecil D. Andrus as Secretary of the Interior, Griffin B. Bell as Attorney General, Juanita Krepps as Secretary of Commerce, Rep. Bob Bergland (D Minn.) as Secretary of Agriculture, Harold Brown as Secretary of Defense, F. Ray Marshall as Secretary of Labor, and Patricia Roberts Harris as Secretary of Housing and Urban Development.

1977

Jan. 4. Carter issues a strict set of guidelines on ethics to be followed by presidential appointees. The guidelines cover three basic areas: public disclosure of financial assets, divestiture of assets that could lead to a conflict of interest, and certain restrictions on employment of appointees after they leave the government.

Jan. 6. Jimmy Carter is formally elected 39th President of the United States and Walter F. Mondale Vice President at the traditional Joint Session of Congress held to count the electoral vote. The final count for President is Carter 297, Ford 240 and Reagan one. In the separate tally for Vice President, Mondale receives 297 votes to 241 for Dole. Reagan's vote came from a "faithless" elector, who though pledged to Ford, bolted his party's choice to cast a symbolic protest vote.

Jan. 7. Carter announces the broad outlines of his economic stimulus plan. The package includes permanent and temporary tax cuts for individuals and business, as well as government spending for jobs.

Jan. 17. Theodore Sorensen, Carter's original choice to be CIA director, withdraws his nomination when it becomes apparent that he does not have sufficient support in the Senate.

Jan. 20. Carter is sworn in as the 39th President of the United States, taking the oath of office as "Jimmy," rather than as James Earl Jr., his formal name. Chief Justice Warren E. Burger administers the oath two minutes after noon before a crowd estimated at 150,000. Carter begins his 14-minute inaugural address by paying tribute to his predecessor, Gerald R. Ford. He calls in his speech for a "new national spirit of unity and trust" and for government leadership "both competent and compassionate." That afternoon, in a break with tradition reflecting his desire for informality, Carter forsakes the presidential limousine and instead walks with his family the mile-and-a-half down Pennsylvania Avenue from the Capitol to the White House.

Text of Candidate Carter's Acceptance Speech

Following is the text, as delivered, of Jimmy Carter's July 15 speech accepting the Democratic presidential nomination.

My name is Jimmy Carter, and I'm running for President. It's been a long time since I said those words the first time, and now I've come here, after seeing our great country, to accept your nomination.

I accept it in the words of John F. Kennedy: "With a full and grateful heart—and with only one obligation—to devote every effort of body, mind and spirit to lead our party back to victory and our nation back to greatness."

It's a pleasure to be with all you Democrats and to see that our Bicentennial celebration and our Bicentennial convention has been one of decorum and order, without any fights or free-for-alls. Among Democrats, that could only happen once every 200 years.

With this kind of a united Democratic Party, we are ready and eager to take on the Republicans, whichever Republican Party they decide to send against us in November.

1976 will not be a year of politics as usual. It can be a year of inspiration and hope. And it will be a year of concern, of quiet and sober reassessment of our nation's character and purpose—a year when voters have already confounded the experts.

And I guarantee you that it will be the year when we give the government of this country back to the people of this country.

There's a new mood in America.

We have been shaken by a tragic war abroad and by scandals and broken promises at home.

Our people are searching for new voices and new ideas and new leaders.

Although government has its limits and cannot solve all our problems, we Americans reject the view that we must be reconciled to failures and mediocrity, or to an inferior quality of life.

For I believe that we can come through this time of trouble stronger than ever. Like troops who've been in combat, we've been tempered in the fire—we've been disciplined and we've been educated. Guided by lasting and simple moral values, we've emerged idealists without illusions, realists who still know the old dreams of justice and liberty—of country and of community.

This year we have had 30 state primaries, more than ever before, making it possible to take our campaign directly to the people of America—to homes and shopping centers, to factory shift lines and colleges, to beauty parlors, and barber shops, to farmers' markets and union halls.

This has been a long and personal campaign—a kind of humbling experience, reminding us that ultimate political influence rests not with the powerbrokers, but with the people. This has been a time for learning and for the exchange of ideas, a time of tough debate on the important issues facing our country. This kind of debate is part of our tradition, and as Democrats we are heirs to a great tradition.

I have never met a Democratic president, but I've always been a Democrat.

Years ago, as a farm boy sitting outdoors with my family on the ground in the middle of the night, gathered close around a battery radio connected to the automobile battery, and listening to the Democratic conventions in far-off cities, I was a long way from the selection process then. I feel much closer to it tonight.

Ours is the party of the man who was nominated by those distant conventions, and who inspired and restored this nation in its darkest hours—Franklin D. Roosevelt.

Ours is the party of a fighting Democrat who showed us that a common man could be an uncommon leader—Harry S Truman.

Ours is the party of a brave young President who called the young in heart, regardless of age, to seek a New Frontier of national greatness—John F. Kennedy.

And ours is also the party of a great-hearted Texan, who took office in a tragic hour and who went on to do more than any other President in this century to advance the cause of human rights—Lyndon Johnson.

Now our party was built out of the sweatshops of the old Lower East Side, the dark mills of New Hampshire, the blazing hearths of Illinois, the coal mines of Pennsylvania, the hardscrabble farms of the southern coastal plans and the unlimited frontiers of America.

Ours is a party that welcomed generations of immigrants—the Jews, the Irish, the Italians, the Poles, and all the others—enlisted them in its ranks, and fought the political battles that helped bring them into the American mainstream—and they have shaped the character of our party.

That is our heritage. Our party has not been perfect. We've made mistakes and we've been disillusioned. We've seen a wall of leadership and compassion and progress.

Our leaders have fought for every piece of progressive legislation from RFD and REA to Social Security and civil rights. In times of need, the Democrats were there.

But in recent years, our nation has seen a failure of leadership. We've been hurt and we've been disillusioned We've seen a wall go up that separates us from our own government.

We've lost some precious things that historically have bound our people and our government together.

We feel that moral decay has weakened our country, that it's crippled by a lack of goals and values. And that our public officials have lost faith in us.

We've been a nation adrift too long. We've been without leadership too long. We've had divided and deadlocked government too long. We've been governed by veto too long. We've suffered enough at the hands of a tired and worn-out administration without new ideas, without youth or vitality, without visions, and without the confidence of the American people.

There is a fear that our best years are behind us, but I say to you that our nation's best is still ahead.

Our country has lived through a time of torment. It's now a time for healing.

We want to have faith again!

We want to be proud again!

We *just* want the truth again!

It's time for the people to run the government, and not the other way around.

It's time to honor and strengthen our families and our neighborhoods, and our diverse cultures and customs.

We need a Democratic President and a Congress to work in harmony for a change, with mutual respect for a change, in the open for a change and next year we are going to have that new leadership. You can depend on it.

It's time for America to move and to speak, not with boasting and belligerence, but with a quiet strength—to depend in world affairs not merely on the size of an arsenal but on the nobility of ideas—and to govern at home not by confusion and crisis but with grace and imagination and common sense.

Too many have had to suffer at the hands of a political and economic elite who have shaped decisions and never had to account for mistakes nor to suffer from injustice. When unemployment prevails, they never stand in line looking for a job. When deprivation results from a confused and bewildering welfare system, they never do without food or clothing or a place to sleep. When the public schools are inferior or torn by strife, their children go to exclusive private schools. And when the bureaucracy is bloated and confused, the powerful always manage to discover and occupy niches of special influence and privilege. An unfair tax structure serves their needs. And tight secrecy always seems to prevent reform.

All of us must be careful not to cheat each other.

Too often, unholy, self-perpetuating alliances have been formed between money and politics, and the average citizen has been held at arm's length.

Each time our nation has made a serious mistake, the American people have been excluded from the process. The tragedy of Vietnam and Cambodia, the disgrace of Watergate, and the embarrassment of the CIA revelations could have been avoided if our government had simply reflected the sound judgment and good common sense and the high moral character of the American people.

It's time for us to take a new look at our own government, to strip away the secrecy, to expose the unwarranted pressure of lobbyists, to eliminate waste, to release our civil servants from bureaucratic chaos, to provide tough management and always to remember that in any town or city, the mayor, the governor and the President represent exactly the same constituents.

As a governor, I had to deal each day with the complicated and confused and overlapping and wasteful federal government bureaucracy. As President, I want you to help me evolve an efficient, economical, purposeful and manageable government for our nation. Now I recognize the difficulty, but if I'm elected, it's going to be done, and you can depend on it.

We must strengthen the government closest to the people.

Business, labor, agriculture, education, science education, government should not struggle in isolation from one another, but should be able to strive toward mutual goals and shared opportunities.

We should make major investments in people and not in buildings and weapons. The poor, the aged, the weak, the afflicted must be treated with respect and compassion and with love.

Now I have spoken a lot of times this year about love, but love must be aggressively translated into simple justice.

The test of any government is not how popular it is with the powerful, but how honestly and fairly it deals with those who must depend on it.

It's time for a complete overhaul of our income tax system. I still tell you it's a disgrace to the human race. All my life I have heard promises of tax reform, but it never quite happens. With your help, we are finally going to make it happen and you can depend on it.

Here is something that can really help our country.

It's time for universal voter registration.

It's time for a nationwide, comprehensive health program for all our people.

It's time to guarantee an end to discrimination because of race or sex by full involvement in the decision-making processes of government by those who know what it is to suffer from discrimination, and they'll be in the government if I'm elected.

It's time for the law to be enforced. We cannot educate children, we cannot create harmony among our people, we cannot preserve basic human freedom unless we have an orderly society. Now crime and a lack of justice are especially cruel to those who are least able to protect themselves. Swift arrest and trial, and fair and uniform punishment should be expected by anyone who would break our laws.

It's time for our government leaders to respect the law no less than the humblest citizen, so that we can end once and for all a double standard of justice. I see no reason why big shot crooks should go free and the poor ones go to jail.

A simple and a proper function of government is just to make it easy for us to do good and difficult for us to do wrong.

Now as an engineer, a planner and a businessman, I see clearly the value to our nation of a strong system of free enterprise based on increased productivity and adequate wages. We Democrats believe that competition is better than regulation. And we intend to combine strong safeguards for consumers with minimal intrusion of government in our free economic system.

I believe that anyone who is able to work ought to work—and ought to have a chance to work. We'll never end the inflationary spiral, we'll never have a balanced budget, which I am determined to see, as long as we have eight or nine million Americans out of work who cannot find a job.

Now any system of economics is bankrupt if it sees either value or virtue in unemployment. We simply cannot check inflation by keeping people out of work.

The foremost responsibility of any President above all else is to guarantee the security of our nation—a guarantee of freedom from the threat of successful attack or blackmail and the ability with our allies to maintain peace.

But peace is not the mere absence of war. Peace is action to stamp out international terrorism. Peace is the unceasing effort to preserve human rights. And peace is a combined demonstration of strength and good will. We'll pray for peace and we'll work for peace, until we have removed from all nations for all time the threat of nuclear destruction.

America's birth opened a new chapter in mankind's history. Ours was the first nation to dedicate itself clearly to basic moral and philosophical principles:

That all people are created equal and endowed with inalienable rights to life, liberty and the pursuit of happiness; and that the power of government is derived from the consent of the governed.

This national commitment was a singular act of wisdom and courage, and it brought the best and the bravest from other nations to our shores.

It was a revolutionary development that captured the imagination of mankind.

It created the basis for a unique role for America—that of a pioneer in shaping more decent and just relations among people and among societies.

Today, 200 years later, we must address ourselves to that role both in what we do at home and how we act abroad—among people everywhere who have become politically more alert, socially more congested and increasingly impatient with global inequities, and who are now organized as you know, into some 50 different nations.

This calls for nothing less than a sustained architectural effort to shape an international framework of peace within which our own ideals gradually can become a global reality.

Our nation should always derive its character directly from the people and let this be the strength and the image to be presented to the world—the character of the American people.

To our friends and allies I say that what unites us through our common dedication to democracy is much more important than that in which occasionally divides us on economics or politics.

To the nations that seek to lift themselves from poverty, I say that America shares your aspirations and extends its hand to you.

To those nation-states that wish to compete with us, I say that we neither fear competition nor see it as an obstacle to wider cooperation.

And to all people I say that after 200 years America still remains confident and youthful in its commitment to freedom and equality, and we always will be.

During this election year, we candidates will ask you for your votes, and from us will be demanded our vision.

My vision of this nation and its future has been deepened and matured during the 19 months that I have campaigned among you for President.

I've never had more faith in America than I do today.

We have an America that, in Bob Dylan's phrase, is busy being born, not busy dying.

We can have an American government that's turned away from scandal and corruption and official cynicism and is once again as decent and competent as our people.

We can have an America that has reconciled its economic needs with its desire for an environment that we can pass on with pride to the next generation.

We can have an America that provides excellence in education to my child and your child and every child.

We can have an America that encourages and takes pride in our ethnic diversity, our religious diversity, our cultural diversity knowing that out of this pluralistic heritage has come the strength and the vitality and the creativity that made us great and will keep us great.

We can have an American government that does not oppress or spy on its own people, but respects our dignity and our privacy and our right to be left alone.

We can have an America where freedom on the one hand and equality on the other hand are mutually supportive and not in conflict, and where the dreams of our nation's first leaders are fully realized in our own day and age.

And we can have an America which harnesses the idealism of the student, the compassion of the nurse or the social worker, the determination of the farmer, the wisdom of a teacher, the practicality of the business leader, the experience of the senior citizen and the hope of a laborer to build a better life for us all, and we can have it and we are gonna have it.

As I've said many times before, we can have an American President who does not govern with negativism and fear of the future, but with vigor and vision and aggressive leadership—a President who's not isolated from the people, but who feels your pain and shares your dreams, and takes his strength and his wisdom and his courage from you.

I see an America on the move again, united, a diverse and vital and tolerant nation, entering our third century with pride and confidence—an America that lives up to the majesty of our Constitution and the simple decency of our people.

This is the America we want.

This is the America that we will have.

We'll go forward from this convention with some differences of opinion, perhaps, but nevertheless united in a calm determination to make our country large and driving and generous in spirit once again, ready to embark on great national deeds. And once again, as brothers and sisters, our hearts will swell with pride to call ourselves Americans.

Thank you very much.

Text of President Carter's Inaugural Address

Following is the text of President Carter's inaugural address, as it was delivered on Jan. 20:

For myself and for our nation, I want to thank my predecessor for all he has done to heal our land.

In this outward and physical ceremony we attest once again to the inner and spiritual strength of our nation.

As my high school teacher, Miss Julia Coleman, used to say, "We must adjust to changing times and still hold to unchanging principles."

Here before me is the Bible used in the inauguration of our first President in 1789, and I have just taken the oath of office on the Bible my mother gave me just a few years ago, opened to a timeless admonition from the ancient prophet Micah:

"He hath showed thee, o man, what is good; and what doth the Lord require of thee, but to do justly, and to love mercy, and to walk humbly with thy God." (Micah 6:8)

New Spirit

This inauguration ceremony marks a new beginning, a new dedication within our government, and a new spirit among us all. A President may sense and proclaim that new spirit, but only a people can provide it.

Two centuries ago our nation's birth was a milestone in the long quest for freedom, but the bold and brilliant dream which excited the founders of this nation still awaits its consummation. I have no new dream to set forth today, but rather urge a fresh faith in the old dream.

Ours was the first society openly to define itself in terms of both spirituality and human liberty. It is that unique self-definition which has given us an exceptional appeal—but it also imposes on us a special obligation—to take on those moral duties which, when assumed, seem invariably to be in our own best interests.

You have given me a great responsibility—to stay close to you, to be worthy of you, and to exemplify what you are. Let us create together a new national spirit of unity and trust. Your strength can compensate for my weakness, and your wisdom can help to minimize my mistakes.

Let us learn together and laugh together and work together and pray together, confident that in the end we will triumph together in the right.

The American dream endures. We must once again have full faith in our country—and in one another. I believe America can be better. We can be even stronger than before.

Let our recent mistakes bring a resurgent commitment to the basic principles of our nation, for we know that if we despise our own government we have no future. We recall in special times when we have stood briefly, but magnificently, united; in those times no prize was beyond our grasp.

But we cannot dwell upon remembered glory. We cannot afford to drift. We reject the prospect of failure or mediocrity or an inferior quality of life for any person.

Our government must at the same time be both competent and compassionate.

We have already found a high degree of personal liberty, and we are now struggling to enhance equality of opportunity. Our commitment to human rights must be absolute, our laws fair, our natural beauty preserved; the powerful must not persecute the weak, and human dignity must be enhanced.

We have learned that "more" is not necessarily "better," that even our great nation has its recognized limits, and that we can neither answer all questions nor solve all problems. We cannot afford to do everything, nor can we afford to lack boldness as we meet the future. So together, in a spirit of individual sacrifice for the common good, we must simply do our best.

Example to Others

Our nation can be strong abroad only if it is strong at home, and we know that the best way to enhance freedom in other lands is to demonstrate here that our democratic system is worthy of emulation.

To be true to ourselves, we must be true to others. We will not behave in foreign places so as to violate our rules and standards here at home, for we know that the trust which our nation earns is essential to our strength.

The world itself is now dominated by a new spirit. Peoples more numerous and more politically aware are craving and now demanding their place in the sun—not just for the benefit of their own physical condition, but for basic human rights.

The passion for freedom is on the rise. Tapping this new spirit, there can be no nobler nor more ambitious task for America to undertake on this day of a new beginning than to help shape a just and peaceful world that is truly humane.

We are a strong nation and we will maintain strength so sufficient that it need not be proven in combat—a quiet strength based not merely on the size of an arsenal, but on the nobility of ideas.

We will be ever vigilant and never vulnerable, and we will fight our wars against poverty, ignorance and injustice, for those are the enemies against which our forces can be honorably marshalled.

We are a proudly idealistic nation, but let no one confuse our idealism with weakness.

Because we are free we can never be indifferent to the fate of freedom elsewhere. Our moral sense dictates a clearcut preference for those societies which share with us an abiding respect for individual human rights. We do not seek to intimidate, but it is clear that a world which others can dominate with impunity would be inhospitable to decency and a threat to the well-being of all people.

Arms Race

The world is still engaged in a massive armaments race designed to insure continuing equivalent strength among potential adversaries. We pledge perseverance and wisdom in our efforts to limit the world's armaments to those necessary for each nation's own domestic safety. And we will move this year a step toward our ultimate goal—the elimination of all nuclear weapons from this earth.

We urge all other people to join us, for success can mean life instead of death.

Within us, the people of the United States, there is evident a serious and purposeful rekindling of confidence, and I join in the hope that when my time as your President has ended, people might say this about our nation:

That we had remembered the words of Micah and renewed our search for humility, mercy and justice;

That we had torn down the barriers that separated those of different race and region and religion, and where there had been mistrust, built unity, with a respect for diversity;

That we had found productive work for those able to perform it;

That we had strengthened the American family, which is the basis of our society;

That we had ensured respect for the law, and equal treatment under the law, for the weak and the powerful, for the rich and the poor;

And that we had enabled our people to be proud of their own government once again.

I would hope that the nations of the world might say that we had built a lasting peace, based not on weapons of war but on international policies which reflect our own most precious values.

These are not just my goals. And they will not be my accomplishments, but the affirmation of our nation's continuing moral strength and our belief in an un-diminished, ever-expanding American dream.

Index

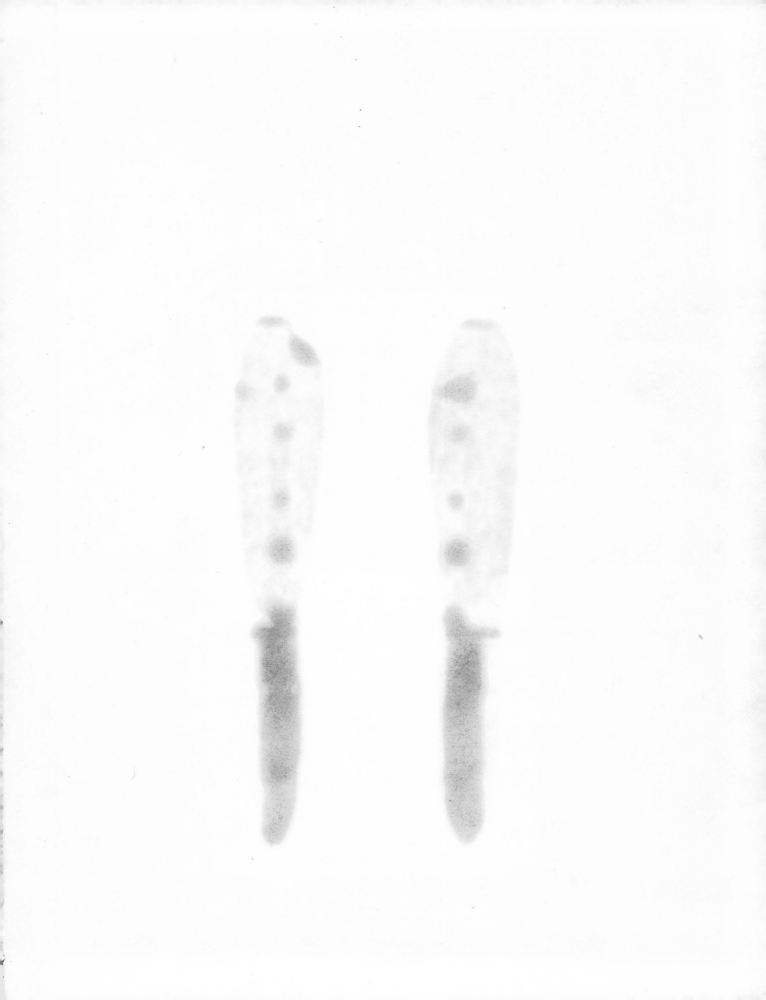

DATE DUE
